CHINESE REFUGEE LAW AND POLICY

This book is the first to systematically examine Chinese refugee law and policy. It provides in-depth legal and policy analysis and makes recommendations to relevant stakeholders, drawing not only on existing legal and policy scholarships but also on empirical information acquired through field visits and interviews with refugees, former refugees, and staff of governmental and non-governmental organisations working with displaced populations. It is a timely response to rapidly growing international interest in and demand for information about Chinese and Asian approaches to refugee protection in academia and the policy sector.

LILI SONG is Lecturer at the Faculty of Law, University of Otago, New Zealand. She holds a PhD in Law from Victoria University of Wellington, a Master's degree in International Law from East China University of Political Science and Law, and a Bachelor's degree in Law from Shanghai University of Finance and Economics. She is a member of the Asia Pacific Refugee Rights Network.

T0381682

CHINESE REFUGEE LAW AND POLICY

LILI SONG
University of Otago, New Zealand

CAMBRIDGE UNIVERSITY PRESS

CAMBRIDGE
UNIVERSITY PRESS

University Printing House, Cambridge CB2 8BS, United Kingdom

One Liberty Plaza, 20th Floor, New York, NY 10006, USA

477 Williamstown Road, Port Melbourne, VIC 3207, Australia

314-321, 3rd Floor, Plot 3, Splendor Forum, Jasola District Centre, New Delhi - 110025, India

103 Penang Road, #05-06/07, Visioncrest Commercial, Singapore 238467

Cambridge University Press is part of the University of Cambridge.

It furthers the University's mission by disseminating knowledge in the pursuit of
education, learning and research at the highest international levels of excellence.

www.cambridge.org
Information on this title: www.cambridge.org/9781009305860
DOI: 10.1017/9781108669474

First published 2020
First paperback edition 2022

A catalogue record for this publication is available from the British Library

ISBN 978-1-108-48398-8 Hardback
ISBN 978-1-009-30586-0 Paperback

CONTENTS

CONTENTS vii

5.2 Current Legal and Policy Framework   138
    5.2.1 Hong Kong's Status under the Refugee Convention and Protocol   138
    5.2.2 Immigration and Human Rights Law   141
    5.2.3 *Non-Refoulement* and the Unified Screening Mechanism   142
5.3 The Role of the Judiciary   145
5.4 The Role of Civil Society   150
5.5 Current Challenges and Opportunities   153

6 **Refugee Law and Policy in Macao**   155
6.1 Macao and Refugees   155
6.2 Current Legal and Policy Framework   157
    6.2.1 Macao's Status under the Refugee Convention and Protocol   157
    6.2.2 Refugee Status Determination in Macao   159
6.3 Current Challenges and Opportunities   164

7 **Conclusion and Recommendations**   166
7.1 China   166
    7.1.1 China's Experience with Refugees   166
    7.1.2 Chinese Refugee Law   167
    7.1.3 Chinese Refugee Policy   169
7.2 Hong Kong and Macao   171
7.3 Recommendations   173

Select Bibliography   176
Index   210

FIGURES

TABLES

ACKNOWLEDGEMENTS

My deepest gratitude goes to the refugees, former refugees and internally displaced persons I met during the course of my research presented in this book. Their determination and resilience have been, and will continue to be, a source of inspiration.

This book is an expansion of my doctoral thesis, which I completed in November 2014 at Victoria University of Wellington, New Zealand. I am indebted to my thesis supervisors, Caroline Sawyer and Marc Lanteigne, for their support and guidance, Emeritus Professor Tony Angelo, then coordinator of the PhD program, for his constant support and never-failing ability to listen patiently, and my thesis examiners, Susan Kneebone, Campbell McLachlan and Vitit Muntarbhorn, for their constructive comments and encouragement. Susan Kneebone has since provided much valuable advice with patience and was my host during my visiting fellowship at the Melbourne Law School from November 2018 to January 2019.

My time at the Michigan Law School as a Grotius research fellow in 2016 was instrumental to the development of this book. James Hathaway's guidance and encouragement were invaluable. I also benefitted greatly from my time at the Oxford Refugee Studies Centre as a visiting research fellow in 2018. I had many inspiring conversations with Jeff Crisp, Gil Loescher, Cathryn Costello, Matthew Gibney, Lilian Tsourdi, Ali Ali, Vladislava Stoyanova, Felix Bender, Jacqi Mosselson and many other colleagues there. I fondly remember their warmth, genuineness and a fantastic party they threw at the end of the term.

I would also like to thank the Australian Center on China in the World at the Australian National University for hosting me as an Australian Endeavour postdoctoral fellow in 2015 and the Northwestern University Center for Forced Migration Studies in Evanston, Illinois and the Melbourne Law School for hosting me as a visiting fellow in 2014 and 2018–19 respectively. My heartfelt thanks go to colleagues I met at these institutes, especially Galya Ben-Arieh, the late Barbara Harrell-Bond,

Jane Golley, Linda Javin, Elisa Nesossi, Geremie Barmé, Luigi Tomba, Benjamin Penny, Rebecca Fabrizi, Paul Farrelly, Jinghong Zhang, Yujie Zhu, Ying Qian, Erika Feller, Michelle Foster, Sarah Biddulph and Wendy Ng. I would also like to thank Kirsteen Lau, Ambrose Chiu, Isaac Shaffer, Mark Daly and Carol Tong Thi Xuan, who took time out of their busy schedules to have email discussions with me about refugee protection in Hong Kong.

I have gratefully received the following grants in support of portions of the research presented in this book: a Victoria University of Wellington Doctoral Scholarship (2011–2014), an Australian Endeavour Research Fellowship (ERF-PDR-4851-2015), a Human Rights and Asia Fellowship awarded by the Human Rights Centre, Seoul National University (2015) and a University of Michigan Grotius Research Fellowship (2016). I am fortunate enough to have published earlier versions of portions of this book in the following articles: "Who Shall We Help? The Refugee Definition in a Chinese Context" (2014) *Refugee Survey Quarterly* 33(1) 44–58, "Refugees or Border Residents from Myanmar? The Status of Displaced Ethnic Kachins and Kokangs in Yunnan Province, China" (2017) *International Journal of Refugee Law* 29(3) 466–487, "Forced Migration of Ethnic Kachins from Myanmar to China: Law and Politics behind China's Response" (2018) *Asian and Pacific Migration Journal* 27 (2) 190–208 and "China and the International Refugee Protection Regime: Past, Present, and Potentials" (2018) *Refugee Survey Quarterly* 37(2) 139–161.

My gratitude also goes to my editors at Cambridge University Press, Joe Ng and Finola O'Sullivan, for their support and patience. Otago University Faculty of Law research assistants Jonathon Yeldon and Andrew Snoddy provided research and proofreading assistance, for which I am grateful.

Last but not least, I thank my family and friends, whose love and company made my journey in writing this book a rewarding one.

Lili Song
June 2019

LIST OF ABBREVIATIONS

AALCO	Asian–African Legal Consultative Organisation
BEEA	Chinese Bureau of Exit and Entry Administration
BSB	Chinese Border Security Bureau
BCD	Chinese Border Control Department
BCP	Burma Communist Party
CAT	Convention against Torture and Other Cruel, Inhuman or Degrading Treatment or Punishment
CIHRDPRK	Commission of Inquiry on Human Rights in the Democratic People's Republic of Korea
CPA	UN Comprehensive Plan of Action
DPRK	Democratic People's Republic of Korea
GDP	gross domestic product
HRW	Human Rights Watch
ICCPR	International Covenant on Civil and Political Rights
IDP	internally displaced person
IOM	International Organisation for Migration
IRO	International Refugee Organisation
KIA	Kachin Independence Army
KIO	Kachin Independence Organisation
MCA	Chinese Ministry of Civil Affairs
MFA	Chinese Ministry of Foreign Affairs
MNDAA	Myanmar National Democratic Alliance Army
MPS	Chinese Ministry of Public Security
NGO	non-governmental organisation
NIA	Chinese National Immigration Administration
NLD	Myanmar National League for Democracy
NPC	Chinese National People's Congress
OCF	Overseas Chinese Farm
PSB	Chinese Public Security Bureau
RSD	Refugee Status Determination
SCIO	Chinese State Council Information Office
SCO	Shanghai Cooperation Organisation

TCAB	Hong Kong Torture Claims Appeal Board
UN	United Nations
UNCEDW	United Nations Committee on the Elimination of Discrimination against Women
UNHCR	United Nations High Commissioner for Refugees
UNHCR ExCom	UNHCR Executive Committee
USM	Hong Kong Unified Screening Mechanism
UNICEF	United Nations Children's Fund

1

Introduction

Traditionally, the People's Republic of China (China) has been an origin, and not a destination, of refugees, and Chinese refugee law and policy have largely escaped international attention.[1] As China has risen as a world power in the past few decades, it is emerging as a destination and transit country for refugees and asylum seekers. Since 1978, China has experienced at least five large-scale refugee inflows from Vietnam, North Korea and Myanmar. In addition, the number of refugees and asylum seekers in non-mass influx situations has also been on the rise since the mid-1990s.

China has land borders with fourteen countries. Several of China's neighbours are well-known refugee-producing countries, including North Korea, Myanmar, Vietnam, Afghanistan and Pakistan. Thus China's potential exposure to future large-scale refugee influxes from neighbouring countries should not be underestimated. As China's economic strength and political influence continue to grow, it is also likely to attract more refugees and asylum seekers from other parts of the world in the years to come.

As noted by Betts and Loescher, China is one of the countries that are most potentially influential on the global refugee regime.[2] As the second largest economy in the world, a party to the 1951 Convention relating to the Status of Refugees (the Refugee Convention) and its 1967 Protocol (the Refugee Protocol, collectively the Refugee Convention and Protocol), a member of the United Nations (UN) Security Council and a member of the Executive Committee of the United Nations High Commissioner for

---

[1] For the purposes of this book, unless otherwise expressed or implied by the context, China refers to the Mainland of the People's Republic of China, excluding the Hong Kong Special Administrative Region (Hong Kong), Macao Special Administrative Region (Macao) and Taiwan.

[2] Alexander Betts and Gil Loescher "Introduction: Continuity and Change in Global Refugee Policy" (2014) 33(1) *Refugee Survey Quarterly* 1 at 6.

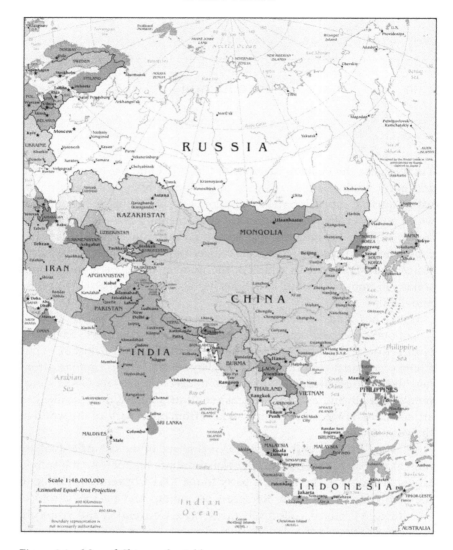

Figure 1.1   Map of China and neighbours
Source: The United States Central Intelligence Agency <https://www.cia.gov/library/publications/
the-world-factbook/attachments/images/large/asia-political.jpg?1547145648>

Refugees (UNHCR), China has the potential to significantly influence and
contribute to the global refugee protection regime.

In recent years, there has been increasing international interest in
further engaging China in the global effort to respond to refugee crises.

For example, in October 2015, the German Chancellor Angela Merkel asked China to help solve the refugee crisis in Europe.[3] In September 2017, Malaysia sought China's assistance in tackling the Rohingya refugee crisis in Bangladesh.[4] The UN High Commissioner for Refugees Filippo Grandi, during his visit to China in June 2017, noted that China could play a key role in solving refugee crises.[5] The Chinese Government has shown an unprecedented interest in refugee matters in recent years. For example, China included a clause on the treatment of refugees in its domestic law for the first time in 2012. Its contribution to UNHCR has grown dramatically since 2011. In November 2017, China even offered to mediate between Myanmar and Bangladesh and proposed a 'three-phase solution' to the Rohingya refugee crisis.[6]

However, China's refugee law and policy have rarely been systematically considered. In this context, this book aims to provide systematic, empirically informed critical analysis of China's refugee law and policy. Chapter 2 provides a brief historical review of refugees in imperial Qing China and the Republic of China and an overview of the People's Republic of China's experience with refugees. It also examines how refugees have been perceived by the public in China in recent years. Chapter 3 provides a systematic review of the legal, policy and institutional framework for refugee status determination and refugee protection in China. Chapter 4 critically analyses China's treatment of refugees, especially its response to five refugee influxes between 1949 and 2018, namely the influx of refugees from Vietnam between 1978 and 1982, the continuous arrivals of North Korean escapees, the influxes of displaced ethnic Kokangs from Myanmar in 2009 and since 2015, and the influx of displaced ethnic Kachins from Myanmar since 2011.

Chapters 5 and 6 of this book examine refugee law and policy in Hong Kong and Macao, two special administrative regions which are under

---

[3] Arne Delfs and Patrick Donahue "Merkel Seeks China's Support on Refugees as Crisis Follows Her" *Bloomberg* (30 October 2015) <www.bloomberg.com/news/articles/2015-10-29/merkel-seeks-china-s-support-on-refugees-as-crisis-follows-her>.

[4] Adrian Lai "Malaysia asks China to Help Tackle Rohingya Refugee Crisis in Bangladesh" *The New Strait Times* (27 September 2017) <www.nst.com.my/news/nation/2017/09/284599/update-malaysia-asks-china-help-tackle-rohingya-refugee-crisis-bangladesh>.

[5] Vivian Tan "China Can Play Key Role in Solving Refugee Crises – UNHCR Chief" (8 June 2017) <www.unhcr.org/en-au/news/latest/2017/6/593946b64/china-play-key-role-solving-refugee-crises-unhcr-chief.html>.

[6] Xinhua "China Proposes Three-Phase Solution to Rakhine Issue in Myanmar: FM" (20 November 2017) <http://news.xinhuanet.com/english/2017-11/20/c_136764392.htm>.

Chinese sovereignty but have high autonomy with independent judicial powers. The Refugee Convention and Protocol have not been extended to Hong Kong. Macao has been bound by those instruments since 1999 and has conducted its own refugee status determination (RSD) since 2004. Chapters 5 and 6 discuss the historical background, the current legal and policy framework, and the current challenges and opportunities for refugee protection in Hong Kong and Macao respectively.

In conclusion, Chapter 7 evaluates China's refugee law and policy, contrasts refugee protection in China with that in Hong Kong and Macao, and makes recommendations to the relevant stakeholders.

This book draws upon existing literature as well as the author's field work in Myanmar, South Korea and China. In March and April 2013, the first seventeen interviews were conducted with refugees, former refugees and humanitarian workers in Kachin State, Myanmar, Yunnan province and Guangxi Zhuang autonomous region, China and Seoul, South Korea. Another three interviews were conducted with refugees and humanitarian workers in Yunnan province, China in December 2014. Three more interviews were conducted in Beijing, China in August 2015.

Twenty-two interviewees were recruited through non-governmental organisations (NGOs) and individual humanitarian workers,[7] including one refugee from Vietnam who arrived in China between 1978 and 1982, two former North Korean escapees,[8] ten displaced Kachin civilians who fled to Yunnan between June 2011 and December 2014,[9] seven humanitarian workers and employees of international organisations, and two officials of the Kachin Independence Organisation (KIO). All interviewees have been anonymised in this book. All interviews were semi-structured and face-to-face, except for one email interview with an employee of an international organisation, and were conducted in English, Mandarin Chinese, Cantonese or Kachin (with Kachin–Chinese or Kachin–English interpreters). No interviewees received any payment or reimbursement for participation.

This book also benefits from my conversations with two Asian–African Legal Consultative Organisation (AALCO) officials in New Delhi, India in 2015, and a number of internally displaced Kachin civilians in Kachin State, Myanmar in April 2013.

---

[7] One interviewee, who was a humanitarian worker, was interviewed twice, in April 2013 and again in December 2014.
[8] Both had left China at the time of interview.
[9] Nine had left China at the time of interview.

I

Mainland China

Refugees and Other Displaced Foreigners in China

2.1 Historical Background

Protection for displaced aliens is not an unheard-of practice in Chinese history. In the Spring and Autumn period (approximately 770–476 BC) and the Warring States period (approximately 475–221 BC), when China was still divided into a group of smaller kingdoms, many intellectuals and politicians fled political turmoil and received protection in another kingdom.[1] In the late eighteenth century, the Qing imperial Chinese Government gave asylum to the king of Annam.[2]

During the First World War, more than 300,000 ethnic Kazakhs, Uzbeks, Kyrgyzs and Russians fled from Tsarist Russia to Xinjiang in Northwest China to escape military service or oppression by the Russian Government.[3] Following the Russian Revolution in 1917, tens of thousands of Russian exiles made their way to China, living mainly in Manchuria and Xinjiang. By mid-1924, about 60,000 Russian exiles were in China.[4] Throughout the 1920s and in the early 1930s, escapees from Russia continued to arrive in China for both political and economic

---

[1] See eg Wang Li *Xianqin Waijiao Ciling Tanjiu* (World Knowledge Press, Beijing, 2008) at 15 (translation: *Research on Pre-Qin Diplomatic Languages*); Richard Louis Walker *The Multi-State System of Ancient China* (Shoe String Press, Hamden (Conn), 1953) at 24–25.

[2] Peter Perdue "Embracing Victory, Effacing Defeat: Rewriting the Qing Frontier Campaigns" in Diana Lary (ed) *The Chinese State at the Borders* (UBC Press, Vancouver, 2007) 105 at 120.

[3] Tacheng Municipality "Tacheng de waiguo qiaomin" (20 July 2011) <www.xjtcsh.gov.cn/tcgk/rwsl/201107/t4028a8ab3145442001314701c94f04dd.html> (translation: "Foreign Sojourners in Tacheng"); Jianhua Huang and Wenhua Ma "Yang Zhengxin yu eguo nanmin cuanrao Xinjiang shijian" (1994) 4 *Yili shifan xueyuan xuebao* 74 (translation: "Yang Zhengxin and the Influx of Russian Refugees in Xinjiang" *Journal of Yili Teachers' College*).

[4] Michael Marrus *The Unwanted: European Refugees in the Twentieth Century* (Oxford University Press, Oxford, 1985) at 60.

reasons.[5] From 1933 to 1941, about 30,000 Jews escaping Nazi persecution and the Holocaust in Europe found refuge in Shanghai.[6]

The Government of the Republic of China (1911–1949 in Mainland China) was generous with these displaced aliens. In the late 1930s, when many countries refused Jewish immigration in the wake of the global economic depression, Shanghai was the only major city in the world which allowed desperate Jewish refugees from Europe to enter without a visa.[7] Those fleeing Russia entered China with little difficulty and settled well into the local community. Some even assumed important civil service jobs in the local Xinjiang Government.[8]

It was not out of pure altruism that the Republic of China treated displaced foreign nationals kindly. After China was forced to open its doors to Western powers after the First Opium War (1839–1842), it did not fully regain the power to control the entry and exit of aliens, especially those from Europe, or to regulate aliens on its soil until the early 1940s. The Republic of China introduced the first regulations requiring foreigners' passports to be inspected upon entry in 1930.[9] It was only on 14 November 1944, the eve of the Chinese victory over the Japanese, that the Republic of China introduced legal requirements for aliens to apply for a residence permit to live in China.[10]

From the mid-nineteenth century to the early 1940s, as a consequence of a series of unequal treaties, Europeans in China enjoyed many

---

[5] Tacheng Municipality, above n 3. According to a report by the administrative head of Tacheng, Ruhai Li, on 23 December 1929, poor crop harvest and food shortage that autumn in the Soviet Union had driven many Russians into Tacheng. Li also noticed that there were a significant number of persons who fled to Tacheng for political reasons. Before and after 1930, the agricultural collectivisation movement in the Soviet Union also led to many escapes to China.

[6] The history of Jewish refugees in Shanghai during the 1930s and 1940s has been covered by many books and articles, eg David Kranzler *Japanese, Nazis and Jews, the Jewish Refugee Community of Shanghai 1938–1945* (Yeshiva University Press, New York, 1976); Pamela Rotner Sakamoto *Japanese Diplomats and Jewish Refugees: A World War II Dilemma* (Praeger, Westport (Conn), 1998); Felix Gruenberger "The Jewish Refugees in Shanghai" (1950) 12 *Jewish Social Studies* 329; Suzanne D Rutland "'Waiting Room Shanghai': Australian Reactions to the Plight of the Jews in Shanghai after the Second World War" (1987) 32 *The Leo Baeck Institute Year Book* 407; Guang Pan *Shanghai: A Haven for Holocaust Victims* (The Holocaust and the United Nations Outreach Programme, Discussion Papers Series vol II, Discussion paper #6) <www.un.org/en/holocaustremembrance/docs/paper15.shtml>.

[7] Pan, above n 6.

[8] Tacheng Municipality, above n 3.

[9] Guofu Liu *Chinese Immigration Law* (Ashgate, Farnham (UK), 2011) at 5.

[10] At 5.

privileges over Chinese citizens. European refugees in China also had a status superior to that of Chinese citizens on the social ladder. Felix Gruenberger, who himself was a Jewish refugee in Shanghai, described how European refugees in Shanghai were ranked lower socially than other foreigners but higher than Chinese citizens:[11]

> Apart from the Japanese occupation forces, there were three social groups in Shanghai. (1) The foreigners. These were the wealthy white Europeans, protected by their consulates, who made up a well-integrated group and who looked down upon anyone who had to do work which was lower than the standard for the white population. (2) The refugees. These consisted first of the Russian refugees and later of the central Europeans. These people were forced by their condition to accept work usually considered unfit for the "whites". (3) The native Chinese. They did the lowest chores and received the lowest wages.

By the time the People's Republic of China was established in October 1949, there were still more than 20,000 refugees in China, including persons of Austrian, Czech, Estonian, Greek, Hungarian, Latvian, Lithuanian, Norwegian, Polish, Romanian, Russian, Spanish, Ukrainian and Yugoslav backgrounds.[12] The majority were ethnic Russians who had fled the Soviet Union in the 1920s.[13] Most of them would be resettled to a third country by the International Refugee Organisation (IRO) and then UNHCR in the 1950s.[14]

2.2   Refugees and Other Displaced Foreigners in China

From 1949 to 1978, China received few refugees or other displaced foreigners. On the one hand, its economic backwardness and socialist political system may not have been attractive to outsiders. On the other hand, China had strictly limited the entry of aliens in general, and there was ubiquitous distrust and hostility towards foreigners in China during this period.

---

[11] Gruenberger, above n 6, at 331.
[12] Glen Peterson "The Uneven Development of the International Refugee Regime in Post-war Asia: Evidence from China, Hong Kong and Indonesia" (2012) 25 *Journal of Refugee Studies* 326 at 328 and 331. Between 1952 and 1969, around 20,000 refugees exited China with the help of the United Nations High Commissioner for Refugees (UNHCR); prior to that, the International Refugee Organisation (IRO) resettled about 19,000 to a third country between 1947 and 1952.
[13] Peterson, above n 12, at 329.
[14] At 329.

However, China did provide political asylum to a few foreigners during this period. The most well-known individual who received asylum in China is probably King Norodom Sihanouk of Cambodia. China granted him political asylum when he was deposed and sentenced to death in a coup led by the American-backed General Lon Nol in 1970.[15] Norodom Sihanouk lived in China for about five years before returning to Cambodia in 1975.

A Japanese Communist Party leader, Kyuichi Tokuda, was granted asylum in China in the early 1950s. Tokuda had participated in the formation of the Japanese Communist Party in the early 1920s and was later elected Secretary General of the Central Committee of the Japanese Communist Party and a member of the House of Representatives.[16] After he was purged from public office in 1950 by the supreme commander for the Allied Powers during the Allied occupation of Japan, he went into exile in China and died in Beijing in 1953.[17]

The Chinese Government also provided asylum to an Indonesian Ambassador to China, Djawoto, in April 1966 in the midst of intensifying diplomatic and political tension between Beijing and Jakarta.[18] Djawoto later assumed the position of Secretary General of the Afro-Asian Journalists' Association in Beijing and lived there for more than a decade.

In the 1960s, China gave refuge to a group of Malayan Communist Party members, who set up and ran the Suara Revolusi Malaya (the Voice of the Malayan Revolution) radio station in China's southern Hunan province.[19] From 1961 to 1980, Chen Pin (also known as Pin Cheng or Chin Peng), a Malayan Communist Party leader, also lived in exile in China after the Malayan Emergency (1948–1960).[20]

---

[15] Michael Colaresi *Scare Tactics: The Politics of International Rivalry* (Syracuse University Press, Syracuse, 2005) at 197.

[16] National Diet Library, Japan "Tokuda, Kyuichi" <www.ndl.go.jp/portrait/e/datas/407 .html?cat=119>.

[17] Sohu News "waiguoren ruhe dedao zhongguo 'bihu'" (18 December 2013) <http://news .sohu.com/s2013/dianji-1291/> (translation: "How Can Foreigners Receive Asylum in China?"); National Diet Library, above n 16.

[18] David Mozingo *Chinese Policy toward Indonesia, 1949–1967* (Cornell University Press, Ithaca, 1976) at 250.

[19] Sohu News, above n 17; Archives Portal Europe "Malayan People's Army 10th Regiment Archives" <www.archivesportaleurope.net/ead-display/-/ead/pl/aicode/NL-AmISG/type/fa/ id/http_COLON__SLASH__SLASH_hdl.handle.net_SLASH_10622_SLASH_ARCH02799>.

[20] Yinghong Cheng "magong zongshuji Chen Ping de chuanqi rensheng" *Phoenix Weekly* (online ed, Hong Kong, 16 October 2013) (translation: "The Legendary Life of the Former Secretary General of the Malayan Communist Party, Chen Ping").

In July 1979, at the height of the ideological rift between China and Vietnam, Hoàng Văn Hoan, then Deputy Chairman of the Vietnamese National Assembly and former Vietnamese Ambassador to China, who had been known for his strong pro-Chinese sentiments, escaped to China when his plane from Hanoi to East Berlin stopped to refuel in Karachi, Pakistan.[21] It was only a few months after the Sino-Vietnam War in February 1979; Hoàng was well received by China and spent the rest of his life there.

China had to deal with large-scale refugee influxes for the first time during the Indochinese refugee crisis. In the late 1970s and early 1980s, China received more than 260,000 refugees from Vietnam, Cambodia and Laos.[22] About 98 per cent of them were ethnic Chinese from Vietnam.[23] Most of the Indochinese refugees were locally settled on state-owned farms in rural south and southwest China and are now well integrated into the local communities.[24]

Except for the Indochinese refugees who settled locally, the number of refugees in China remained under 100 until 2003. Muntarbhorn noted that non-Indochinese asylum seekers in China numbered fewer than fifty in 1990 and that "little is heard of their fate, but generally they have been treated on a case-by-case basis with the knowledge of UNHCR".[25] UNHCR noted that as of 1 January 1996, there were only forty-five non-Indochinese refugees in China, including twenty-eight Somalis, eight Burundians, four Rwandans, three Iranians, one Sri Lankan and one Sudanese.[26]

The number of non-Indochinese refugees registered with UNHCR in China (UNHCR refugees) began to increase notably from 2003 (Figure 2.1a). The increased curve in UNHCR refugees and asylum seekers roughly matches that of the growth in China's gross domestic

[21] Tai Sung An "Vietnam: the Defection of Hoàng Văn Hoan" (1980) 7 *Asian Affairs* 288 at 288.

[22] Shuying Liang *guoji nanmin fa* (Intellectual Property Publishing House, Beijing, 2009) at 272 (translation: *International Refugee Law*).

[23] Jing Song "Vietnamese refugees well settled in China, await citizenship" (10 May 2007) UNHCR <www.unhcr.org/464302994.html>.

[24] Tom Lam "The Exodus of Hoa Refugees from Vietnam and their Settlement in Guangxi: China's Refugee Settlement Strategies" (2000) 13 *Journal of Refugee Studies* 374 at 378.

[25] Vitit Muntarbhorn *The Status of Refugees in Asia* (Clarendon Press, Oxford, 1992) at 66.

[26] *Update on Regional Developments in Asia and Oceania* UN Doc EC/46/SC/CRP.44 (19 August 1996) at [74].

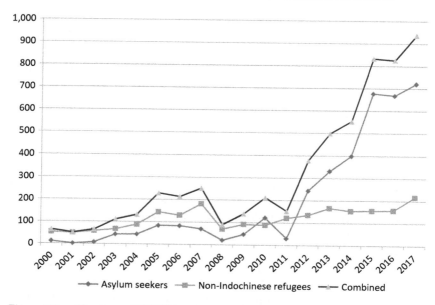

Figure 2.1a   Numbers of UNHCR refugees and asylum seekers in China, 2000–2017
Source: UNHCR Population Statistics Database <http://popstats.unhcr.org/en/persons_of_concern>

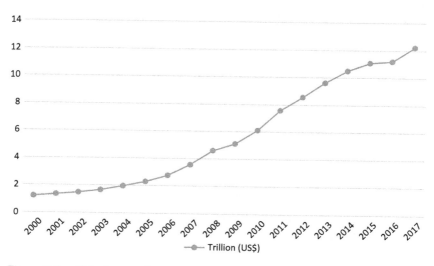

Figure 2.1b   China's gross domestic product, 2000–2017
Source: The World Bank "China" <https://data.worldbank.org/country/china>

product (GDP) (Figure 2.1b). As of mid-2018, 243 UNHCR refugees and 685 asylum seekers were living in China.[27]

The numbers shown in Figure 2.1a includes only refugees and asylum seekers to whom UNHCR had access; thus excluding North Korean escapees and displaced ethic Kokangs and Kachins from Myanmar to whom the Chinese authority has denied refugee status and blocked UNHCR's access. In the mid-1990s, when a severe famine hit North Korea, large numbers of North Koreans entered China in search of food. The famine eased in the late 1990s, but the exodus continues to the present day.[28] As the Chinese authority regards them as illegal economic migrants, North Korean escapees in China do not have legal status and have to live in hiding. Many of them have sought to travel clandestinely to a third country. There are no official statistics for the number of North Korean escapees in China. Estimates vary from 5,000 to 300,000 at different points.[29]

Displaced ethnic Kokangs from the Kokang Special Region in Shan State, Myanmar first fled to China's Yunnan province in 2009. On 8 August 2009, approximately 37,000 civilians flooded into Yunnan province,[30] as a result of a military stand-off and clashes between Myanmar Government troops (the Tatmadaw) and the Myanmar National Democratic Alliance Army (MNDAA), an ethnic Kokang military group that exercised actual control of the Kokang Special Region for decades.

---

[27] UNHCR "Mid-Year Trends 2018" (January 2019) <www.unhcr.org/en-au/statistics/unhcrstats/5c52ea084/mid-year-trends-2018.html>.

[28] For discussion on North Koreans' motivations to leave North Korea, see eg Stephan Haggard and Marcus Noland *Witness to Transformation: Refugee Insights into North Korea* (Peterson Institute for International Economics, Washington (DC), 2011) at 29; Human Rights Watch (HRW) *The Invisible Exodus: North Koreans in the People's Republic of China* (vol 14, no 8(C), November 2002) at 9 <www.hrw.org/reports/2002/northkorea/>; Rhoda Margesson, Emma Chanlett-Avery and Andorra Bruno *North Korean Refugees in China and Human Rights Issues: International Response and US Policy Options* (Congressional Research Service, Order Code RL34189, 26 September 2007) at 6 <www.fas.org/sgp/crs/row/RL34189.pdf>.

[29] James D Seymour *China: Background Paper on the Situation of North Koreans in China* (January 2005) at 15 <www.refworld.org/docid/4231d11d4.html>; Haggard and Noland, above n 28, at 2. See also eg Congressional-Executive Commission on China *2013 Annual Report* (10 October 2013) at 118 <www.cecc.gov/publications/annual-reports/2013-annual-report>.

[30] State Council Information Office of the People's Republic of China (SCIO) "Yunnan Sheng zhengfu jiu dangqian zhongmian bianjing jushi juxing xinwen fabuhui" (31 August 2009) on file with author (translation: "Yunnan Government Holds Press Conference on Situation on China–Myanmar Border"). The figure was given by the Chinese authority and includes both ethnic Kokang Myanmar nationals and Chinese nationals returning home from the Kokang Special Region.

They returned to Myanmar in early September 2009 as the conflict in the Kokang Special Region eased.[31] In February 2015 and in March 2017 respectively, the resumption of armed conflict between the Tatmadaw and the MNDAA in the Kokang Region drove about 60,000 and about 20,000 displaced civilians into China's Yunnan province.[32] As recently as August 2018, more than 10,000 displaced Kokangs remained in Yunnan, receiving little attention and assistance from within China or the international community.[33]

Like the ethnic Kokangs, displaced ethnic Kachins from Myanmar have fled to China's Yunnan province to escape armed conflicts. On 9 June 2011, armed conflict broke out between the Tatmadaw and the Kachin Independence Army (KIA), an ethnic Kachin military group that exercised actual control of many areas in Kachin State, Myanmar, forcing tens of thousands of ethnic Kachins to flee towards the Myanmar–China border.[34] While most of the displaced Kachins were accommodated in internally displaced persons (IDP) camps in Kachin State near the Chinese border, many of them crossed into the neighbouring Yunnan province of China. By late June 2012, about 10,000 displaced Kachins had entered Yunnan.[35] Since then, many displaced Kachins have continued

---

[31] Shan Nan "Beijing chaichu yingdi qianfan guogan nanmin" (1 September 2009) *Asia News* <www.asianews.it/news-zh/%E5%8C%97%E4%BA%AC%E6%8B%86%E9%99%9A4%E8%90%A5%E9%9C%B0%E9%81%A3%E8%BF%94%E6%9E%9C%E6%95%A2%E9%9A%BE%E6%B0%91-16205.html> (translation: "Beijing Removed Camps and Repatriated Kokang Refugees").

[32] Xinhua "Over 60,000 Myanmar refugee arrivals in China since conflict outbreak" (7 March 2015) <https://reliefweb.int/report/china/over-60000-myanmar-refugee-arrivals-china-conflict-outbreak>.

[33] Huagang Li "liuluo de guogan – 2018 zhongmian bianjing guogan nanmin shengcun kunjing" (26 Aug 2018) <www.kokang123.com/thread-37177-1-1.html> (translation: "Kokang in Exile – Difficult Life of Kokang Refugees on the Chinese-Myanmar Border in 2018").

[34] Kachin News "Kachin IDPs Reach over 40,000 due to Civil War in Northern Burma" (2 September 2011) <www.kachinnews.com/news/2040-kachin-idps-reach-over-40000-due-to-civil-war-in-northern-burma.html>.

[35] The New Humanitarian "Displaced Kachins in China in Need" (27 June 2012) <www.irinnews.org/news/2012/06/27>. The figure was provided by the IDPs and Refugees Relief Committee based in Laiza. HRW estimated that 7,000–10,000 displaced Kachins had entered China's Yunnan province (HRW *Isolated in Yunnan: Kachin Refugees from Burma in China's Yunnan Province* (June 2012) at 36). Others estimated that between 20,000 and 25,000 displaced Kachin fled to Yunnan (Chenggang Fan and Shiwei Shao "dao zhongguo qu: zhongmian bianjingxianshang de shiwan keqin nanmin" (17 January 2013) *Southern Weekly* <www.infzm.com/content/85250> (translation: "Go to China: The 100 Thousand Displaced Kachins on the China–Myanmar Border")).

to flee to and remain in Yunnan.[36] As of June 2019, the KIA and the Myanmar Government had not reached a new ceasefire agreement; clashes between the two parties continued,[37] and the inflow of displaced Kachins into Yunnan is likely to continue.

2.3   Chinese Public Perception of Refugees

Refugees and asylum have been sensitive topics in China in the past few decades.[38] Such sensitivity probably stems, in part, from the fact that China has been a refugee-producing country since 1949 and that Chinese refugee issues have been involved in some of the most politically sensitive events in China. The exodus of hundreds of thousands of Mainland Chinese residents to Hong Kong from 1949 to the early 1980s is seen by the Chinese authority as people voting with their feet against the Communist Government and was a forbidden topic in China for decades.[39] Following the Dalai Lama's departure from China to India in the 1950s, large numbers of Tibetans sought refuge in India and Nepal. After the Tiananmen Square incident in 1989, many Chinese students received asylum in the West. Since the mid-1990s, the potential geopolitical impacts relating to the status of North Korean escapees in China have also added to the political sensitivity of the topic of refugees.

As a result of the sensitivity of these topics, Chinese-language public information about refugees – be it refugees in China or Chinese nationals

---

[36] See eg Lianhe Zaobao "weibi zhanhuo mianbei pingmin fentao yunnan" (14 January 2017) <www.zaobao.com.sg/news/sea/story20170114-713261> (translation: "Escaping Warfare: Civilians from Northern Myanmar Fled to Yunnan Province"); Radio Free Asia "mianbei zhanhuo chongran dapi nanmin taowang zhongguo" (21 November 2016) <www.rfa.org/cantonese/news/myanmar-civilwar-11212016083635.html> (translation: "Armed Conflict Resumed in North Myanmar: Large Numbers of Refugees Fled to China"); Lawi Weng "Analysis: A Window Opens for China to Nudge Myanmar Army Forward on Peace Process" (23 November 2017) Irrawaddy <www.irrawaddy.com/news/burma/analysis-window-opens-china-nudge-myanmar-army-forward-peace-process.html>.

[37] Lawi Weng "Army Shelling Seen Signaling Start of New Offensive in Kachin, Shan States" (14 December 2017) Irrawaddy <www.irrawaddy.com/news/burma/army-shelling-seen-signaling-start-new-offensive-kachin-shan-states.html>.

[38] Liu, above n 9, at 91; Lihong Lan and Xiuxia Shi "Reflection on the Latest Progress in Chinese Legislation on International Migration" (2013) 8 *Frontiers of Law in China* 618 at 635.

[39] HX Liu "zhenjing zhongyang de 'dataogang' fengchao" *People's Daily Online* (1 August 2010) <www.people.com.cn/GB/198221/198819/198857/12308776.html> (translation: "'The Great Escape to Hong Kong' that Shocked the Chinese Central Government").

granted asylum in other countries – has traditionally been sparse. Besides, as the Indochinese refugees in China mainly live on state-owned farms in rural areas in six provinces and autonomous regions in southern China and UNHCR refugees in China have limited freedom of movement,[40] most Chinese will have little opportunity to meet a refugee.

In the past ten years, frequent influxes of displaced Kokangs and Kachins from Myanmar have received relatively more coverage from mainstream Chinese media and stirred up some discussion on China's refugee policy in newspapers and among netizens. In February 2012, the website of China's national television station published an article about acceptance of refugees and conducted an online survey on two questions: (1) "what is your view of refugees?", and (2) "what is your view of illegal immigrants (feifa rujingzhe)?"[41] Each question came with three options which readers were invited to choose from. That survey was one of the first, if not the first, of Chinese public opinion of refugees in China. More than three-quarters of the respondents agreed that refugees' human rights should be protected, although China's state interest should also be taken into consideration, and about 46 per cent of the respondents viewed illegal immigrants as refugees with some needs.[42] Although the number of responses to the survey was relatively small, the results of the survey indicate, to some extent, the sympathy for refugees and asylum seekers from members of the Chinese general public.

In the past few years, as refugee issues have become a top concern for the international community, there has been increasing international interest in further engaging China in international refugee affairs and, at the same time, the Chinese Government has demonstrated growing interest in playing a greater role in international refugee governance.[43] In May 2016, Amnesty International released a Refugee Welcome Index based on a survey it had commissioned. China was ranked as the most

---

[40] See Section 4.1.

[41] Hansen Li (ed) "jiena guoji nanmin: chuyu liyi, yuanyu daoyi" (27 February 2012) <http://news.cntv.cn/special/thinkagain/refugee/index.shtml> (translation: "Acceptance of International Refugees: Out of Interest, Originated in Humanity").

[42] This is based on the results as of 30 June 2019. The results of the survey can be viewed by clicking the "View Results" button at <http://news.cntv.cn/special/thinkagain/refugee/index.shtml>.

[43] See Lili Song "Strengthening Responsibility Sharing with South–South Cooperation: China's Role in the Global Compact on Refugees" (2019) 30(4) International Journal of Refugee Law 687.

welcoming country for refugees.[44] Of the 1,055 Chinese surveyed, 94 per cent would personally accept refugees into China and 86 per cent agreed that the Chinese Government should do more to help refugees fleeing war or persecution; 46 per cent were willing to open their homes to refugees.[45] The representativeness of the Amnesty International Survey with respect to the Chinese attitude towards refugees has been questioned.[46] A Chinese state-run newspaper, the *Global Times*, was quick to doubt the 2016 Amnesty International Refugee Welcome Index and started a survey on its own website on 19 May 2016. More than 90 per cent of respondents to the *Global Times* survey said they were not willing to open their homes to refugees, and nearly 80 per cent said they did not want to accept refugees in their city or as their neighbours.[47]

On World Refugee Day in 2017, UNHCR posted in Chinese on Sina Weibo, a popular Chinese blog platform, about a public film screening it hosted "to pay tribute to the world's 65.6 million people who are displaced and homeless, and to pay tribute to all those who support and care for the refugees".[48] UNHCR's goodwill Ambassador in China, actress and celebrity blogger Chen Yao, who had more than 80 million followers on Sina Weibo, shared UNHCR's post. Chinese netizens soon poured negative comments onto Yao, criticising her for supporting refugees from

---

[44] Amnesty International "Refugees Welcome Survey 2016 – The Results" (19 May 2016) <www.amnesty.org/en/latest/news/2016/05/refugees-welcome-survey-results-2016/>.

[45] Amnesty International and GlobeScan *Refugees Welcome Survey 2016: Views of Citizens Across 27 Countries – Topline Report from GlobeScan* (May 2016) <www.amnesty.org/download/Documents/ACT3041002016ENGLISH.PDF>.

[46] Gwynn Guilford and Hanna Kozlowska "Is China Really the Most Welcoming Country for Refugees?" (19 May 2016) <https://qz.com/687518/is-china-really-the-most-welcoming-country-for-refugees/>; Merriden Varrall and Zixin Wang "How China views the plight of refugees" (5 July 2017) <www.lowyinstitute.org/the-interpreter/how-china-views-plight-refugees>; Diandian Guo "Amnesty International Claims China Most Welcoming to Refugees, Chinese Netizens Don't Agree" (May 20, 2016) <www.whatsonweibo.com/amnesty-international-claims-china-welcoming-refugees-chinese-netizens-dont-agree/>.

[47] "zhongguren zui huanying nanmin diaocha zaozhiyi jiucheng wangyou buyuanyi jieshou nanmin" *Global Times* (online ed, 20 May 2016) <https://new.qq.com/cmsn/20160520013125> (translation: "Doubts Raised about Survey Ranking the Chinese the Most Welcoming to Refugees: Ninety Per Cent Netizens Unwilling to Accept Refugees"). As of June 2019, the online poll is open, but the results cannot be viewed: "*Global*'s Poll: Are You Willing to Accept Refugees at Home?" (19 May 2016) <http://opinion.huanqiu.com/survey/2016-05/8952416.html?agt=15422>.

[48] Manya Koeste "Chinese Netizens on World Refugee Day: 'Don't Come to China'" (23 June 2017) <www.whatsonweibo.com/chinese-netizens-world-refugee-day-dont-come-china/>.

the Middle East to come to China.[49] The topic "Should China accept refugees?" became one the week's biggest topics on Sina Weibo.[50] Yao eventually shut down the comment function on her blog and denied having called for acceptance of more refugees into China.[51] At the same time, an online survey on whether China should take in refugees opened on Sina Weibo and attracted 210,000 responses, more than 97 per cent of which opposed China taking in refugees.[52] A similar survey on Weibo in June 2018 yielded similar results.[53]

Chinese netizens opposing China accepting refugees cited reasons such as potential negative impacts on social stability, alleged links between refugees and Islam and terrorism, and the poverty that still exists in many parts of China.[54] Some also argued that if large numbers of refugees were to be resettled in China, their own generation's sacrifice as a result of the one-child policy would be rendered worthless.[55] Others echoed Chinese state media's argument that the West, which was to be blamed for the conflict that caused displacement in the Middle East, should take the refugees.[56]

In sum, current public sentiment in China towards refugees is, at best, mixed. Nevertheless, it should be pointed out that Chinese communities that have interacted with refugees and asylum seekers seem to have demonstrated notable sympathy and kindness towards them. The Indochinese refugees were generously hosted by local residents upon their arrival at the Chinese border and later were generally accepted by local communities when they were resettled.[57] Korean Chinese communities in northeast China have sheltered and assisted North Korean escapees in the border area despite disapproval from the Government.[58] The

---

[49] Zhang Hui "Famous People Are Quitting Their Social Media Accounts to Avoid Abuse from Netizens" (19 September 2018) <www.globaltimes.cn/content/1120244.shtml>.

[50] Koeste, above n 48.

[51] Koeste, above n 48.

[52] Max Walden "Online polls show 97pc of Chinese Reject Accepting Refugees" (22 June 2018) <https://asiancorrespondent.com/2018/06/online-polls-show-97pc-of-chinese-reject-accepting-refugees/>.

[53] Ruohan Li "97% of Chinese would reject receiving refugees: online poll" (20 June 2018) <www.globaltimes.cn/content/1107731.shtml#.W0PeY6hoR9Q.twitter>.

[54] Koeste, above n 48; Varrall and Wang, above n 46; Guo, above n 46.

[55] Koeste, above n 48.

[56] Li, above n 53.

[57] See Liang, above n 22, at 277.

[58] See eg Haggard and Noland, above n 28, at 34; Ju Hui Judy Han "Beyond Safe Haven: A Critique of Christian Custody of North Korean Migrants in China" (2013) 45 *Critical Asian Studies* 533; Seymour, above n 29, at 15.

displaced Kokangs were well received by residents in China's Yunnan province; many Chinese nationals not only called for support to the displaced Kokangs but also volunteered at the temporary camps set up for them.[59] Chinese civilians from Yunnan province and other parts of China also provided accommodation, food and clothes to the displaced Kachins and helped Kachin community leaders to negotiate with Chinese Government officials to optimise the displaced Kachins' chances of staying in China.[60]

---

[59] Piaobotanggula "guogan, jinye wumian weini qidao" (28 August 2009) <http://bbs .tianya.cn/post-news-141112-1.shtml> (translation: "Kokang, Praying for You in This Sleepless Night"); Shanghai Jiaotong University "jiaoda zhiyuanzhe zai Yunnan bianchun anquan duguo guogan zhanshi" (24 September 2009) <http://topics.sjtu.edu.cn/newsnet/ shownews.php?id=22669> (translation: "Jiaotong University Volunteers Survived Kokang War").

[60] Interviews conducted by the author (April 2013).

The Framework: Law, Policy and Institutions

3.1 Legal Framework for Refugee Protection in China

3.1.1 Introduction

China does not have a Western-style separation of powers, where the legislative, executive and judicial branches stand independently to restrain each other. In China, the legislative power is shared by more than one organ.[1] The National People's Congress (NPC) is the highest legislative organ in China. It is vested with the authority to amend the Constitution and to establish and amend basic laws governing criminal offences, civil affairs, the state organs and other matters in China.[2] The People's Congresses at local level are authorised to enact local legislation. The State Council is the Central Government of China. It is empowered to formulate administrative regulations. Governments at local level are authorised to make local regulations.

According to the 2000 Chinese Law on Legislation,[3] Chinese legislation can be divided into three tiers.[4] Top-tier legislation consists of laws (*falü*) made by the NPC or its Standing Committee;[5] second-tier legislation consists of administrative regulations (*xingzheng fagui*) made by the State Council;[6] and third-tier legislation includes local regulations

---

[1] Ronald Keith and Zhiqiu Lin "Judicial Interpretation of China's Supreme People's Court as 'Secondary Law' with Special Reference to Criminal Law" (2009) 23 *China Information* 223 at 246; China Net "China's Current Legislation Structure" (2003) <www.china.org.cn/english/kuaixun/76212.htm>.

[2] Constitution of the People's Republic of China 1982, arts 62(1) and (3). An English version of the 1982 Constitution is available at <www.npc.gov.cn/englishnpc/Constitution/node_2825.htm>.

[3] The official English version of the 2000 Chinese Legislation Law is available at <www.npc.gov.cn/englishnpc/Law/2007-12/11/content_1383554.htm>.

[4] Art 79.

[5] Art 7.

[6] Art 56.

(*difangxing fagui*),[7] autonomous regulations (*zizhi tiaoli*), separate regulations (*danxing tiaoli*)[8] and rules (*guizhang*).[9] In this book, unless otherwise indicated or implied by the context, the term Chinese law refers to Chinese legislation in general rather than just the laws made by the State Council.

China's legal system is generally based on a civil law model. In theory, a decision of a Chinese court will not bind another Chinese court, but in practice, judges of lower courts usually try to follow the interpretations of the law decided by the Supreme People's Court.[10] From time to time, the Supreme People's Court, the highest court in China, issues so-called judicial interpretations, which contain the Supreme People's Court's opinion on legal matters. These judicial explanations are generally considered to serve as a source of law,[11] and are hence binding on lower courts. Until 2013, Chinese courts, including the Supreme People's Court, generally did not publish their decisions. The Supreme People's Court reports its work to the NPC and its Standing Committee and is generally considered to be non-independent.[12]

---

[7] The People's Congress or its Standing Committee at provincial and municipal levels are authorised to make local regulations (art 63).

[8] The People's Congresses of autonomous regions at provincial, prefectural or county level are authorised to formulate autonomous regulations and separate regulations (art 66). There are five autonomous regions at the provincial level, namely the Guangxi Zhuang Autonomous Region, the Tibet Autonomous Region, the Xinjiang Uighur Autonomous Region, the Inner Mongolia Autonomous Region and the Ningxia Hui Autonomous Region.

[9] Ministries and Commissions of the State Council, the People's Bank of China, the State Audit Administration and the other organs endowed with administrative functions directly under the State Council are authorised to formulate rules (art 71).

[10] Susanna Fischer "A Brief Introduction to the Legal System of China" (2002) <http://faculty.cua.edu/fischer/ComparativeLaw2002/bauer/China-main.htm>.

[11] See eg Keith and Lin, above n 1, at 224; Jinrong Wang "On the Judicial Interpretation of China's Supreme People's Court" (1995) 3 *China L* 9, cited in Li Wei "Judicial Interpretation in China" (1997) 5 *Willamette Journal of International Law and Dispute Resolution* 87 at 87, n 1; Shibing Cao "The Legal Status of Decisions and Judicial Interpretations of the Supreme Court of China" (2008) 3(1) *Frontiers of Law in China* 1 at 2. Both Wang and Cao were working for the Supreme Court of China when they wrote their articles.

[12] The Supreme People's Court of China "Introduction" (16 July 2017) <http://english.court.gov.cn/2015-07/16/content_21299713.htm>. For discussion about Chinese judicial independence, see Randall Peerenboom (ed) *Judicial Independence in China: Lessons for Global Rule of Law Promotion* (Cambridge University Press, Cambridge, 2009); Ting Gong "Dependent judiciary and unaccountable judges: Judicial corruption in contemporary China" (2004) 4(2) *China Review* 33; United States Congressional-Executive Commission on China "Judicial Independence in the PRC" <www.cecc.gov/judicial-independence-in-the-prc>.

China has ratified most of the core human rights treaties, but has not ratified the International Covenant on Civil and Political Rights (ICCPR), which it signed in 1998. Scholars have noted that China is slow in embracing traditional international human rights values.[13] Although the Chinese Government has made notable efforts to incorporate international human rights standards into its domestic human rights law,[14] effective enforcement of these human rights standards in China remains a challenge in various ways.[15]

Prior to China's reform and opening-up in 1979, the law had often been neglected or abused for decades, and the governance of the country had relied heavily on the policy of the Chinese Communist Party, especially during the Cultural Revolution (1966–1976). For example, the Chinese Ministry of Justice was dismantled in 1959 and was re-established only in 1979. In the past few decades, China has made notable progress in moving away from the primarily "rule of man" governance approach of traditional China and Maoist China, and is gradually developing elements of a rule of law society.[16] However, China has yet to fully establish a rule of law system, in which law acts to impose

---

[13] See Sonya Sceats and Shaun Breslin, *China and the International Human Rights System* (Chatham House, London, October 2012) <www.chathamhouse.org/sites/default/files/public/Research/International%20Law/r1012_sceatsbreslin.pdf>; Ted Piccone *China's Long Game on Human Rights at the United Nations* (The Brookings Institute, Washington, 2018) <www.brookings.edu/wp-content/uploads/2018/09/FP_20181009_china_human_rights.pdf>; Ann Kent, *China, the United Nations, and Human Rights: The Limits of Compliance* (University of Pennsylvania Press, Philadelphia, 1999).

[14] See Lingliang Zeng, *guoji renquan guoyue de shishi he zhongguo de shijian* (Wuhan University Press, Wuhan, 2015) (translation: *Internatonal Human Rights Treaties and China's Practice*).

[15] Ming Wan "Human Rights Lawmaking in China: Domestic Politics, International Law, and International Politics" (2007) 29(3) *Human Rights Quarterly* 727; Sanzhuan Guo "Implementation of Human Rights Treaties by Chinese Courts: Problems and Prospects" (2009) 8(1) *Chinese Journal of International Law* 161; Ahl, Björn "Exploring Ways of Implementing International Human Rights Treaties in China" (2010) 28(3) *Netherlands Quarterly of Human Rights*, September 361; Na Jiang *China and International Human Rights: Harsh Punishments in the Context of the International Covenant on Civil and Political Rights* (Springer, Berlin, 2014); Eva Pils *China's Human Rights Lawyers: Advocacy and Resistance* (Routledge, Oxon, 2014); Eric Kolodner "Religious Rights in China: A Comparison of International Human Rights Law and Chinese Domestic Legislation" (1994) 16(3) *Human Rights Quarterly* 455.

[16] Jamie P. Horsley "The Rule of Law in China Incremental Progress" in C. Fred Bergsten and others (eds) *The China Balance Sheet in 2007 and Beyond* (Center for Strategic and International Studies and the Peterson Institute for International Economics, Washington, 2007) 93 at 94.

meaningful restraints on the Government and private power rather than being used as a tool as the Government sees fit.[17] It is in this context that the discussion in the rest of this chapter should be understood.

3.1.2 The Status of the Refugee Convention and Protocol in China

3.1.2.1   China's Accession to the Refugee Convention and Protocol

China acceded to both the Refugee Convention and the Refugee Protocol on 24 September 1982.[18] It made reservations on the following articles: (1) the latter half of art 14 of the Refugee Convention, which concerns artistic rights and industrial property,[19] (2) art 16(3) of the Refugee Convention, which concerns access to courts,[20] and (3) art 4 of the Refugee Protocol, which concerns settlement of disputes.[21]

China was one of the first Asian state parties to these key legal instruments on refugee protection.[22] It was also one of the first communist countries to accede to these instruments.[23] The following historical

---

[17] See generally Randall Peerenboom *China's Long March toward Rule of Law* (Cambridge University Press, Cambridge, 2002); Weifang He *In the Name of Justice: Striving for the Rule of Law in China* (The Brookings Institution, Washington, 2012); Wei Pan "Toward a consultative rule of law regime in China" (2003) 12(34) *Journal of Contemporary China* 3; Eric W Orts "The rule of law in China" (2001) 34 *Vanderbilt Journal of Transnational Law* 43; Karen Turner, James Feinerman and R Kent Guy (eds) *The Limits of the Rule of Law in China* (University of Washington Press, Washington, 2015); Mary Gallagher "Mobilizing the Law in China: 'Informed Disenchantment' and the Development of Legal Consciousness" (2006) 40(4) *Law and Society Review* 783.

[18] Convention relating to the Status of Refugees 189 UNTS 137 (opened for signature 28 July 1951, entered into force 22 April 1954); Protocol relating to the Status of Refugees 606 UNTS 267 (opened for signature 31 January 1967, entered into force 4 October 1967).

[19] United Nations Treaty Collection "Convention relating to the Status of Refugees" <https://treaties.un.org/Pages/ViewDetailsII.aspx?src=TREATY&mtdsg_no=V-2&chapter=5&Temp=mtdsg2&clang=_en>.

[20] United Nations Treaty Collection, above n 19.

[21] United Nations Treaty Collection "Protocol relating to the Status of Refugees" <https://treaties.un.org/Pages/ViewDetails.aspx?src=IND&mtdsg_no=V-5&chapter=5&clang=_en>.

[22] Japan acceded to the Convention and Protocol in 1981 and 1982 respectively. The Philippines acceded to both instruments in 1981. UNHCR Bureau for Asia and the Pacific, *Fact Sheet* (September 2014) at 7, available at <www.unhcr.org/5000139a9.pdf>.

[23] Jerzy Sztucki "Who is a Refugee? The Convention Definition: Universal or Obsolete?" in Frances Nicholson and Patrick Twomey (eds) *Refugee Rights and Realities* (Cambridge University Press, Cambridge, 1999) at 55.

events need to be highlighted against the background of China's accession to the Refugee Convention and Protocol. First, in late 1978 and early 1979, China adopted a reform and opening-up policy. As a result, the Chinese Government desired to integrate into the international community, and there was a revival of interest in international law in China. In the early 1980s, China ratified a series of international treaties. Of the twenty-seven human rights instruments to which China was a party in 2012, eight were ratified or acceded to between 1981 and 1984, including the Refugee Convention and Protocol.[24] It is likely that China's accession to the Refugee Convention and Protocol was partly driven by Beijing's desire to integrate into the international community.

Second, prior to 1971, the State of China was represented by Taiwan (the Republic of China) at the UN and China was excluded from the UN. As a result, China was not involved in the drafting of the Refugee Convention or the Refugee Protocol. Even after China's entry into the UN in 1971, China, which was carrying out the Cultural Revolution (1966–1976), refrained from actively participating in activities of UNHCR and a few other UN bodies for ideological reasons until the late 1970s.[25]

The Indochinese refugee influx into China beginning in 1978 proved a crucial opportunity for UNHCR to engage with China, and UNHCR played a key role in introducing China to the international refugee protection regime. In 1978, when large numbers of refugees were arriving from Vietnam, Chinese officials did not even know "what a refugee is".[26] In response to the Vietnamese refugee influx, China agreed for UNHCR to establish a task office in Beijing and provide assistance to Indochinese refugees in China. On 1 September 1979, the Chinese Minister of Foreign Affairs wrote in a reply to UNHCR that China agreed to "consider

---

[24] Chinese State Council Information Office "2012 zhongguo renquan shiye de jinzhan" (14 May 2012) <http://news.xinhuanet.com/politics/2013-05/14/c_115758619.htm> (translation: "2012 Progress of Human Rights in China"); China Human Rights Studies Association "zhongguo jiaru le naxie guoji renquan gongyue he yidingshu" (27 March 2006) <http://theory.people.com.cn/GB/49150/49152/4239175.html> (translation: "Which International Human Rights Treaties and Protocols Has China Ratified?").

[25] Qing Ling *cong Yan'an dao lianheguo* (Fujian People's Press, Fuzhou, 2008) at 173 and 178 (translation: *From Yan'an to the United Nations*) cited in Jiancheng Zheng "From Nanqiao to Refugee: The Formation of China's Policy toward Indochinese Refugees, 1978–1979" (PhD Thesis, Ji'nan University, 2015) at 88.

[26] Jing Zhang "Zhongguo weishenme bushe nanminying" *China Society Magazine* (May 2002) 58 at 58 (translation: "Why China Did Not Establish Refugee Camps").

carefully" the invitation from UNHCR to become a party to the Refugee Convention and Protocol.[27]

Former director of UNHCR's Regional Bureau for Asia and Oceania Alexander Casella, who was one of the earliest staff at UNHCR's Beijing Office, recalled discussing with and persuading the Chinese to accede to the instruments:[28]

> Over the previous year [1980] I had discussed at length with the Chinese the subject of them joining the Refugee Conventions and their constant reply was "why", to which I would answer "why not". My main argument was that they had nothing to lose.

Casella's "main selling point" was that the obligations they entailed could be easily circumvented and all the signatories did so with gusto.[29] He also argued that as all the Western countries had adhered to them and as all Soviet bloc countries were opposed to them on principle, adhesion by China would be a good cosmetic move that would further illustrate how far they were from the Soviet system.[30] He further noted that China, as it was in the early 1980s, was unlikely to receive mass influxes of refugees.[31] According to Casella:[32]

> I [Casella] did not expect anything to come from these exchanges and was therefore totally caught by surprise when ... as if it was a matter of no great importance, one of the Chinese in our group turned to [UN High Commissioner for Refugees] Hartling and mentioned off-hand that China had decided to adhere to the 1951 Refugee Conventions. I saw Hartling's face light up. As far as refugee law was concerned, he had made history.

Whatever political calculations prompted China's decision to accede to the Refugee Convention and Protocol, it is most likely that the Chinese leadership at that time did not foresee that China, a Third World communist country continuously producing large numbers of refugees since its founding in 1949, would face increasing refugee issues in just twenty years' time.

---

[27] Chinese State Council *Public Announcement 1982 NO14 Proposal on Reviewing, Discussing the Decision to accede to the Convention relating to the Status of Refugees and the Protocol relating to the Status of Refugee* (10 June 1982).

[28] Alexander Casella *Breaking the Rules* (Editions du Tricorne, Geneva, 2011) at 222.

[29] At 222.

[30] At 222.

[31] At 223.

[32] At 222.

3.1.2.2   The Status of the Refugee Convention
and Protocol in China

In theory, by acceding to the Refugee Convention and Protocol, China is bound by the provisions of these instruments; it also has the obligation to perform the Refugee Convention and Protocol in good faith according to the principle of *pacta sunt servanda* enshrined in art 26 of the 1969 Vienna Convention on the Law of Treaties,[33] to which China is a party. In reality, generally speaking, a treaty can only be enforced domestically in China after the adoption of a Chinese law transforming the treaty into domestic Chinese law or authorising direct application of the treaty in China.[34] The Chinese Constitution is silent on the legal status of international treaties ratified by China within the Chinese domestic legal system; no consensus has emerged among jurists and scholars on the subject.[35] According to Judge Hanqin Xue of the International Court of Justice and Qian Jin, strictly speaking, treaties ratified by China do not automatically become part of Chinese domestic law and therefore do not automatically become enforceable in China.[36]

As of June 2019, China has incorporated few provisions of the Refugee Convention and Protocol into its domestic law and has not established a national mechanism for RSD. Domestic Chinese law contains no provisions on who qualifies as a refugee, which organisation or government body is responsible for RSD, or how an application for refugee status can be made.

Since very few provisions of the Refugee Convention and Protocol have been incorporated into Chinese law and direct application of these two instruments has not been authorised by any Chinese law, almost

---

[33] Vienna Convention on the Law of Treaties 1155 UNTS 331 (opened for signature 23 May 1969, entered into force 27 January 1980.

[34] Hanqin Xue and Qian Jin "International Treaties in the Chinese Domestic Legal System" (2009) 8(2) *Chinese Journal of International Law* 299 at 322; Guoqing Jiang "guojifa yu guojitiaoyue de jigewenti" (29 April 2000) <www.npc.gov.cn/npc/xinwen/2000-04/29/content_1459914.htm> (translation: "Several Issues of International Law and International Treaties"). The exceptions are bilateral cooperation agreements and memoranda of understanding between governments, which qualify as international treaties under Chinese law.

[35] For discussions on domestic implementation of treaties in China, see eg Xue and Jin, above n 34, at 300; Sanzhuan Guo "Implementation of Human Rights Treaties by Chinese Courts: Problems and Prospects" (2009) 8(1) *Chinese Journal of International Law* 161; Yongwei Liu "guoji tiaoyue zai zhongguo shiyong xinlun" (2007) 2 *Jurists Review* 143 (translation: "New Thoughts on Application of International Treaties in China").

[36] Xue and Jin, above n 34.

none of the provisions of the Refugee Convention and Protocol is enforceable in China. As a result, refugees generally are not able to bring a case to a Chinese court to enforce the provisions of the Refugee Convention and Protocol.

Despite the lack of relevant national legislation, the Chinese Government has repeatedly asserted that it has duly implemented the Refugee Convention and Protocol. For example, in a 2008 report to the UN, it claimed that "China has been implementing the convention [relating to the Status of Refugees] in real earnest".[37] In another report to the UN in 2010, it stated that:[38]

> China is a state party to the 1951 Convention relating to the Status of Refugees and the 1967 Protocol relating to the Status of Refugees . . . [It] has provided international protection to refugees within its capacity, guaranteed their legitimate rights and interests to the greatest extent . . .

In fact, in the first decade following China's accession to the Refugee Convention and Protocol, the Chinese authority did not seem to show a good understanding of or adequate respect for the provisions of these instruments. For example, in 1989, seven years after China's accession to the Refugee Convention and Protocol, a provincial office submitted an enquiry to the Chinese Ministry of Public Security (MPS) regarding the Indochinese refugees' eligibility for Chinese identity cards. In the enquiry, the provincial office referred to the Vietnamese refugees as *guiguo nanmin*, which means "refugees who returned to China", seemingly confusing the concept of refugees and that of overseas Chinese nationals returning to China.[39] In its reply, the MPS stated:[40]

---

[37] People's Republic of China *10th to 13th Periodic Reports on the Implementation of the International Convention on the Elimination of All Forms of Racial Discrimination* UN Doc CERD/C/CHN/13 (24 June 2008) at [142].

[38] Committee on Economic, Social and Cultural Rights *Implementation of the International Covenant on Economic, Social and Cultural Rights: Second periodic reports submitted by States parties under articles 16 and 17 of the Covenant – China* UN Doc E/C.12/CHN/2 (6 July 2012) at [23].

[39] Between the 1950s and 1970s, due to anti-Chinese movements in Malaysia, Indonesia and India, several waves of overseas Chinese nationals returned from those countries on ships sent by the Chinese Government to collect them. Most Indochinese refugees in China ethnic Chinese, and they received treatment on par with those Chinese nationals returning from Indonesia and India. This is probably the cause of the Jiangxi Office's confusion.

[40] Ministry of Public Security (MPS) *Security Management Bureau Reply to Jiangxi Province Resident ID Card Issuance Office's Enquiry about Whether to Issue ID Card to Refugees Returning to China* 1989 (GONGSAN[1989]NO350).

> Regarding people who reside in China as a "refugee", their nationality should be identified first. Refugees should refer to persons who, due to reasons of race, politics and religion, etc., stay outside of their country of origin, and are unable or unwilling to receive protection from that country, including stateless persons who, due to such reasons, are unable to stay in their country of habitual residence, and unable or unwilling to return to that country.

In comparison, the Refugee Convention defines a refugee as any person who:[41]

> As a result of events occurring before 1 January 1951 and owing to well-founded fear of being persecuted for reasons of race, religion, nationality, membership of a particular social group or political opinion, is outside the country of his nationality and is unable or, owing to such fear, is unwilling to avail himself of the protection of that country; or who, not having a nationality and being outside the country of his former habitual residence as a result of such events, is unable or, owing to such fear, is unwilling to return to it.

The definition of a "refugee" given by the MPS omitted the requirement of well-founded fear for persecution, which is central to the definition of a refugee under the Refugee Convention. In addition, the reply did not mention membership of a particular social group, which is a ground for fear of persecution recognised in the Convention refugee definition, and used the term "politics" (*zhengzhi*) rather than "political opinion" (*zhengzhi jianjie*) as a ground for refugee status.

In 1992, the MPS issued a notice on handling aliens illegally entering or overstaying in China (1992 Notice) to provincial public security authorities.[42] The 1992 Notice mentioned that the number of Pakistanis, Iranians and Afghans overstaying in China was increasing year by year and that most of these people, "using the excuse of escaping wars, applied for refugee status with UNHCR's office in China, and after having registered with UNHCR, lived on charity provided by UNHCR".[43] The Notice required local-level public security authorities to repatriate all aliens who entered illegally or were overstaying in China "regardless of

---

[41] Refugee Convention, above n 18, art 1A(2).
[42] MPS *Notice on Taking Legal Actions Against Illegal Entry and Illegal Stay of Aliens* (GONGTONGZI [1992] NO39, 9 April 1992).
[43] 1992 Notice, above n 42.

whether they have registered with UNHCR".[44] In 1992, China repatriated 172 aliens who allegedly entered China illegally or were overstaying in China, including more than thirty UNHCR refugees.[45] Before the 2008 Olympic Games in Beijing, China again deported fifteen UNHCR refugees,[46] over which UNHCR issued a statement of concern.[47]

3.1.3   The Chinese Constitution

The concept of asylum has been included in all five constitutional documents of the People's Republic of China. The first constitutional document of the People's Republic of China, the 1949 Common Program of the Chinese People's Political Consultative Conference (1949 Common Program),[48] provided in art 60 that:

> The People's Republic of China should grant the right of residence to foreigners who are persecuted by the government of their home country because of their participation in peace and democracy movements for the interest of the people and seek asylum in China.

Article 99 of the 1954 Constitution stipulated that:

> The People's Republic of China grants the right of residence to any foreigner who is persecuted because of her support for justice, participation in peace movements or conduct of scientific work.

Cohen and Chiu noted that art 99 of the 1954 Chinese Constitution was similar to that contained in the constitutions of the Soviet Union and the East European socialist countries.[49] Similar provisions can be found in

---

[44] 1992 Notice, above n 42.

[45] Chengdu Liu "dui gongan churujing guanli bumen jiaqiang nanmin guanli de jidian sikao" (2000) 4 *Journal of Beijing People's Police College* 46 at 47 (translation: "Several Thoughts on Improving Refugee Administration by Border Exit and Entry Administration Department of Public Security System").

[46] Stephanie Nebehay "China deports refugees ahead of Olympics: UN" (9 April 2008) <www.reuters.com/article/2008/04/08/us-china-un-refugees-idUSL086328120080408>; UNHCR "China: Concerns over deportation" (8 April 2008) <www.unhcr.org/47fb4ed42.html>.

[47] UNHCR, above n 46.

[48] The 1949 Common Program of the Chinese People's Political Consultative Conference served as an interim Constitution. Since 1949, four Constitutions have been promulgated by the People's Republic of China successively on 20 September 1954, 17 January 1975, 5 March 1978 and 4 December 1982.

[49] Jerome Alan Cohen and Hungdah Chiu *People's China and International Law: A Documentary Study* (Princeton University, Princeton, 1974) vol 1 at 508.

art 29 of the 1975 Constitution and art 59 of the 1978 Constitution, both of which provided that:

> The People's Republic of China grants the right of residence to any foreigner who is persecuted because of her support for justice, participation in revolutionary movements or conduct of scientific work.

The Constitution currently in force was promulgated on 4 December 1982, about a month after China's accession to the Refugee Convention and Protocol. Article 32(2) of the 1982 Constitution provides that "[t]he People's Republic of China may grant asylum to foreigners who request it for political reasons". Article 32(2) of the 1982 Constitution is the only existing provision in Chinese domestic law that contains criteria for granting asylum in China,[50] and the Chinese Government and Chinese scholars have referred to it as a legal ground for China's admission of refugees.[51]

Compared to the provisions in previous Chinese constitutional documents, art 32(2) of the 1982 Constitution is different in a few ways. First, the notion of persecution, which was mentioned in corresponding articles in all previous Chinese constitutional documents, is absent from art 32(2) of the 1982 Constitution. Second, unlike all previous Chinese constitutional documents, which gave relatively specific descriptions of the reasons for which the foreigner could receive asylum, the 1982 Constitution mentioned "political reasons" (*zhengzhi yuanyin*) as the only ground for a foreigner's request for asylum. Third, while the 1949 Common Program stated that China "should grant" the right of residence to persecuted foreigners and the 1954, 1975 and 1978 Constitutions provided that China "grants the right of residence" to persecuted

---

[50] There was a similar provision in the 1985 Law on Administration of Entry and Exit of Aliens, which was replaced by the 2012 Law on Exit and Entry Administration on 1 July 2013.

[51] See eg UN Committee on the Elimination of Discrimination against Women (UNCEDW) *Consideration of Reports Submitted by States Parties under Article 18 of the Convention on the Elimination of All Forms of Discrimination against Women: Combined Seventh and Eighth Periodic Report of States Parties – China* UN Doc CEDAW/C/CHN/7-8 (17 January 2013) at [224]; Shuying Liang *guoji nanmin fa* (Intellectual Property Publishing House, Beijing, 2009) at 259 (translation: *International Refugee Law*); Guofu Liu *zhongguo nanminfa* (World Affairs Press, Beijing, 2015) at 4 (translation: *Chinese Refugee Law*); Vitit Muntarbhorn *The Status of Refugees in Asia* (Clarendon Press, Oxford, 1992) at 61; Yuanjun Wang "guanyu jianli woguo nanmin baohu falv zhidu de jidian sikao" (2005) 12 *Public Security Research* 46 at 46 (translation: "Several Thoughts on Establishment of Refugee Protection Mechanism in China"); Liu, above n 45, at 46.

foreigners, the 1982 Constitution only stipulates that China "may grant" asylum. This seems to show a decreasing commitment of the Chinese Government to provide asylum to aliens in its constitutional documents from 1949 to 1982.

More importantly, there is a gap between art 32(2) of the 1982 Constitution and the definition of a refugee under the Refugee Convention and Protocol. Despite the fact that the 1982 Constitution was promulgated after China's accession to the Refugee Convention and Protocol and that China began to consider acceding these two instruments in 1979, art 32 (2) does not seem to take into consideration the Convention refugee definition. On the one hand, whereas the requirement of persecution is essential to the Convention refugee definition, art 32(2) of the 1982 Constitution removes the requirement of persecution, even though it was included in asylum clauses in earlier Chinese constitutional documents.[52] In this sense, art 32(2) could be seen as less restrictive than the Convention refugee definition.

On the other hand, while the Convention refugee definition recognises race, nationality, religion, political opinion and membership of a particular social group as grounds for a refugee's fear of persecution, the only ground for requesting asylum under art 32(2) of the 1982 Constitution is "political reasons". The term "political reasons" is not defined in the 1982 Constitution. As of June 2019, no definition of the term can be found in published Chinese laws or judicial decisions.

A few examples of "political reasons" have been given in Chinese administrative and judicial documents. According to the Ministry of Finance 2007 Interim Implementation Rules for Management of State-Owned Assets by Institutes Operating Abroad, "political reasons" include armed conflicts and riots in the host country and bilateral relations between China and the host country.[53] In a 1985 judicial explanation, the People's Supreme Court of China mentioned that the claimant was unable to claim her property right for "political reasons", referring to the fact that her father-in-law was suppressed during the land reform and

---

[52] Public information provides little explanation as to why the element of persecution was removed from art 32(2) of the 1982 Constitution. The element was included in the asylum article in all previous Chinese constitutional documents.

[53] *The People's Republic of China Ministry of Finance Interim Implementation Rules for Management of State-owned Assets by Institutes Functioning Abroad* (CAIXING [2007]NO559), art 26. A Chinese version of the Rules is available at <www.mof.gov .cn/zhengwuxinxi/caizhengwengao/caizhengbuwengao2008/caizhengbuwengao20082/ 200805/t20080519_29058.html>.

her husband was put through a labour camp.[54] Asset management and real property rights are legal disciplines considerably different from asylum and immigration law or human rights law. Therefore, the examples of "political reasons" given in these two documents may be of relatively modest significance to the interpretation of art 32 of the 1982 Constitution.

It may be helpful to look at the ordinary meaning of the term "political reasons" in Chinese language. Generally, "political reasons" can be understood as any reason relating to politics. The *Contemporary Chinese Language Dictionary*, an authoritative Chinese language dictionary, defines the term "politics" (*zhengzhi*) as activities of classes, political parties, social groups and individuals in domestic and international relations.[55] Chengdu Liu from the Beijing Public Security Bureau's Border Exit and Entry Sector suggested in his article published in the *Journal of Beijing People's Police College* that political asylum may be given to the following types of persons: (1) high-level state officials; (2) high-level officials of the UN, other internal organisations and foreign NGOs; (3) employees of foreign embassies; (4) influential leaders of opposite parties, politicians and well-known figures; (5) science and technology experts, famous scholars, military personnel and social activists; (6) persons who have made outstanding contribution to China's scientific research, economic development or cultural exchange; and (7) the family and relatives of the above and other foreigners.[56]

In light of the above, the term "political reasons" under art 32 of the 1982 Constitution seems to leave considerable room for interpretation. If interpreted broadly, art 32 may be capable of covering people fleeing persecution for reasons of the five grounds mentioned in the Convention refugee definition. However, if interpreted restrictively, its coverage could be as narrow as suggested by Liu from the Beijing Public Security Bureau.

---

[54] The Supreme People's Court of China *Reply regarding the Real Estate Dispute between Fang Yishun, Fang Shengeng and the Central Production Team of Hengfeng Village, Wufeng Region, Qimen County* (28 March 1985), available at <www.law-lib.com/law/law_view.asp?id=3137>.

[55] Chinese Academy of Social Science Institute of Linguistics Dictionary Department *xiandai hanyu cidian* (The Commercial Press, Beijing, 1996) at 1609 (translation: *Contemporary Chinese Language Dictionary*). When used in conjunction with another noun, the Chinese term *zhengzhi* can also mean 'political', functioning as an adjective. In art 32 (2) of the 1982 Constitution, the term 'political reasons' is *zhengzhi yuanyin* in Chinese, *yuanyin* meaning 'reason(s)'.

[56] Liu, above n 45, at 48.

There is no evidence that art 32(2) of the 1982 Constitution has been litigated before Chinese courts. As rightly noted by Kellogg, the provisions of the Chinese Constitution are more or less ignored and the Chinese Constitution has rarely been litigated.[57] The Chinese Constitution primarily concerns itself with state organisational structure rather than the protection of fundamental rights of individuals.[58] Indeed, art 32(2) essentially provides only for the power of the Chinese authority to grant asylum, not the right of aliens to access asylum in China. Further, the right of citizens or organisations to challenge the constitutionality of government actions is not mentioned in the 1982 Constitution. However, emerging constitutional cases in China show that the Chinese Constitution is litigable,[59] and it remains to be seen whether future development in constitutional litigation in China will open up opportunities for improving refugee rights in China through a constitutional case grounded in art 32(2).

3.1.4   The Law on Exit and Entry Administration

Generally speaking, a state's immigration law is of particular relevance to refugee protection in that state. At the time of writing, China does not have a codified immigration law. Chinese immigration rules are scattered among a number of laws and regulations.[60] Prior to 1 July 2013, China regulated the exit and entry of aliens in the 1985 Law on Administration of the Entry and Exit of Aliens (Alien Exit–Entry Law).[61] The Alien Entry–Exit Law, which was promulgated on 22 November 1985 by the Standing Committee of the NPC and entered into force on 1 February 1986, stated in art 15: "Aliens who seek asylum for political reasons shall be permitted to reside in China upon approval by the competent authorities of the Chinese Government". Prior to 1 July 2013, this article,

---

[57] See eg Thomas E Kellogg "Constitutionalism with Chinese characteristics? Constitutional development and civil litigation in China" (2009) 7(2) *ICON* 215.

[58] Jianfu Chen "Constitutional Judicialisation and Popular Constitutionalism in China: Are We There Yet?" in Guanghua Yu (ed) *The Development of the Chinese Legal System* (Routledge, Oxon, 2011) 3 at 4.

[59] See eg Keith Hand "Resolving Constitutional Disputes in Contemporary China" (2011) 7 *University of Pennsylvania East Asia Law Review* 51.

[60] See generally Guofu Liu *Chinese Immigration Law* (Ashgate, Farnham (UK), 2011).

[61] The official English translation is available at <http://newyork.china-consulate.org/eng/lsqz/laws/t42216.htm>.

together with art 32(2) of the 1982 Constitution, was often referred to as a legal ground for refugee protection in China.[62]

On 1 July 2013, the Alien Entry–Exit Law was superseded by the 2012 Exit and Entry Administration Law (Exit–Entry Law), which was promulgated by the Standing Committee of the NPC on 30 June 2012. Article 46 of the Exit–Entry Law provides:[63]

> Foreigners applying for refugee status may, during the screening process, stay in China on the strength of temporary identity certificates issued by public security organs; foreigners who are recognized as refugees may stay or reside in China on the strength of refugee identity certificates issued by public security organs.

This is the first time China included provisions regarding the treatment of refugees and asylum seekers in its domestic law.[64] Article 46 of the Exit–Entry Law represents a step forward from art 15 of the Alien Entry–Exit Law in two ways. First, it explicitly recognises the right of refugees and asylum seekers to stay and live legally in China. Before the Exit–Entry Law, refugees' right to remain in China was not clearly stated under Chinese law. The Chinese Government did not issue identity documents to UNHCR refugees or asylum seekers awaiting UNHCR's decision on their applications; the legal status of UNHCR travel documents issued to refugees is unclear in China.[65] Although in practice China allows UNHCR refugees and asylum seekers awaiting decision to stay in China temporarily, their stay in China lacked sufficient legal protection under domestic Chinese law prior to the Exit–Entry Law. The precarious situation of UNHCR refugees is exemplified by China's forced repatriation of more than thirty UNHCR refugees along with illegal migrants in the early 1990s.[66] Article 46 of the Exit–Entry Law provides a legal safeguard against arbitrary repatriation of refugees and asylum seekers in China.

---

[62] See eg UNCEDW, above n 51, at [224]; Liang, above n 51, at 259; Liu, above n 51, at 4; Muntarbhorn, above n 51, at 61; Wang, above n 51, at 46; Liu, above n 45, at 46.

[63] The official English translation is available at <http://english.gov.cn/archive/laws_regula tions/2014/09/22/content_281474988553532.htm>.

[64] Human Rights Liaison Unit, Division of International Protection, UNHCR *Submission by the United Nations High Commissioner for Refugees For the Office of the High Commissioner for Human Rights' Compilation Report – Universal Periodic Review: People's Republic of China* (March 2013) at 1, available at <www.refworld.org/pdfid/5135b0cb2.pdf>.

[65] Jerry Z Li and Sanzhuan Guo "China" in Dinah Shelton (ed) *International Law and Domestic Legal Systems: Incorporation, Transformation, and Persuasion* (Oxford University Press, Oxford, 2011) 158 at 160; Wang, above n 51, at 47.

[66] Liu, above n 45, at 47.

Second, art 46 of the Exit–Entry Law identifies the Chinese authority in charge of issuing identity certificates to refugees and asylum seekers. Neither art 32(2) of the 1982 Constitution nor art 15 of the Alien Entry–Exit Law specifies which authorities are responsible for dealing with refugee matters. As Wang pointed out, the lack of clear designation and distribution of responsibilities to Chinese authorities to handle refugee matters had hindered refugee protection and management in China.[67] By stipulating that Chinese public security authorities are responsible for issuing identity certificates to refugees, art 46 of the Exit–Entry Law removes one obstacle to the protection of refugees in China.

The Exit–Entry Law, however, is silent on who qualifies as a refugee, which authorities are responsible for handling applications for refugee status or conducting RSD, or what the RSD procedures are. According to UNHCR, which has been advocating for national refugee protection legislation in China, a national asylum regulation should in principle follow to facilitate the implementation of art 46.[68] As of June 2019, the Chinese authorities had not promulgated a national asylum regulation or implementation rules in relation to art 46.

Given that art 46 covers only refugees whose status has been recognised and asylum seekers whose applications are being processed, the exercise of the right under this article is possible only when a claimant of refugee status has access to RSD procedures. In the absence of a national RSD mechanism, UNHCR is the only organisation that currently conducts RSD in China (see Section 3.4). North Korean escapees and displaced Kokangs and Kachins in Yunnan who cannot access UNHCR's RSD procedures will find themselves excluded from the protection provided by art 46.

The Exit–Entry Law seems to leave room for the possibility of temporary and humanitarian protection. Under art 31, foreigners on short-term visas may apply for Chinese residence on the ground of humanitarian reasons. Additionally, art 20 allows foreigners "who need to enter China urgently for humanitarian reasons" to obtain a so-called "port visa" (*kou'an qianzheng*) at Chinese borders, exempting them from the requirement of applying for a normal visa at Chinese embassies or consulates as required by art 15 of the Exit–Entry Law. A port visa is

[67] Wang, above n 51, at 47.
[68] UNHCR *Regional Representation for China and Mongolia: Fact Sheet* (September 2013), on file with author.

valid for a single entry and a stay of no longer than thirty days. Additionally, art 23 allows aliens who "need to enter China temporarily due to *force majeure* or other urgent reasons" to enter without a visa. Once admitted under art 23, they are allowed to stay in China for up to fifteen days. These provisions, if constructively interpreted, may well serve as the legal basis for allowing asylum seekers to enter China in humanitarian emergencies and for granting residence to displaced foreigners who do not qualify for refugee status but are in need of international protection. However, the terms "humanitarian reasons", "force majeure" and "urgent reasons" in arts 31, 20 and 23 are not defined in the Exit–Entry Law and, at the time of writing, it is unclear how they are interpreted and applied in practice by Chinese authorities.[69]

3.1.5   The Counterterrorism Law and the Extradition Law

On 1 January 2016, the Counterterrorism Law of the People's Republic of China entered into force.[70] Article 2 cl 2 of the Counterterrorism Law states: "The State does not make compromises to terrorist organisations or offer asylum or give refugee status to any terrorist personnel". In art 3, "terrorist personnel" (*kongbu huodong renyuan*) is defined as "people who carry out terrorist activities and members of terrorist organisations". A "terrorist organisation" is defined in art 3 as "a criminal organisation of three persons or more which has been formed to carry out terrorist activities". "Terrorist activities", also defined in art 3, refer to the following "acts of terrorist nature":

> (1) Activities that seriously harm society such as organising, planning, preparing for, or carrying out any of the following conduct so as to cause injuries to persons, major property damage, damage to public facilities, or havoc in public order;

---

[69] For more discussion about humanitarian clauses in the Exit–Entry Law, see Lili Song "zhongguo chujingrujingfa zhong de rendaozhuyi tiaokuan tanxi" in Huiyao Wang and Guofu Liu (eds) *liudong yu zhili: quanqiu rencai yimin yu yiminfa* (World Knowledge Press, Beijing, 2019) 162 (translation: "Exploring the Humanitarian Clauses in the Chinese Exit–Entry Administration Law" in *Mobility and Governance: Global Talents, Migrants and Migration Law*).

[70] Counterterrorism Law of the People's Republic of China 2015 (China), amended on 27 April 2018. The Chinese version is available at <www.npc.gov.cn/npc/xinwen/2018-06/12/content_2055871.htm>. An unofficial English translation is available at <www.uschina.org/china-hub/unofficial-translation-counter-terrorism-law-peoples-republic-china>.

(2) Advocating terrorism, inciting others to commit terrorist activities, unlawfully possessing items that advocate terrorism, or compelling others to wear or bear clothes or symbols that advocate terrorism in a public place;

(3) Organising, leading, or participating in a terrorist organisation;

(4) Providing information, capital, funding, labor, technology, venues or other support, assistance or facilitation for terrorist organisations, terrorist activity personnel, or the commission of terrorist activities;

(5) Other terrorist activities.

Article 2 cl 2 is the first, and only, provision in Chinese law about exclusion from refugee protection. Its provision of excluding persons engaged in terrorist activities from receiving asylum or refugee status seems to reflect China's obligation under two multilateral conventions of the Shanghai Cooperation Organisation (SCO), an intergovernmental regional organisation headquartered in Beijing. Article 23 of the 2009 SCO Convention against Terrorism,[71] and art 21 of the 2017 SCO Convention on Combating Extremism,[72] to both of which China is a party, identically provide that "[t]he Parties shall take necessary measures to prevent granting the refugee status and providing documents confirming it to persons involved in offences covered by this Convention". It is worth noting that China appears to have invoked art 23 of the 2009 SCO Convention against Terrorism. In May 2011, China successfully requested Kazakhstan, a SCO member state, to extradite an ethnic Uighur Chinese national who China claimed was "a major terrorist suspect" and whose refugee status was revoked by UNHCR.[73]

A few months after the Counterterrorism Law entered into force, the NPC Standing Committee's Legislative Affairs Commission published a *Commentary on the Counterterrorism Law of the People's Republic of China*.[74] The commentary itself is not legally binding, but given that its

---

[71] Convention of the Shanghai Cooperation Organisation against Terrorism 2815 UNTS 69 (concluded 16 June 2009, entered into force 14 January 2012), <https://treaties.un.org/doc/Publication/UNTS/Volume%202815/Part/volume-2815-I-49374.pdf>.

[72] Convention of the Shanghai Cooperation Organisation on Combating Extremism (concluded 9 June 2017), <https://read.un-ilibrary.org/international-law-and-justice/international-instruments-related-to-the-prevention-and-suppression-of-international-terrorism_106718f3-en#page1>.

[73] Hannah Beech "China's Uighur Problem: One Man's Ordeal Echoes the Plight of a People" (28 July 2011) <http://world.time.com/2011/07/28/chinas-uighur-problem-one-mans-ordeal-echoes-the-plight-of-a-people/>; Radio Free Asia "UNHCR Refuses to Shed Light" (6 June 2011) <www.rfa.org/english/news/uyghur/refugees-06062011190817.html>.

[74] Sheng Lang and Aili Wang *Commentary on the Counterterrorism Law of the People's Republic of China* (Law Press, Beijing, 2016) at 8.

authors are government officials "who participated in the legislative work of the Counterterrorism Law",[75] it gives an authoritative account of what was on the legislators' minds when the Counterterrorism Law was made. With regard to art 2 cl 2, the commentary first notes "some countries such as Russia have included similar provisions in their counterterrorism law".[76] This indicates that the legislators were aware of the practice of some other countries, especially Russia, relating to exclusion of terrorists from refugee protection.

It is generally accepted that exclusion clauses under art 1F of the Refugee Convention are exhaustive and should be interpreted restrictively and applied with caution.[77] Although acts of terrorism potentially amount to the crimes or acts mentioned in art 1F,[78] not every act labled as terrorism will necessarily meet the definitions of the crimes and acts numerated in art 1F, and membership of an organisation labled as terrorist organisation should not automatically disqualify a person from refugee protection,[79] especially in light of the absence of an

---

[75] At 2.

[76] At 8.

[77] Andreas Zimmermann and Philipp Wennholz "Article 1F 1951 Convention" in Andreas Zimmermann (ed) *The 1951 Convention Relating to the Status of Refugees and Its 1967 Protocol: A Commentary* (Oxford University Press, Oxford, 2011) 579 at 602; Guy S Goodwin-Gill and Jane McAdam *The Refugee in International Law* (3rd ed, Oxford University Press, Oxford, 2007) at 190; Geoff Gilbert "Current Issues in the Application of the Exclusion Clauses" in Erika Feller, Volker Türk and Frances Nicholson (eds) *Refugee Protection in International Law: UNHCR's Global Consultations on International Protection* (Cambridge University Press, Cambridge, 2003) 425 at 439; Michael Kingsley Nyinah "Exclusion under Article 1F: Some Reflections on Context, Principles and Practice" (2000) 12 (special issue) *International Journal of Refugee Law* 295 at 310; *Al-Sirri v Secretary of State for the Home Department* [2012] UKSC 54, [2013] 1 AC 745; *DD (Afghanisatan) v Secretary of State for the Home Department* [2012] UKSC 54, [2013] 1 AC 745; UNHCR *Guidelines on International Protection: Application of the Exclusion Clauses: Article 1F of the 1951 Convention relating to the Status of Refugees* UN Doc HCR/GIP/03/05 (4 September 2003) at [25]–[29].

[78] Art 1F of the Refugee Convention provides: 'The provisions of this Convention shall not apply to any person with respect to whom there are serious reasons for considering that: (a) he has committed a crime against peace, a war crime, or a crime against humanity, as defined in the international instruments drawn up to make provision in respect of such crimes; (b) he has committed a serious non-political crime outside the country of refuge prior to his admission to that country as a refugee; (c) he has been guilty of acts contrary to the purposes and principles of the United Nations.'

[79] Sarah Singer *Terrorism and Exclusion from Refugee Status in the UK: Asylum Seekers Suspected of Serious Criminality* (Brill, Leiden, 2015) at 26; Cornelis Wounters "Reconciling National Security and Non-refoulement: Exceptions, Exclusion and Diplomatic Assurance" in Ana Salinas de Frías, Katja Samuel, Nigel White (eds) *Counter-Terrorism:*

internationally accepted definition of "terrorism". Blanket exclusion from refugee protection of persons who are labelled as terrorists without assessing the individual's situation in accordance with established standards relating to art 1F and appropriate procedural guarantees would entail undue risk of unlawful *refoulement*.[80] The Counterterrorism Law allows persons who are identified as terrorist personnel to apply for a review by the same government institution which is responsible for identifying terrorist personnel,[81] but does not allow the remedy of external or judicial review. In light of this, the Counterterrorism Law does not provide sufficient procedural safeguard to prevent arbitrary exclusion from refugee status.

The NPC commentary further states that:[82]

> when foreigners or stateless persons apply for asylum or refugee status, the relevant authority should, in accordance with laws such as the Exit–Entry law, take appropriate measures including investigation to make sure that the applicant for asylum or refugee status has not carried out terrorist activities . . .

The commentary does not specify which authority is the relevant authority. China has not established its national mechanism for RSD. As will be discussed in more detail below, since 1980 UNHCR has been the only organisation in China that processes refugee status applications, and the Chinese authority has not involved itself substantively in the RSD procedure administered by UNHCR. In accordance with arts 12 and 16 of the Counterterrorism Law, the competent authorities to identify a terrorist or a terrorist organisation are China's national counterterrorism authority and the Chinese courts. As the Chinese authority has not involved itself substantively in the RSD procedure administered by UNHCR, whether and how art 2 cl 2 of the Counterterrorism Law will

---

International Law and Practice (Oxford University Press, Oxford, 2012) 579 at 583; *Bundesrepublik Deutschland and Vertreter des Bundesinteresses beim Bundesverwaltungsgericht (intervening) v B*, judgment of 9th November 2010, Case C-57/09, Case C-101/09 (2010) ECR I-10979.

80 Goodwin-Gill and McAdam, above n 79, at 197; James C Hathaway and Michelle Foster *The Law of Refugee Status* (2nd ed, Cambridge University Press, Cambridge, 2014) at 593.

81 Counterterrorism Law, art 15: "Organizations and personnel designated as terrorist that are dissatisfied with the designation, may apply for a review through the administrative body of the national leading institution for counter-terrorism efforts. The national leading institution for counter-terrorism efforts shall promptly conduct a review and make a decision to sustain or revoke the designation. Review decisions are final".

82 Lang and Wang, above n 74, at 8.

be effectively enforce is to be seen. As of June 2019, there was no evidence that art 2 cl 2 has been invoked against a refugee or an asylum seeker whose asylum claim was being considered by UNHCR in China.

The commentary also notes that China may grant asylum and refugee status to foreigners in accordance with the Refugee Convention and Protocol as well as Chinese law,[83] and that according to art 8 of the Chinese Extradition Law (further discussed below),[84] China should not extradite any foreigner to whom China has granted asylum.[85] This indicates that the legislators had these provisions in mind when drafting art 2 cl 2 of the Counterterrorism Law. Art 8 of the Extradition Law provides the circumstances under which the Chinese Government shall refuse a request by a foreign state for extradition, including:

> (3) the request for extradition is made for a political offence, or the People's Republic of China has granted asylum to the person sought;

Article 8(3) of the Extradition Law could be seen as a legal guarantee of *non-refoulement* of refugees in the event of extradition. As art 2 cl 2 of the Counterterrorism Law excludes persons identified as terrorists from asylum and refugee status, such persons are excluded from the protection provided by art 8(3) of the Extradition Law. Nevertheless, art 8 of the Extradition Law also prohibits extradition when:

> (4) the person sought is one against whom penal proceedings instituted or punishment may be executed for reasons of that person's race, religion, nationality, sex, political opinion or personal status, or that person may, for any of those reasons, be subjected to unfair treatment in judicial proceedings;
>
> . . .
>
> (7) the person sought has been or will probably be subjected to torture or other cruel, inhuman or humiliating treatment or punishment in the Requesting State; . . .

Thus arts 8(4) and (7) provide some protection against *refoulement* to asylum seekers who are denied refugee status, including those excluded from refugee protection under art 2 cl 2 of the Counterterrorism Law. It must be noted that the protection afforded by art 8 of the Extradition Law is limited to the situation of extradition, and does not apply to

---

[83] Lang and Wang, above n 74, at 8.

[84] Extradition Law of the People's Republic of China 2000. An unofficial English translation is available at <www.oecd.org/site/adboecdanti-corruptioninitiative/39776447.pdf>.

[85] Lang and Wang, above n 74, at 8.

non-extradition situations, and as of June 2019 there was no evidence that art 8(3), (4) or (7) has been litigated.

3.1.6   A National Refugee Law on the Horizon?

Since the 1990s, the Chinese Government has been working on drafting a national refugee law with the assistance of UNHCR.[86] Several symposiums were held jointly by the Chinese Government and UNHCR between 2004 and 2007 to discuss issues such as state sovereignty and refugee protection, RSD mechanism and procedure, treatment of refugees, cooperation between the Chinese Government and UNHCR and the experience of other Asia-Pacific countries. In a symposium in September 2012 jointly organised by UNHCR and the Ministry of Foreign Affairs (MFA), an international refugee law expert from New Zealand was invited to present the national refugee legislation of New Zealand as a case study.[87]

According to UNHCR, a draft refugee regulation with input from relevant ministries was submitted to the State Council for deliberation in 2008, but the draft was not adopted.[88] In a report submitted to the UN Committee on the Elimination of Discrimination against Women (UNCEDW) in early 2012, China stated that it had drafted Rules for Identification and Administration of Refugees.[89] The draft rules contain provisions on the definition of a refugee, authorities in charge of refugee affairs, RSD, temporary settlement and repatriation of refugees and loss of refugee status.[90] China also claimed to have been making efforts to finalise the legislative work as soon as possible, but no timeline was provided.[91] In 2015, Liu, a Chinese immigration law expert of Beijing Institute of Technology, discussed extensively the relevance and feasibility of a national refugee law in China and proposed a forty-seven-article draft Refugee Regulation in a Chinese book written and published under UNHCR sponsorship.[92] As of June 2019, China had not enacted a national refugee law.

[86]   UNCEDW, above n 51, at [225].
[87]   UNHCR, above n 68, at 2.
[88]   UNHCR, above n 64, at 2.
[89]   UNCEDW, above n 51, at [225].
[90]   At [225].
[91]   At [225].
[92]   Liu, above n 51, at 324.

The fact that the Chinese authority has been working on a national refugee regulation to some extent indicates political willingness to improve refugee protection in China. The delay in the process, however, suggests that such political willingness is still not strong enough to provide a legal guarantee for the protection and rights of refugees under Chinese law. Liu pointed out three reasons for such delay.[93] First, China has not developed a culturally diverse and tolerant society. Second, there are political considerations involving neighbouring countries. Third, there are concerns of attracting more refugees. Liang, the author of China's first book on international refugee law, noted in a 2017 interview that as China was a developing country with a burdensome large population, the Chinese Government would be unlikely to take in many refugees.[94]

Although the Refugee Convention and Protocol do not impose a legal obligation on state parties to establish a national RSD mechanism, it is in line with the spirit of these instruments for state parties to establish a fair and effective RSD mechanism.[95] Considering that the number of refugees and asylum seekers in China has been increasing quickly in recent years, China should do its best to accelerate the legislative process of its national refugee law.

3.2   The Chinese Government's Expressed View on Refugee Protection

3.2.1   Benevolence and Otherness in Traditional Chinese Philosophy

The idea of benevolence occupies an important place in traditional Chinese philosophical thinking. An important school of ancient Chinese philosophy, Mohism, emphasises the concept of *Jian'ai*, which can be translated as inclusive care or universal love. According to Mohists, benevolence involves an extension to outsiders of attitudes and conduct

---

[93] Guofu Liu "zhongguo weilai raobuguo nanmin yiti" (23 February 2012) <http://news.xinhuanet.com/world/2012-02/23/c_122744895.htm> (translation: "China Cannot Avoid Refugee Issues in the Future").

[94] Fang Haochen "zhongguo weihe hui jieshou guoji nanmin? Tamen guode zenmeyang?" (26 June 2017) <www.ims.sdu.edu.cn/info/1014/8699.htm> (translation: "Why Does China Accept International Refugees? How Is Their Life in China?").

[95] UNHCR *Fair and efficient asylum procedures: a non-exhaustive overview of applicable international standards* (2 September 2005) <www.refworld.org/docid/432ae9204.html>.

normally found within the family.[96] The concept of *ren*, which can be translated as benevolence, kindness and philanthropy, is central to Confucian thoughts.[97] According to Confucian teaching, "the benevolent loves others" (*ren zhe ai ren*). However, unlike Mohists, Confucianists believe in love with differentiation or graded love, according to which the love for family and relatives is superior to the love for friends and acquaintances, which is in turn superior to the love for strangers.[98] Chen, of China's Sun Yat-Sen University School of Philosophy, has argued that China's refugee policy should be guided by the Confucian philosophy of graded love.[99] According to Chen, refugees are strangers who need help and China should act to help them in accordance with the teaching of benevolence.[100] However, to what extent China should help a particular refugee or a particular group of refugees depends on the strength of the refugees' links to China and the Chinese people, as well as China's capacity to help.[101] This, Chen argued, would create a foundation for stable and sustainable love rather than cause problems in the host society.[102]

There is a Chinese saying from the classic Chinese narrative history *The Commentary of Zuo*: "Those who are not of our kin are sure to be of a different heart". The idea embodied in this saying is that persons of a different race or ethnicity are not to be fully trusted. Scholars have noted that the thinking embodied in this saying has influenced the Chinese Government's foreign policy, nationality policy and domestic ethnic policy.[103] The influence of such thinking on the Chinese Government,

---

[96] Chris Fraser *The Philosophy of the Mozi: The First Consequentialists* (Columbia University Press, New York, 2016) at 136.

[97] Hanna B Krebs *Responsibility, legitimacy, morality: Chinese humanitarianism in historical perspective* (Overseas Development Institute, Humanitarian Policy Group Working Paper, September 2014) at 3.

[98] Generally, Botian Liu "Equal Care versus Graded Love" (Master's Thesis, Duke University, 2017).

[99] Shaoming Chen "rujia lunli yu guoji nanmin wenti" (May 2017) <www.sohu.com/a/281382650_720102> (translation: "Confucian Ethics and the International Refugee Problem").

[100] Chen, above n 99.

[101] Chen, above n 99.

[102] Chen, above n 99.

[103] See eg Shiyuan Hao (translated by Xiaohua Tong) *How the Communist Party of China Manages the Issue of Nationality: An Evolving Topic* (Springer, Berlin, 2016) at 96; Shuo Wang and Susan Shirk "The Media" in Nina Hachigian (ed) *Debating China: The US–China Relationship in Ten Conversations* (Oxford University Press, Oxford, 2015) 67 at 82; Zonggui Li *Between Tradition and Modernity: Philosophical Reflections on the*

as well as the traditional Chinese mistrust of foreigners,[104] provides a context for understanding the Chinese Government's view on refugee protection discussed below.

3.2.2   The Chinese Government's Expressed View on Refugee Protection

As mentioned earlier, refugees have been a sensitive topic in China. The Chinese Government has not published any official document regarding its policy towards refugees and asylum seekers in China. Nevertheless, bits and pieces of the Chinese Government's view on refugee protection in general can be found in Chinese delegates' statements at UN meetings, Chinese Government press conferences, China's state reports to international organisations, high-ranking Chinese officials' speeches at international conferences and academic articles written by government employees.

A most notable point that China consistently stresses is the importance of addressing the root causes of refugee crises, which according to the Chinese Government include inter alia poverty and underdevelopment. At a UNHCR meeting on 28 June 1979, the Chinese representative stated that the Chinese Government supported the proposal of then British Prime Minister, Margaret Thatcher, to convene an international meeting on Indochinese refugees but objected to a meeting that would only discuss refugee resettlement without discussing the root causes of the Indochinese refugee exodus.[105] The Chinese delegate argued that discussing resettlement without discussing the root causes would only encourage Vietnam to expel more refugees.[106] Again in 1984, China argued that the main problem with the lengthy Indochinese refugee crisis was that "none of the root causes of outflows had been eliminated".[107]

Modernization of Chinese Culture (Chartridge Books, Oxford, 2014) at 170; Qiang Fang "Struggling for a Better Solution: Chinese Communist Party and Minorities" in Xiaobing Li and Patrick Fuliang Shan (eds) *Ethnic China: Identity, Assimilation, and Resistance* (Lexington Books, Lanham, 2015) 199 at 200.

[104] Margaret Pearson, *China's New Business Elite: The Political Consequences of Economic Reform* (University of California Press, Berkeley, 1999) 103.

[105] "huyu guojishang youxiao zhizhi yuenan shuchu nanmin" *People's Daily* (Beijing, 30 June 1979) at 5 (translation: "Calling the International Community to Effectively Stop Vietnam from Exporting Refugees").

[106] *People's Daily*, above n 105.

[107] Sara Davies *Legitimising Rejection: International Refugee Law in Southeast Asia* (Martinus Nijhoff, Leiden, 2008) at 177.

In more recent years, on various occasions where high-ranking Chinese diplomats talked about refugee issues, they consistently emphasised the need to address the root causes of refugee flows and often highlighted that poverty and underdevelopment were among those causes.[108] In December 2001, China's then Vice Foreign Minister, Wang Guangya, proposed four points to address the refugee problem at a ministerial meeting of state parties to the Refugee Convention, the first point being "to safeguard world peace, [and] promote common development" in order to "prevent the emergence of refugees at the root".[109] At the 61st UNHCR Executive Committee (ExCom) meeting in 2010, then Chinese Ambassador to the UN in Geneva stated that the "focus should be on root causes and prevention" and that the international community should "encourage dialogue and reconciliation to resolve disputes through non-violent means and to develop economy and build a lasting peace".[110] The Chinese Foreign Minister, Wang Yi, stated in 2015 and 2017 that poverty is one of the root causes of the Syrian refugee issue and emphasised that the root causes must be addressed in order to solve the issue.[111] At the UN Summit for Refugees and Migrants in 2016, the

---

[108] See eg Shaojun Yao "Statement by Counsellor YAO Shaojun during the General Debate on the Item of Refugees at the Third Committee of the 72nd Session of the General Assembly" (2 November 2017) <www.china-un.org/eng/hyyfy/t1507214.htm>; Permanent Mission of the People's Republic of China to the United Nations Office at Geneva and Other International Organizations in Switzerland (CPMG) "Ma Zhaoxu Called for Durable Solution to the Global Issue of Refugees" (5 October 2016) <www.china-un.ch/eng/dbtzyhd/t1403595.htm>; Ministry of Foreign Affairs of the People's Republic of China (MFA) "Dai Bingguo Meets with UN High Commissioner for Refugees Guterres" (3 September 2010) <www.fmprc.gov.cn/eng/wjb/zzjg/gjs/gjsxw/t738076.shtml>; Luo Cheng "Statement by Mr LUO Cheng of the Chinese Delegation at the Third Committee of the 64th Session of the UN General Assembly, on Refugees (Item 41)" (3 November 2009) <www.china-un.org/eng/hyyfy/t624524.htm>; Guangya Wang "Statement by HE Mr Wang Guangya, Vice Foreign Minister of the People's Republic of China, at the Ministerial Meeting of States Parties to the 1951 Convention Relating to the Status of Refugees (12 December 2001)" (25 November 2003) <http://pg.china-embassy.org/eng/zt/rqwt/t46963.htm>; Guangya Wang "Remarks by HE Mr Wang Guangya, Vice Minister of Foreign Affairs of China, at the Opening Ceremony of the Third APC Mekong Sub-regional Meeting on Refugees, Displaced Persons and Migrants" (8 August 2002) <www.fmprc.gov.cn/eng/wjdt/zyjh/t25088.htm>.

[109] Wang (2001), above n 108.

[110] Yafei He "Statement by Ambassador Yafei HE on the 61st UNHCR Excom" (4 October 2010) <www.china-un.ch/eng/hom/t758725.htm>.

[111] MFA "Wang Yi Talks about Issue of Refugees in the Middle East" (24 June 2017) <www.fmprc.gov.cn/mfa_eng/zxxx_662805/t1473802.shtm>; MFA "Wang Yi: Both Temporary and Permanent Solutions Should Be Adopted to Eliminate Root Causes in

Chinese Premier, Li Keqiang, noted that conflict, poverty and under-development were among the root causes of migration.[112] In September 2017, the "three-phase solution" China proposed to solve the Rohingya refugee crisis also appears to reflect China's focus on root causes, with the first phase focusing on achieving a ceasefire "so that local residents can no longer be displaced" and the third phase focusing on poverty allevi-ation as "a long-term solution".[113]

China's emphasis on root causes and its view that poverty and under-development are among the main root causes of refugee crises may be linked to its experience in handling the exodus of hundreds of thousands of Mainland Chinese to Hong Kong in the 1950s through the early 1980s. The Chinese authority at that time had strict border control and sent the Chinese People's Liberation Army to the Shenzhen–Hong Kong frontier to stop people from leaving.[114] The exodus, however, continued for more than thirty years. In the late 1970s, Deng Xiaoping pointed out that the exodus was not a problem that could be solved by sending soldiers to the frontier,[115] and that the economic gap between Mainland China and Hong Kong was a main cause of the continuous exodus.[116] One of the measures the Chinese authority took to narrow the economic gap was to establish a special economic zone in Shenzhen city, which borders Hong Kong, in 1979.[117] The Shenzhen Special Economic Zone soon proved to be an economic success. The number of people fleeing to Hong Kong quickly declined in the mid-1980s, ending the "Great Escape to Hong Kong". Nowadays, the Chinese leadership has called China's battle to end the "Great Escape to Hong Kong" an important historic lesson that must not be forgotten.[118]

Addressing Syrian Refugee Issue" (28 October 2015) <www.fmprc.gov.cn/mfa_eng/zxxx_662805/t1310429.shtml>.

[112] *General Assembly Adopts Declaration for Refugees and Migrants, as United Nations, International Organization for Migration Sign Key Agreement* UN Doc GA/11820 (19 September 2016) <www.un.org/press/en/2016/ga11820.doc.htm>.

[113] Xinhua "China Proposes three-phase solution to Rakhine issue in Myanmar: FM" (20 November 2017) <http://news.xinhuanet.com/english/2017-11/20/c_136764392.htm>.

[114] HX Liu "zhenjing zhongyang de 'dataogang' fengchao" *People's Daily Online* (1 August 2010) <www.people.com.cn/GB/198221/198819/198857/12308776.html> (translation: "'The Great Escape to Hong Kong' that Shocked the Chinese Central Government").

[115] Liu, above n 114.

[116] Liu, above n 114.

[117] Liu, above n 114.

[118] Xinhua "mingji 'yongjiao toupiao' de lishi jingshi" (4 November 2013) <http://news.xinhuanet.com/politics/2013-11/04/c_117988157.htm> (translation: "Remembering the Historic Lesson of 'Voting with Foot'").

Another point the Chinese Government has repeatedly made is the need to prevent abuse of the refugee protection mechanism.[119] For example, in 2001 then Chinese Vice Foreign Minister suggested drawing "a clear line between the refugee issue and others, preventing the abuse of the protection regime and asylum policies as prescribed in the Convention".[120] In 2007, a high-ranking Chinese diplomat stated that the Chinese Government "believes that effective improvement of the efficiency of refugee protection also calls for effective measures to keep the protection regime from being abused by various illegal migrants and criminals" and called on "all the parties concerned to strictly abide by the provisions of the Convention on Refugees and prevent the refugee protection regime from being abused".[121] In 2009, at the Third Committee of the 64th Session of the UN General Assembly on Refugees, the Chinese delegation again urged that "effective measures should be taken to safeguard the integrity of the international refugee protection mechanism to prevent its abuse".[122] In 2016, at the general debate of the 67th Session of the UNHCR ExCom, the Chinese Ambassador stated that "[i]t is important to adhere to the humanitarian nature and avoid politicizing or abusing the refugee protection mechanisms".[123] In 2017, the Chinese Ambassador to the UN similarly called for the international community to "adhere to the principle of objectivity and neutrality, avoid interfering in the internal affairs of the countries concerned and prevent the politicization and abuse of international refugee protection mechanisms".[124]

It is relevant to note that the Chinese Government has repeatedly claimed or implied that recognition or assistance of certain Chinese

---

[119] See eg Yao, above n 108; Cheng, above n 108; Yousheng Ke "Statement by Mr. KE Yousheng, Adviser of the Chinese Delegation, at the Third Committee of the 62nd Session of the General Assembly, on the Report of UNHCR (Item 42)" (8 November 2007) <www.china-un.org/eng/xw/t380695.htm>; Wang (2001), above n 108; He, above n 110; Yafei He "Statement by HE Ambassador HE Yafei at the intergovernmental event at the ministerial-level of Member States of the United Nations to commemorate the 60th anniversary of the 1951 Convention relating to the Status of Refugees and the 50th anniversary of the 1961 Convention on the Reduction of Statelessness" (9 December 2011) <www.china-un.ch/eng/hom/t885656.htm>.

[120] Wang (2001), above n 108.

[121] Ke, above n 119.

[122] Cheng, above n 108.

[123] CPMG, above n 108.

[124] Shaojun, above n 108; Wu Haitao "Statement by Ambassador WU Haitao at the Security Council Briefing by the United Nations High Commissioner for Refugees" (2 November 2017) <www.china-un.org/eng/hyyfy/t1511072.htm>.

refugees constituted abuse of the refugee protection mechanism. For example, in 1972 it insisted that Chinese Mainlanders who fled to Hong Kong and Tibetans who fled to India and Nepal were not refugees and that UNHCR's assistance to them was "illegal".[125] More recently, China has sought forced repatriation of Chinese nationals, who had been recognised as refugees or prima facie qualified for refugee status, from other countries such as Thailand,[126] Nepal,[127] Cambodia,[128] Kazakhstan,[129] and Albania,[130] claiming that these Chinese nationals were not refugees. In 2009, when a Chinese MFA spokesperson was asked whether China had pressured Cambodia to deport twenty-two ethnic Uighurs whose applications for refugee status were under review by UNHCR's office in Cambodia, she replied by saying that the twenty-two Uighurs were suspected of criminal offences and that criminals should not be allowed to take advantage of the UN refugee protection system.[131] China's constant calls for the prevention of abuse of the international refugee protection mechanism and its criticism of international protection of certain Chinese refugees probably suggest that the Chinese Government is cautious, if not wary, about the existing international refugee protection mechanism.

Lastly, the Chinese Government has expressed the view that voluntary repatriation is the best solution for refugees. At a UNHCR meeting in

---

[125] Jerome Alan Cohen and Hungdah Chiu *People's China and International Law: A Documentary Study* (Princeton University Press, Princeton, 1974) vol 2 at 1386.

[126] Amy Sawitta Lefevre and Pairat Temphairojana "UN agency protests Thailand's deportation of Chinese refugees" (19 November 2015) <www.reuters.com/article/us-china-thailand-refugees/u-n-agency-protests-thailands-deportation-of-chinese-refugees-idUSKCN0T70J720151118>; Edward Wong and Poypiti Amatatham "Ignoring Protests, Thailand Deports about 100 Uighurs Back to China" *The New York Times* (10 July 2015) <http://cn.nytimes.com/asia-pacific/20150710/c10uighur/enus/>.

[127] Human Rights Watch (HRW) "Nepal: Increased Pressure from China Threatens Tibetans – Authorities Increase Surveillance and Abuses Against Refugees" (1 April 2016) <www.hrw.org/news/2014/04/01/nepal-increased-pressure-china-threatens-tibetans>.

[128] Seth Mydans "20 Uighurs Are Deported to China" *The New York Times* (19 December 2009) <www.nytimes.com/2009/12/20/world/asia/20uighur.html?_r=0>.

[129] Hannah Beech "China's Uighur Problem: One Man's Ordeal Echoes the Plight of a People" *Time* (online ed, 28 July 2011) <http://world.time.com/2011/07/28/chinas-uighur-problem-one-mans-ordeal-echoes-the-plight-of-a-people/>.

[130] Ian Jeffries, *Political Developments in Contemporary China: A Guide* (Routledge, Abingdon, 2010) at 329.

[131] Edward Wong "China Is Disputing Status of Uighurs in Cambodia" *The New York Times* (17 December 2009) <www.nytimes.com/2009/12/18/world/asia/18xinjiang.html>.

1996, speaking of the refugees from Vietnam who had locally settled in China, a Chinese representative stated:[132]

> China regarded voluntary repatriation as the most appropriate solution to the refugee problem ... With the conclusion of the Comprehensive Plan of Action in South-East Asia and the resulting solution to the problem of Vietnamese refugees in Southeast Asia, the repatriation of the Vietnamese refugees in China had become a matter of urgency.

In May 2001, at the first UNHCR expert panel meeting of worldwide consultation on the international protection of refugees, the Chinese Ambassador said that voluntary repatriation is "the best way recognized by the international community to resolve the refugee problem and represents the natural termination of the refugee status".[133] He further urged the international community to make an effort to address the root causes of refugees to pave the way for voluntary repatriation and spoke against "the idea and practice of pressurizing the asylum country to have refugees naturalized in the name of permanently resolving the refugee problem".[134]

Although China has generally maintained a low profile in the international discourse on refugee governance, it has shown a growing ambition to play a greater role in international refugee protection in recent years.[135] For example, in a statement to the UN General Assembly on 2 November 2017, counsellor of the Chinese mission to the UN, Yao Shaojun, stated:[136]

> China advocates the establishment of a new type of international relations based on mutual respect, fairness, justice and win-win cooperation, and the building of a community of shared future for mankind. This concept serves as an important guide to the improvement of the global effort to address the refugee problem.

---

[132] UHCR Executive Committee (ExCom), *Summary Record of the 509th Meeting* UN Doc A/AC.96/SR.509 (8 January 1997).

[133] CPMG "China's Relationship with United Nations High Commissioner for Refugees (UNHCR)" (16 April 2004) <www.china-un.ch/eng/rqrd/jblc/t85094.htm>.

[134] CPMG, above n 133.

[135] See Lili Song "Strengthening Responsibility Sharing with South–South Cooperation: China's Role in the Global Compact on Refugees" (2019) 30(4) *International Journal of Refugee Law* 687; Lili Song "China and the International Refugee Protection Regime" (2018) 37(2) *Refugee Survey Quarterly* 139.

[136] Yao, above n 108.

China's aspiration for a greater role in refugee affairs may lead to opportunities for introducing new development in China's refugee law and policy. Indeed, if China is to achieve its aspiration to be a leader in global refugee governance, it will have to convince the international community that it upholds the core principles of refugee protection and protects refugees within its own borders in compliance with international standards. It is unlikely that any country that does not do so will be able to earn leadership in the field of global refugee governance.

3.3   Chinese Government Bodies Involved in Refugee Matters

China has not established a national RSD mechanism. UNHCR is the only organisation that processes individual refugee status applications in China.[137] However, the Chinese Government has restricted UNHCR from accessing and assisting North Korean escapees and displaced Kokangs and Kachins from Myanmar and handled these groups with little or no involvement of UNHCR.

Three government bodies have dealt with refugee matters in China: the MPS, the Ministry of Civil Affairs (MCA) and the MFA. Prior to March 2018, China did not have a government department specifically tasked with immigration or refugee management, and immigration administrative functions were distributed between the MPS and the MFA.[138]

The MPS is China's principle police and security authority, responsible for a broad spectrum of matters such as policing, exit–entry administration, border security, household registration and identity card administration. The MPS's involvement in refugee matters is mainly because of its policing and border control roles. First, the MPS has interacted with refugees through its nationwide system of public security bureaus (PSBs), which serve as police stations in China. The PSBs are responsible for household registration and, according to art 46 of the 2012 Exit–Entry Law, for issuing refugee identity cards to refugees and temporary identity cards to asylum seekers. Refugees and asylum seekers registered with UNHCR have to report to the PSBs regularly. The PSBs are also responsible for handling illegal migrants. North Korean escapees in urban areas

---

[137] See eg Cui Jia "Refugees Look to End Life in Limbo" *China Daily* (online ed, 1 June 2016) <www.chinadaily.com.cn/a/201601/01/WS5a2b8c3ca310eefe3e9a1204.html>.

[138] 2012 Exit–Entry Law, art 4. These ministries have branches at provincial and municipal levels.

have been questioned and repatriated without being assessed for refugee status by the PSBs.[139]

Second, the MPS has dealt with refugees because of its border control functions. Prior to April 2018, this function was performed through the Bureau of Exit and Entry Administration (BEEA), the Border Security Bureau (BSB) and the PSBs. The BEEA primarily takes care of immigration control at nine major cities (Beijing, Shanghai, Tianjin, Guangzhou, Shenzhen, Zhuhai, Shantou, Haikou and Xiamen),[140] while the BSB's armed border security force is responsible for guarding land and coastal borders elsewhere. According to art 58 of the 2012 Exit–Entry Law, the BEEA, the BSB and the PSBs at county level or above are authorised to investigate, detain and repatriate illegal border crossers. During the Kokang incident in 2009, then Minister of Public Security, Meng Jianzhu, was sent to Yunnan in response to the incident. The Yunnan provincial PSB held a press conference on 31 August 2009 to comprehensively explain the situation of the displaced Kokangs in China.

On 3 April 2018, the Chinese Government established the new National Immigration Administration (NIA) under the MPS. It is the first time that China had established a national immigration administration. The BEEA and the BSB have since merged under the umbrella of the NIA.[141] The NIA is tasked with, inter alia, refugee administration, repatriation of illegal migrants and nationality administration.[142] As the NIA is a relatively new agency, it remains to be seen whether and how it will change the current refugee administration system in China.

The MCA was established in 1978. The predecessor of the MCA is the Ministry of Internal Affairs, established in 1949, which was mainly responsible for providing disaster relief and strengthening the institutional system of the newly founded People's Government. The MCA played a leading role in China's reception, local settlement and

---

[139] HRW *The Invisible Exodus: North Koreans in the People's Republic of China* (vol 14, no 8 (C), November 2002) at 16 <www.hrw.org/reports/2002/northkorea/>.

[140] Bureau of Exit and Entry Administration of the MPS "churujing bianfang jiancha zongzhan ji xiashu churujing bianfang jianchazhan" (3 July 2008) <www.mps.gov.cn/n16/n84147/n84165/1291480.html> (translation: "Exit–Entry Inspection Head Station and Exit–Entry Stations under It").

[141] Xinhua "zhonggong zhongyang yinfa shenhua dang he guojia jigou gaige fang'an" (21 March 2018) <www.gov.cn/zhengce/2018-03/21/content_5276191.htm#allContent> (translation: "The Central Committee of the Chinese Communist Party Issues Plan for Deepening State and Party Institutional Reform").

[142] China Daily "China to provide more efficient immigration services" *China Daily* (online ed, 24 January 2019) <www.china.org.cn/china/2019-01/24/content_74404689.htm>.

repatriation of the Indochinese refugees. The State Council Office of Reception and Settlement of Indochinese Refugees, established in 1979, was headed by the Minister of Civil Affairs and physically housed at the MCA.[143] The MCA then served as UNHCR's implementing partner for local settlement and voluntary repatriation of the Lao and Cambodian refugees in the 1980s and 1990s.[144] The MCA also provided assistance to the displaced Kokangs in 2009. The Chinese characters for "civil disaster relief" were printed on the tents and blankets provided to the Kokangs by Chinese authority.[145]

According to the MCA website, the MCA's main functions also include "participating in drafting administration rules on international refugees in China, and jointly taking charge of temporary settlement and repatriation of international refugees in China with other relevant departments".[146] As mentioned earlier, the MCA was tasked with drafting the Detailed Rules for Refugee Identification and Administration. With the establishment of the NIA in April 2018, it remains to be seen whether the drafting of the national refugee regulation will be transferred to the NIA.

The MFA is responsible for foreign relations between China and other countries as well as international organisations. It is stated on the MFA's website that one of the MFA's main functions is to "handle global and regional security, political, economic, human rights, social, refugee and other diplomatic affairs in the United Nations and other multilateral fora".[147] However, in 2002, when seven North Korean escapees attempted to lodge their application for refugee status to the MFA, they were immediately taken away and investigated by Chinese police (see section 4.3.1).

---

[143] Liang, above n 51, 259.

[144] ExCom *UNHCR Activities Financed by Voluntary Funds: Report for 1993–1994 and Proposed Programmes and Budget for 1995 – Part II Asia and Oceania – Section 4 – China* UN Doc A/AC.96/825/Part II/4 (16 August 1994) at [9].

[145] See Nancy Shwe (translated by Sarah Jackson-Han) "Kokang Fighters Flee to China" (31 August 2009) <www.rfa.org/english/news/myanmar/kokang-08312009061953.html>.

[146] Ministry of Civil Affairs of the People's Republic of China *minzhengbu zhuyao zhize* <www.mca.gov.cn/article/zwgk/jggl/zyzz/> (translation: "Main Duties and Responsibilities of Ministry of Civil Affairs").

[147] MFA *Main Responsibilities of the Ministry of Foreign Affairs of the People's Republic of China* <www.fmprc.gov.cn/eng/wjb/zyzz/>.

3.4 UNHCR in China

3.4.1 Relations between UNHCR and China

UNHCR first operated in China in January 1952, resettling European refugees in China to third countries through an office in Shanghai, a task it took over from the IRO.[148] When a refugee had an offer of resettlement from a third country, the Chinese Government would issue an exit visa to the refugee and the China Travel Service would arrange for the refugee to travel to Shanghai and from there to the China–Hong Kong Border.[149] Since Beijing did not have diplomatic relations with most other countries, Hong Kong – then still British Hong Kong – served as a transit point of the refugee's journey to the resettlement destination. UNHCR's Office in Shanghai was closed in 1956 and its functions were assumed by the official Chinese People's Relief Association.[150]

UNHCR re-established its presence in China in February 1980, when it opened a task office in Beijing in response to the Vietnamese refugee influx to China.[151] On 1 December 1995, the task office in Beijing was upgraded to a branch office,[152] which was further upgraded to a regional office in May 1997. At present, the work of the UNHCR Beijing Office includes advocating for respect for the principle of *non-refoulement*, undertaking RSD under UNHCR mandate, identifying durable solutions for all persons of concern and lobbying for the enactment of national refugee legislation and policies in accordance with international refugee law; the Office is also responsible for providing life-sustaining assistance to refugees pending the implementation of appropriate durable solutions,

---

[148] Before 1956, China issued exit visas on the condition that the refugee had obtained an entry visa for his or her resettlement country. From spring 1956 onwards, exit visas were issued without precondition (Glen Peterson "The Uneven Development of the International Refugee Regime in Postwar Asia: Evidence from China, Hong Kong and Indonesia" (2012) 25 *Journal of Refugee Studies* 326 at 331).

[149] At 330.

[150] At 331.

[151] UNHCR Hong Kong "Regional Representation in China" (10 March 1999) <www.unhcr.org/hk/en/134-china-2.html>.

[152] Agreement on the upgrading of the UNHCR Mission in the People's Republic of China to UNHCR branch office in the People's Republic of China, UNHCR–China 1899 UNTS 61 (signed 1 December 1995, entered into force 1 December 1995) <www.nkfreedom.org/UploadedDocuments/UNHCR-China1995Treaty.pdf>.

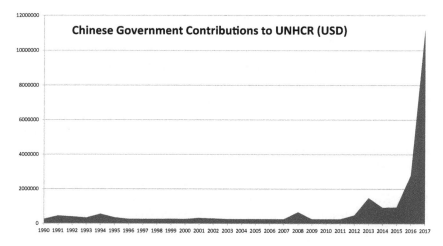

Figure 3.1 Chinese Government contributions to UNHCR (USD), 1990–2017
Source: Shuying Liang *guoji nanmin fa* (Intellectual Property Publishing House, Beijing, 2009) at
254, n 1 (translation: *International Refugee Law*); UNHCR, Contributions to UNHCR for each
budget year 2010-2017, available at <www.unhcr.org>

including accommodation, living allowances and access to basic
healthcare.[153]

The Chinese Government claims to have maintained a cooperative
relationship with UNHCR.[154] Since the 1980s, China and UNHCR have
worked together to support the Indochinese refugees in China. UNHCR
provides training for Chinese Government officials every year and has
held several symposiums jointly with the Chinese Government on refugee protection issues.[155] China has donated annually to UNHCR since
1990.[156] Before 2009, its annual donation was USD 250,000 in most
years.[157] Since 2012, China's financial contribution to UNHCR has
increased significantly (Figure 3.1). In 2013, China's contribution to
UNHCR was nearly USD 1,500,000, representing a more than 210 per

---

[153] UNHCR "The People's Republic of China: Fact Sheet" (December 2015) <www.unhcr
.org/protection/operations/5000187d9/china-fact-sheet.html>.
[154] CPMG, above n 133; Ke Yousheng "Statement by Mr KE Yousheng, Adviser of the
Chinese Delegation, at the Third Committee of the 62nd Session of the General Assembly, on the Report of UNHCR (Item 42)" (8 November 2007) CPMUN <www.fmprc
.gov.cn/ce/ceun/eng/xw/t380695.htm>.
[155] Interview with UNHCR officials (the author, Beijing, August 2015).
[156] Liang, above n 51, at 254, n 1.
[157] Liang, above n 51, n 1.

cent increase from 2012 and a nearly 500 per cent increase from 2011.[158] In 2014, China announced that it would raise its regular annual donation to UNHCR from USD 250,000 to USD 800,000,[159] and its contribution to UNHCR in that year was USD 929,464.[160] China's contribution to UNHCR further increased in 2015, 2016 and 2017, peaking at USD 11,114,039 in 2017.[161]

Despite the recent increase, China's annual contribution to UNHCR is still significantly lower than that of the United States or Japan. In 2016 and 2015 respectively, China ranked thirty-ninth and fifty-first in terms of annual contribution to UNHCR, while the United States and Japan ranked first and second.[162] Given that China has been the second-largest economy in the world since 2010,[163] its financial contribution to UNHCR does not appear to be commensurate with its economic volume.

The relations between China and UNHCR are not always free from tensions. After China's entry into the UN in 1971, as a policy of the Chinese Government, China refrained from participating in activities of certain UN agencies, including UNHCR, for ideological reasons until 1979.[164] In 1972, it criticised UNHCR for extending assistance to Tibetan refugees and Chinese refugees in Hong Kong and Macao, demanding the UN agency to stop[165]

> all illegal activities on the question of so-called "Tibetan refugees" and "Chinese refugees" in Hong Kong and Macao, [to] abolish the organs for these illegal activities, and [to] delete all the related parts from the report.

Prince Sadruddin Aga Khan, who was the UN High Commissioner for Refugees from 1966 to 1977, had tried to establish a dialogue with China,

---

[158] UNHCR "Government Contributions to UNHCR" (2014) <www.unhcr.org/cgi-bin/texis/vtx/page?page=49e487cd6&submit=GO>.

[159] CPMG "zhongguo daibiao Ren Yisheng gongcan zai lianheguo nanmin zhiweihui di65ci huiyi yibanxing bianlun zhongde fayan" (2 October 2014) <www.china-un.ch/chn/hyyfy/t1197675.htm> (translation: "Statement of Chinese Representative Ren Yisheng at 65th UNHCR ExCom Meeting").

[160] *Contributions to UNHCR: For Budget Year 2014 – As at 31 December 2014* (7 April 2015), available at <www.unhcr.org/536c960a9.pdf>.

[161] UNHCR "Contributions to UNHCR -2017 (as at 14 February 2018, in US dollars)" (14 February 2018) <https://www.unhcr.org/5954c4257.html>.

[162] Above n 161.

[163] David Barboza "China Passes Japan as Second-Largest Economy" *The New York Times* (online ed, 15 August 2010) <www.nytimes.com/2010/08/16/business/global/16yuan.html?pagewanted=all&_r=0>.

[164] Ling, above n 25, at 173 and 178.

[165] Cohen and Chiu, above n 125, at 1386.

which refused his attempts on the ground that UNHCR provided aid to Tibetans in exile.[166]

In recent years, the Chinese authority has publicly expressed disagreement with UNHCR on more than one occasion. For example, in 2013, at a press conference in Beijing a spokesman of the Chinese MFA warned UNHCR not to make "irresponsible comments" about China's treatment of North Korean escapees.[167] In 2015, China accused UNHCR of interfering with China's judicial sovereignty when UNHCR's Bangkok Office tried to prevent the Thai authority from deporting, upon extradition requests from China, two Chinese nationals who had been identified as refugees by UNHCR's Bangkok Office.[168] The Chinese authority summoned UNHCR's representative in China to express China's discontent about UNHCR Bangkok Office's "interference" and demanded the representative report China's concerns to the headquarters of UNHCR in Geneva.[169]

Notably, China deported fifteen UNHCR refugees before the 2008 Olympic Games in Beijing.[170] In response, UNHCR expressed concerns:[171]

> On this occasion as always in the past with similar cases, UNHCR has made it clear to China that any deportation of refugees must scrupulously observe the relevant articles of the 1951 Refugee Convention, to which the People's Republic of China is a party, and depending on the circumstances may well constitute a violation of the *non-refoulement* provision of the Convention.

Indeed, it was not the first time China had forcibly repatriated UNHCR refugees. As mentioned above, in 1992, more than thirty UNHCR refugees were repatriated by the Chinese authority.[172] In the 1992 Notice, the MPS reminded UNHCR that it had no right to intervene in China's

---

[166] Casella, above n 28, at 47.

[167] Terril Yue Jones "China warns UN against 'irresponsible remarks' on North Koreans" (3 June 2013) <www.reuters.com/article/2013/06/03/us-korea-north-china-idUSBRE9 5209W20130603>.

[168] Lingzhi Fan "zhongtai hezuo yindu xianfan zao lianheguo nanminshu ganshe zhongfang ti yanzheng jiaoshe" *The Global Times* (25 November 2015) <http://world.huanqiu .com/exclusive/2015-11/8044932.html> (translation: "China Protested against UNHCR's Interference in Extradition of Criminal Suspects from Thailand to China").

[169] Fan, above n 168.

[170] UNHCR, above n 46.

[171] UNHCR, above n 46.

[172] Liu, above n 45, at 47.

internal affairs.[173] Such a statement indicates that in the early 1990s China probably viewed UNHCR's protection of refugees as potential intervention in China's internal affairs. China's view of UNHCR has probably not changed completely since then. As noted by Margesson, Chanlett-Avery and Bruno in 2007, China was suspicious of UNHCR's intentions and UNHCR could not provide assistance to North Korean escapees in China in an open, transparent manner.[174] China also repeatedly denied UNHCR's requests to access the China–Myanmar border and the displaced ethnic Kokangs and Kachins from Myanmar,[175] even though a few Chinese and Myanmar religious and non-governmental groups were allowed to access and provide assistance to the displaced ethnic Kokangs and Kachins in Yunnan province.[176] This indicates that the Chinese authority probably remains mistrustful of UNHCR.

On the other hand, as Greenhill noted, UNHCR has been criticised by NGOs and media for being "soft" and "powerless" vis-à-vis the Chinese authority, especially on the issue of North Korean escapees in China.[177] In fact, UNHCR's non-confrontational approach may have pragmatic advantages, given the mistrust that the Chinese authority already has of UNHCR. It is worth noting that China's attitude towards international human rights institutions has been described as "engagement and resistance".[178] The Chinese authority is known for its defensive attitude to open criticism on China's domestic human rights issues.[179] Avoiding

---

[173] 1992 Notice, above n 42.

[174] Rhoda Margesson, Emma Chanlett-Avery and Andorra Bruno, *North Korean Refugees in China and Human Rights Issues: International Response and US Policy Options* (United States Congressional Research Service, Order Code RL34189, 26 September 2007) at 11 <www.fas.org/sgp/crs/row/RL34189.pdf>.

[175] Kris Janowski "UNHCR seeks access to North Koreans detained in China" UNHCR (21 January 2003) <www.unhcr.org/3e2d81b94.html>; UNHCR "China: UNHCR calls for access to Myanmar refugees" (4 September 2009) <www.unhcr.org/news/briefing/2009/9/4aa108159/china-unhcr-calls-access-myanmar-refugees.html?query=kokang>; UNHCR "UNHCR reaches Kachins sent back from China" (7 September 2012) <www.unhcr.org/5049cdba9.html>.

[176] The Economist "The Han that Rock the Cradle" (12 March 2015) <www.economist.com/news/asia/21646248-kokang-conflict-causes-problems-china-too-han-rock-cradle>.

[177] Kelly M Greenhill *Weapons of Mass Migration: Forced Displacement, Coercion, and Foreign Policy* (Cornell University Press, Ithaca, 2010) at 238; see also Radio Free Asia "Criticism over Deportation" (5 June 2011) <www.rfa.org/english/news/uyghur/refugee-06052011164247.html>.

[178] Randall Peerenboom *China Modernizes: Threat to the West or Model for the Rest?* (Oxford University Press, New York, 2007) at 83.

[179] See eg Eva Brems *Human Rights: Universality and Diversity* (Kluwer Law International, The Hague, 2001) at 51.

direct confrontation and maintaining a relatively amicable relationship with the Chinese authority may allow UNHCR to build trust with the Chinese authority in the long term and to optimise UNHCR's chance of influencing China on less sensitive issues.

Indeed, UNHCR has been playing a vital role in engaging China in the global discourse on refugee protection. For example, in 2012 UNHCR arranged for an international refugee law expert from New Zealand to present New Zealand's national refugee legislation to China as a case study.[180] In 2015 UNHCR also arranged for a seven-person Chinese delegation to visit the Mahama refugee camps in Rwanda, where the Chinese delegation displayed "special interest in the health clinic and the camp extension site".[181] In his visit to China in June 2017, the UN High Commissioner for Refugees, Filippo Grandi, said China could play a key role in solving refugee crises, noting that "[t]hrough its many development projects, China can help to stabilize areas in conflict and address the root causes of displacement".[182] Achieving a delicate balance between safeguarding the rights of refugees in China and building a constructive relation with the Chinese Government will remain a key challenge for UNHCR in China.

3.4.2   Refugee Status Determination Conducted by UNHCR

In practice, at the time of writing UNHCR is the only organisation that processes refugee status claims in China. UNHCR established an office in Beijing in 1980 and has since then been processing refugee status claims in China.[183] According to the 1995 China–UNHCR Agreement on the Upgrading of the UNHCR Mission in the People's Republic of China to UNHCR Branch Office in the People's Republic of China,[184] UNHCR may, in consultation and cooperation with the Chinese Government, have unimpeded access to refugees at any time.[185] The 1995 Agreement

---

[180] UNHCR, above n 68, at 2.

[181] UNHCR "Rwanda: Emergency Update – Burundi Refugee Influx" (16 June 2015), <https://data2.unhcr.org/ar/documents/download/48364>.

[182] Vivian Tan "China can play key role in solving refugee crises – UNHCR chief" (8 June 2017)   <www.unhcr.org/en-au/news/latest/2017/6/593946b64/china-play-key-role-solving-refugee-crises-unhcr-chief.html>.

[183] UNHCR Hong Kong "Regional Representation in China" <www.unhcr.org/hk/en/134-china.html>.

[184] Agreement on the upgrading of the UNHCR Mission in the People's Republic of China to UNHCR branch office in the People's Republic of China, above n 152.

[185] Art 3(5).

also refers to art 35 of the Refugee Convention, which requires state parties to cooperate with UNHCR in the exercise of its functions, as a basis of cooperation between the Chinese Government and UNHCR.[186] However, the Chinese authority has not allowed UNHCR to access North Korean escapees and displaced Kachins and Kokangs from Myanmar.[187]

The Chinese Government acknowledges the status of the refugees recognised by UNHCR but has had little involvement in the RSD process administered by UNHCR.[188] According to Wang, this is due to the lack of clear legal or administrative provisions on the respective responsibilities of each party.[189] How UNHCR and China handled the first asylum cases in China probably sheds some light on why the current pattern of work between UNHCR and China began in the first place. In December 1981, six members of the Polish Solidarity Trade Union movement, which had been outlawed by the Polish Government of General Jaruzelski, turned up at UNHCR's Beijing Office requesting asylum. According to Casella, who was called by UNHCR's Beijing Office for advice:[190]

> there was no way we could have convinced the Chinese to show some leniency towards a group of opponents to a communist regime ... So Jacques went to the [Chinese] authorities informing them that six foreigners – he deliberately did not mention their nationality – had come to the office and would like their visas prolonged for ten days to do some more sightseeing. The request in itself was innocuous and was met with no objection. Not that the Chinese were duped; they were fully aware of what the whole matter was about but obviously they had decided not to press the issue, at least for the time being. Jacques then went to the Australian Embassy and explained to them what the matter was about. Three days later the six Poles, all holding visas for Australia and air tickets provided by UNHCR, were escorted by Jacques to Beijing airport where they boarded a flight to Sydney, thus bringing the matter to a close. For all concerned it was a win-win situation. The Chinese did not have to turn down an asylum request that, on principle, they could not have granted.

Somehow, UNHCR continues to process asylum claims with little involvement of the Chinese authority. Generally, UNHCR's Beijing Office conducts RSD at its premise located in central Beijing for asylum

---

[186] Art 3(1).
[187] UNHCR "UNHCR reaches Kachins sent back from China", above n 175.
[188] Yuanjun Wang "guanyu jianli woguo nanmin baohu falv zhidu de jidian sikao" (2005) 12 *Public Security Research* 46 at 47 (translation: "Thoughts on Establishment of a Refugee Protection Mechanism in China").
[189] Wang, above n 188.
[190] Casella, above n 28, at 219.

seekers who approach it. Considering the vastness of Chinese territories and that UNHCR has only one office in China's mainland, it can be a challenge for some refugees and asylum seekers to reach UNHCR's Beijing Office. Beijing is by no means close to China's land or sea borders, where many refugees and asylum seekers are likely to enter China. Since refugees and asylum seekers often arrive without proper entry documents and with limited financial resources, it would be difficult for them to make their way to Beijing, because they would be subject to identity document checks on the train, at the airport and at hotels.

According to the UNHCR Procedural Standards for Refugee Status Determination under UNHCR's Mandate (UNHCR Procedural Standards), when it is necessary, UNHCR allows the registration and application form submission procedures to be conducted by approved implementing partners on the condition that it is possible for UNHCR to exercise effective monitoring and supervision and that the approval of relevant UNHCR RSD supervisors is obtained.[191] Usually, NGOs serve as implementing partners in UNHCR RSD procedures. In China, very few, if any, NGOs openly provide assistance to refugees and asylum seekers. There is no evidence that UNHCR's Beijing Office has had any non-governmental implementing partner in Mainland China.[192]

The UNHCR Procedural Standards also provide that interviews of the applicant must be conducted by qualified UNHCR eligibility officers and must not be conducted by implementing partners.[193] Therefore, UNHCR is to "take all feasible steps" to conduct RSD outside UNHCR offices when conditions in the host country make it difficult for asylum seekers to reach a UNHCR office.[194] Officials of UNHCR's Beijing Office have travelled to areas outside Beijing, such as Yunnan province and Guangzhou city, to conduct RSD.[195] Where the applicant is identified as a refugee by UNHCR, the person will obtain a permit from the Chinese

---

[191] *Procedural Standards for Refugee Status Determination under UNHCR's Mandate* (2003) at 3–16 <www.unhcr.org/4317223c9.html>.
[192] See UNHCR, above n 153.
[193] At 1–6.
[194] At 3–16.
[195] Jing Wan "nanmin wenti yizhi zai fasheng, bushi zhe jiushi na" *Southern Weekly* (online ed, China, 8 July 2011) <www.infzm.com/content/61090> (translation: "Refugee Problems Always Happen, Either Here or Elsewhere"). This article includes the transcript of an interview with Choosin Ngaotheppitak, then Head of UNHCR Hong Kong Office, who served for four years in the UNHCR Beijing Office between 2003 and 2007. Login was required for access to the full text of this article as of 30 June 2019.

Government which allows him or her to travel within China; the applicant then travels to Beijing.[196]

However, UNHCR's Beijing Office does not always have access to refugees and asylum seekers. In 1999, UNHCR sent a team to northeast China near the China–North Korea border; the team assessed the situation of North Korean escapees and determined that some of them qualified as refugees.[197] China reprimanded UNHCR for this action[198] and has not allowed UNHCR to access the China–Korea border area since then. More notably, after North Koreans entered UNHCR's Beijing Office to seek asylum in the early 2000s, the Chinese authority tightened security around UNHCR's Beijing Office, intentionally making it more difficult for North Koreans to approach UNHCR. The Chinese Government also declined UNHCR's repeated requests to access the displaced Kokangs and Kachins from Myanmar in Yunnan.

---

[196] Wan, above n 195.
[197] US Committee for Refugees and Immigrants (USCRI) "US Committee for Refugees World Refugee Survey 2002 – China (Including Tibet)" (10 June 2002) <www.refworld .org/docid/3d04c14c10.html>.
[198] USCRI, above n 197.

The Reality: Treatment of Refugees in China

4.1 UNHCR Refugees

The UNHCR Office in Beijing has been processing refugee status claims in China since it was established in 1980. The Chinese Government acknowledges the refugee status of those who are identified as refugees through the RSD process administered by UNHCR's Beijing Office,[1] although it has not substantially involved itself in the UNHCR RSD process. As there are few legal provisions on treatment of refugees and asylum seekers in Chinese law, the treatment of UNHCR refugees and asylum seekers in China has, in reality, largely been a matter of policy.

To date, public information about the situation of UNHCR refugees and asylum seekers in China remains sparse. According to a 2014 article by Sidiki Sheriff, a Liberian who sought asylum in China, UNHCR would issue an "asylum seeker certificate" to the applicant "during the form filling process".[2] This certificate, which according to Sheriff was "a form of identification used just in case you encounter a problem or are threatened with arrest by police", was valid for two to three months and could be renewed for another period.[3] In order to renew the certificate, the applicant must register themselves with the local police in the town or city of their residence and send a notification to UNHCR's Beijing Office.[4] This requirement to register with the local police was introduced a few months before Sheriff wrote his article,[5] not long after the 2012 Exit–Entry Law entered into force on 1 July 2013.

---

[1] For the purposes of this book, the term "UNHCR refugees" does not include the Vietnamese/Indochinese refugees in China. They were recognised as refugees at the 1979 Meeting by the Chinese Government and did not go through the UNHCR RSD process.

[2] Sidiki Sheriff "Asylum Registration in China" (1 March 2014) Rights in Exile <https://rightsinexile.tumblr.com/post/78227619023/asylum-registration-in-china>.

[3] Sheriff, above n 2.

[4] Sheriff, above n 2.

[5] Sheriff, above n 2.

Asylum seekers registered with the local police station would receive a temporary residence permit from the police. In 2017, an asylum seeker in Beijing described his experience in going through the local police registration as "a struggle".[6] Upon informing UNHCR of his request for refugee status, this asylum seeker was told by UNHCR to obtain a temporary residence permit and bring it to his interview. The asylum seeker's first attempt to obtain the temporary residence permit failed because he did not have a landlord or agent with him. He went with an agent the second time around and waited hours, only to be told that his permit was denied again because his name was not on the rental contract. UNHCR then postponed his interview because of his failure to get the permit. He finally got the permit the third time around and attended his interview, following which UNHCR issued a renewable six-month asylum seeker certificate to him.

Asylum seekers recognised as refugees by UNHCR receive a refugee certificate from UNHCR, which will inform the Chinese police about their status.[7] Failed asylum seekers who do not have a legitimate ground to stay in China will be handled by the Chinese public security authority as illegal immigrants.[8] Refugee status claimants who receive a negative decision from UNHCR have no access to judicial review in China.

A few news articles published in the past fifteen years provide a glimpse into who have been recognised as UNHCR refugees in China and what their lives in China were like. A 2004 article mentioned a refugee from Sri Lanka under the pseudonym of Hamai who was a leader of an anti-terrorism organisation in Sri Lanka.[9] Because Hamai organised influential anti-terrorism photo exhibitions around Sri Lanka, he was repeatedly threatened by terrorists and found himself in seriously dangerous situations several times. Hamai left Sri Lanka and was recognised

---

[6] That's Beijing "I'm an Asylum Seeker Living in Beijing. Here's What My Life Is Like" (12 July 2017) <www.thatsmags.com/shanghai/post/19734/an-asylum-seekers-firsthand-account-of-life-in-china>.

[7] UNHCR *Submission by the United Nations High Commissioner for Refugees for the Office of the High Commissioner for Human Rights' Compilation Report: People's Republic of China and the Special Administrative Regions of Hong Kong and Macao* (March 2018) <www.refworld.org/docid/5b56ffde9.html>; Shuchen Fang "zai hebeisheng sanheshi shenghuo de bajisitan nanmin shi zenme huishi" (25 June 2017) <www.sohu.com/a/151888273_354194> (translation: "Facts about Pakistan Refugees Living in Sanhe City, Hebei Province").

[8] Fang, above n 7.

[9] Xiao Shao "shenghuo zai zhongguo de waiguo nanmin" *Baixing* (Beijing, March 2004) at 50 (translation: "Foreign Refugees Living in China" *Ordinary People*).

as a refugee by UNHCR in China. He was living in a big city in China at the time of the article. Another refugee mentioned in this 2004 article is a Burundian man who came to China as an exchange student in the late 1980s. When he was about to return to his country after seven years of study in China, large-scale ethnic conflicts erupted in Burundi. He was recognised as a refugee by UNHCR and allowed to stay in China. He rented an apartment in a Beijing suburb and lived there with his wife and children. However, he was not allowed to work, even though he had a master's degree in industrial design, and had to live on a monthly allowance provided by UNHCR. Eventually, with the help of UNHCR, he moved to Canada a few years later.

A 2013 article in the *Global Times*, a state-owned newspaper in China, introduces the story of a Zimbabwean refugee Taonga, who was an artist.[10] Fleeing discrimination and threats in his native Zimbabwe for being homosexual, Taonga came to China to join his Chinese boyfriend in 2012 on a tourist visa and later registered as a refugee with UNHCR. Taonga was not allowed to work or open a bank account, and could not travel without approval. When he wanted to leave Beijing to attend a friend's wedding in Sichuan province in southwest China, he was advised that it would be better to stay in Beijing because local authorities in Sichuan might not recognise his identity document issued by UNHCR.[11] The article also mentions that a teenage refugee from Pakistan, who fled with his family for religious reasons, had received home tuition from volunteers arranged by UNHCR and was enrolled in a Chinese public school as a result of the Chinese Government's policy decision in November 2012 to allow refugee children to attend public primary schools in five provinces in China.

As illustrated in the above articles, UNHCR refugees are allowed to stay temporarily in China until UNHCR finds a durable solution for them, usually resettlement in a third country.[12] They may choose to live outside Beijing. Unlike the Indochinese refugees who were mainly settled in local communities in rural areas, UNHCR refugees are largely scattered across China's major cities. They hold identity documents issued by

---

[10] Meilian Lin "Home away from home" *Global Times* (online ed, Beijing, 22 December 2013), <www.globaltimes.cn/content/833531.shtml>.

[11] Lin, above n 10.

[12] UNHCR Hong Kong "Regional Representation in China" (10 March 1999) <www.unhcr .org/hk/en/134-china-2.html>.

UNHCR, have no right to work and rely on UNHCR for assistance in terms of food, accommodation, healthcare and child education.[13]

As of June 2019, the Chinese Government did not issue travel documents to UNHCR refugees, despite the fact that they are eligible for Chinese identity cards under art 46 of the Exit–Entry Law. The Chinese Government did not allow them to work and provided little financial assistance.[14] In contrast, the Chinese Government has issued Chinese identity documents to Indochinese refugees and allows them to work. Such differentiated treatment of UNHCR refugees and Indochinese refugees in China is not in line with the principle of non-discrimination set forth in art 3 of the Refugee Convention,[15] which prohibits states from discriminating between and among refugees on the basis of race, religion or country of origin when applying the Convention.[16]

Since November 2012, following a policy decision by the Chinese Government, refugee children residing in five Chinese provinces have been allowed to attend public primary schools under the same conditions as local Chinese children.[17] This is a recent positive development in the treatment of UNHCR refugees in China. China has been a party to the Refugee Convention and Protocol since 1982 and the world's second largest economy since 2010. It has committed more than one billion US dollars to refugee assistance projects outside China under the Belt-and-Road Initiative.[18] It is high time for China to do more to provide refugees in China with the protection and support they deserve under the Refugee Convention and Protocol.

---

[13] UNHCR Hong Kong, above n 12.

[14] UNHCR Hong Kong, above n 12.

[15] Convention relating to the Status of Refugees 189 UNTS 137 (opened for signature 28 July 1951, entered into force 22 April 1954).

[16] Article 3 of the Refugee Convention provides: "The Contracting States shall apply the provisions of this Convention to refugees without discrimination as to race, religion or country of origin".

[17] Vivian Tan "Chinese schools offer primary education for urban refugees" (22 November 2013) <www.unhcr.org/en-au/news/latest/2013/11/528f66086/chinese-schools-offer-primary-education-urban-refugees.html>.

[18] Xinhua "yidaiyilu guojihezuo gaofengluntan chengguo qingdan (quanwen)" (16 May 2017) <www.xinhuanet.com/world/2017-05/16/c_1120976848.htm> (translation: "List of Achievements of the Belt-and-Road Forum for International Cooperation (Full Text)"); Ministry of Commerce, People's Republic of China "China and UNHCR Sign the Assistance Agreement to Meet Refugee Challenges" (30 September 2017) <http://english.mof com.gov.cn/article/newsrelease/significantnews/201710/20171002654087.shtml>.

4.2   From Returning Overseas Chinese to Refugees: Vietnamese Refugees

4.2.1   China's Exceptional Generosity towards Vietnamese Refugees

In April 1978, large numbers of people began to flood into China from Vietnam. The majority of them, hundreds of thousands of people, entered China from Vietnam overland and by boat through Guangxi Zhuang autonomous region, which is a main gateway between China and Vietnam; others crossed into Yunnan province overland.[19] By the early 1980s, about 280,000 people had arrived, most of them from Vietnam with a small portion from Laos.[20]

Upon their arrival at the Chinese border, they were provided with shelter, food, clothes, medicine and a daily allowance by local Chinese authorities. A network of the Office of Reception and Settlement of Indochinese Refugees was established at the state and provincial levels to facilitate and oversee the reception and settlement process.[21] Later, they were transferred from the border area to resettlement places in six provinces and autonomous regions in south and southwest China, including Guangxi Zhuang autonomous region, Guangdong province, Hainan province (part of Guangdong province before mid-1980s), Yunnan province, and Jiangxi province, and the majority of them were given jobs on overseas Chinese farms (OCFs). Guangxi and Guangdong, where many of the refugees or their ancestors were originally from and where a similar climate to Southeast Asia can be found, together hosted around 200,000 refugees.[22] A significant proportion of the refugees, with few occupational qualifications, were settled on existing and newly established OCFs; refugees with a fishing background were provided with suitable facilities to resume their trade in fishing villages; others were absorbed by mines, factories and small township enterprises.[23]

Between April 1978 and 1982, China received and settled locally about 280,000 Indochinese refugees.[24] In addition to those who came directly from Vietnam and Laos, China also offered resettlement to 2,814

---

[19]   Shuying Liang *guoji nanmin fa* (Intellectual Property Publishing House, Beijing, 2009) at 276 (translation: *International Refugee Law*).

[20]   At 272.

[21]   At 272.

[22]   Liang, above n 19, at 280.

[23]   Tom Lam "The Exodus of Hoa Refugees from Vietnam and their Settlement in Guangxi – China's Refugee Settlement Strategies" (2000) 13 *Journal of Refugee Studies* 374.

[24]   Liang, above n 19, at 280.

Indochinese refugees from refugee camps in Thailand between 1980 and 1982,[25] the majority of whom were ethnic Chinese from Laos and Cambodia.[26] In 1991, China and Laos signed an agreement on the repatriation of Lao refugees, following which 3,550 refugees voluntarily returned to Laos between 1991 and 1997.[27] During the same period, more than thirty Cambodian refugees also voluntarily returned to Cambodia as a result of cooperation between the Chinese and Cambodian Governments and UNHCR's assistance. As of March 1999, about 800 Lao refugees and five Cambodian refugee families remained in China.[28]

Those from Vietnam generally remain in China.[29] Nowadays, the number of Vietnamese refugees and their descendants in China has grown to about 300,000.[30] They are well integrated into the local communities.[31] Although they have not been naturalised,[32] most of them have been registered in the Chinese household registration (*hukou*) system, obtained a Chinese identity card,[33] and enjoy socio-economic rights on a par with Chinese citizens.[34] Their local integration in China was praised by the former UN High Commissioner for Refugees António Guterres as "one of the most successful integration programs (of refugees) in the world".[35]

China's policy towards these refugees from Vietnam is notably generous. First, as noted by UNHCR, during the Indochinese refugee crisis in the 1970s and 1980s, China "was virtually alone in the east Asia region in granting not only asylum, but also settlement for the refugees from Vietnam",[36] whereas its neighbours, such as Thailand, Malaysia and

---

[25] David Feith *Stalemate: Refugees in Asia* (Asian Bureau Australia, Parkville, 1988) at Appendix. Cambodia has no land border with China.

[26] At Appendix.

[27] Liang, above n 19, at 306.

[28] UNHCR Hong Kong, above n 12.

[29] A small number of them resettled to third countries through family reunion.

[30] Jing Song "Vietnamese refugees well settled in China, await citizenship" (10 May 2007) UNHCR <www.unhcr.org/464302994.html>.

[31] Lam, above n 23, at 378.

[32] Song, above n 30.

[33] United States Committee for Refugees and Immigrants (USCRI) "World Refugee Survey" (2009) <www.refugees.org/resources/refugee-warehousing/archived-world-refugee-surveys/2009-wrs-country-updates/china.html>; Liang, above n 19, at 265.

[34] UNHCR "UNHCR Regional Representation in China" <www.unhcr.org/hk/en/134-china-2.html>.

[35] Song, above n 30.

[36] UNHCR *The State of the World's Refugees: Fifty Years of Humanitarian Action* (Oxford University Press, Oxford, 2000), at 82 <www.unhcr.org/3ebf9bad0.pdf>.

Singapore, constantly resisted and deterred refugees from Vietnam. Second, the refugees from Vietnam who arrived during the Indochinese refugee crisis enjoy socio-economic rights on a par with Chinese citizens, whereas other recognised refugees in China currently have no right to work, depend on UNHCR support (in terms of food, accommodation, healthcare and children's education) and have not been allowed to settle locally.

Why has China been exceptionally generous towards refugees from Vietnam who arrived during the Indochinese refugee crisis? Muntarbhorn rightly noted in 1992 two important factors to which China's generosity could be attributed.[37] First, during the Indochinese refugee crisis those who fled to China were overwhelmingly ethnic Chinese from Vietnam. Second, China's economic reform in the late 1970s provided a rare historical opportunity for the local settlement of the refugees from Vietnam. In addition to these two factors, the complex issues surrounding their nationality and China's overseas Chinese policy in early to mid-1978 were two other, arguably equally crucial, factors underlying China's readiness to accept the refugees from Vietnam.

4.2.2   Status of the Displaced Persons from Vietnam under Chinese Law, 1978–1979

China officially declared its recognition of the displaced persons from Indochina as refugees in August 1979.[38] On 4 August 1979, the Meeting on the Reception and Settlement of Indochinese Refugees (1979 Meeting) was held in Beijing, co-presided by then Chairman of China Li Xiannian and then Vice-Premier Chen Muhua, and attended by officials from eighteen ministries and Government departments, and five provinces and autonomous regions.[39] The 1979 Meeting laid down four principles for the Indochinese refugee reception and settlement: (1) from the standpoint of political implication and humanity, the reception and settlement work should be handled with care and responsibility; (2) political education of the refugees should be strengthened; (3) the refugees' living conditions should be improved gradually; and (4) publicity

---

[37] Vitit Muntarbhorn *The Status of Refugees in Asia* (Clarendon Press, Oxford, 1992) at 61.

[38] See Jiancheng Zheng "From Nanqiao to Refugee: The Formation of China's Policy toward Indochinese Refugees, 1978–1979" (PhD Thesis, Jinan University, 2015) at 101; Liang, above n 19, at 273.

[39] Liang, above n 19, at 273.

and reporting of the reception and settlement work should be enhanced.[40] Under principle number 4, the 1979 Meeting required "[a]ll the [displaced] people [from Indochina] to be settled should be collectively called refugees".[41]

To fully understand China's response to the Vietnamese refugees, it would be helpful to first examine the relevant legal context in China. Most of the Vietnamese refugees in China arrived between 1978 and 1982.[42] China was not a party to the Refugee Convention until September 1982. Muntarbhorn, Robinson and Liang noted that art 32 of the 1982 Constitution of China, which stipulates that "China may grant asylum to foreigners who request it for political reasons", provides a legal basis for China's acceptance of refugees.[43] Liang did not indicate whether art 32 of the 1982 Constitution was invoked in the case of the Vietnamese refugees. Pointing out that China had not acceded to the Refugee Convention or its 1967 Protocol, she stated that China accepted the Vietnamese refugees on the basis of humanitarian spirit.[44] Muntarbhorn noted – and Robinson agreed with him – that art 32 of the 1982 Constitution "has not generally been invoked for the large-scale influx of Indochinese refugee cases".[45] Indeed, the 1982 Constitution was promulgated and entered into force on 4 December 1982, after most of the Vietnamese refugees had been accepted by and settled locally in China.

The 1978 Constitution, which was in force between March 1978 and December 1982, also contained a provision on asylum. Article 59 of the 1978 Constitution provided that "[t]he People's Republic of China grants the right of residence to any foreigner who is persecuted because of his or her support for justice, participation in revolutionary movements or conduct of scientific work".[46] There is no evidence that the Chinese

---

[40] At 274.

[41] Song Han *A Sunshine Home: Humanitarian Resettlement in Guangdong* (English ed, Lingnan Arts Publishing, Guangzhou, 1999) at 46, as cited in Zheng, above n 38, at 98; see also Liang, above n 19, at 274.

[42] Song, above n 30.

[43] Muntarbhorn, above n 37, at 62; W Courtland Robinson *Terms of Refuge: The Indochinese Exodus & the International Response* (Zed Books, London, 1998) at 282; Liang, above n 19, at 259.

[44] Liang, above n 19, at 273.

[45] Muntarbhorn, above n 37, at 62; Robinson, above n 43, at 282.

[46] The full text is available in Chinese at <www.npc.gov.cn/wxzl/wxzl/2000-12/06/content_4365.htm>. An unofficial English translation is available at <https://commons.wikimedia.org/w/index.php?title=File:People%27s_Republic_of_China_1978_Constitution.pdf&page=3>.

authority had published any legal, policy, or judicial document explaining what constituted "support for justice", "participation in revolutionary movements", or "conduct of scientific work".[47] Between 1949 and 1978, China granted asylum to only a few persons, mainly leaders of communist parties, heads of state and high-ranking diplomats. This suggests that China had a restrictive approach to asylum.

Ninety-nine per cent of the Indochinese refugees China accepted came from Vietnam,[48] and about 98 per cent of the Vietnamese refugees China accepted were ethnic Chinese.[49] They were mainly from North Vietnam and were mostly labourers with little education.[50] It is well recognised that they fled from Vietnam to China because they were persecuted by the Vietnamese authority as a consequence of the political and territorial conflicts between China and Vietnam at that time.[51] There is no evidence that they were targeted by the Vietnamese authority because of their involvement in any revolutionary movement, support for justice or scientific work. Nor has the Chinese authority claimed so. It was the view of the Chinese Government at the 1979 meeting that the refugees from Vietnam were persecuted by the Vietnamese authority because of their Chinese ethnicity.[52] Therefore, it is unlikely that art 59 of the 1978 Constitution was the legal basis of China's acceptance of the Vietnamese refugees.

Since China has treated the Vietnamese as refugees for decades, it is usually taken for granted that they were accepted and settled locally as refugees from the very beginning of the influx. However, China's initial response to the influx of the ethnic Chinese fleeing Vietnam suggests that this was not the case.

---

[47] See Section 3.1.3.

[48] Yu'e Zhou and Jiancheng Zheng "zai hua yinzhi nanmin yu guoji hezuo: yizhong lishi de fenxi he sikao" (2014) 3 *Southeast Asian Affairs* 41 at 45 (translation: "Indochinese Refugees in China and International Cooperation").

[49] Song, above n 30.

[50] See eg Michael Godley "A Summer Cruise to Nowhere: China and the Vietnamese Chinese in Perspective" (1980) 4 *The Australian Journal of Chinese Affairs* 35; Lam, above n 23; Pao-min Chang "The Sino-Vietnamese Dispute over the Ethnic Chinese" (1982) 90 *The China Quarterly* 195.

[51] UNHCR, above n 36, at 82; Liang, above n 19, at 269; Lam, above n 23, at 377; Xiaorong Han "Exiled to the Ancestral Land: The Resettlement, Stratification and Assimilation of the Refugees from Vietnam in China" (2013) 10 *International Journal of Asian Studies* 25 at 27; Jing Zhang "zhongguo weishenme bu she nanminying" *China Society Magazine* (May 2002) at 61 (translation: "Why China Did Not Establish Refugee Camps").

[52] Liang, above n 19, at 272.

4.2.3   Initial Acceptance and Settlement as Chinese Nationals

When large numbers of displaced persons of Chinese ethnicity started to flood into China from Vietnam in April 1978, China promptly charged Vietnam with persecuting Chinese nationals. It claimed that the exodus was a result of the forced naturalisation Vietnam had imposed upon Chinese nationals living in Vietnam,[53] and that in doing so Vietnam had departed from the principle of voluntary naturalisation jointly agreed upon by the two countries in 1955.[54] Vietnam, on the other hand, claimed that there were no "persecuted Chinese" or "Chinese nationals", only "Hoa people" or "Vietnamese of Chinese origin", and counter-charged China with manipulating the Hoa people to leave Vietnam.[55]

Historically, the issue of the nationality of the Chinese people living in Vietnam was a complicated one.[56] In imperial Vietnam and during the French colonisation, the Vietnamese authorities treated Chinese residents in Vietnam as Chinese nationals, not Vietnamese nationals.[57] The 1885 Treaty of Tientsin between China and France provided that the Chinese in Vietnam "shall enjoy, both in their persons and property, the same security as French dependents".[58] On the other hand, Chinese nationality laws passed by the Chinese Qing imperial Government in 1909 and by the Government of the Republic of China in 1912, 1914, and 1929 applied the principle of *jus sanguinis* to male lineage as the major basis for acquiring Chinese nationality, regardless of the country of birth, and prohibited naturalisation without the Chinese Government's

---

[53] Spokesman of the Overseas Chinese Affairs Office of the State Council "Statement on Viet Nam's Expulsion of Chinese Residents" *Beijing Review* (Beijing, 2 June 1978) at 16.

[54] At 16.

[55] Godley, above n 50, at 50; Pao-min Chang, *Beijing, Hanoi, and the Overseas Chinese* (University of California Institute of East Asian Studies, Berkeley, 1982) at 39.

[56] See Godley, above n 50, at 50; Tung-Pi Chen "The Nationality Law of the People's Republic of China and the Overseas Chinese in Hong Kong, Macao and Southeast Asia" (1984) 5 *New York Law School Journal of International & Comparative Law* 281; Leo Suryadinata "China's Citizenship Law and the Chinese in Southeast Asia" in M Barry Hooker (ed) *Law and the Chinese in Southeast Asia* (Institute of Southeast Asian Studies, Singapore, 2002).

[57] Tang Lay Lee "Stateless Persons, Stateless Refugees and the 1989 Comprehensive Plan of Action – Part 2: Chinese Nationality and the People's Republic of China" (1995) 7 *International Journal of Refugee Law* 481 at 485; Luong Nhi Ky "The Chinese in Vietnam: A Study of Vietnamese-Chinese Relations with Special Attention to the Period 1862–1961" (PhD Thesis, University of Michigan, 1963) at ch 7.

[58] Treaty of Peace, Friendship and Commerce between France and China (9 June 1885), art 1 <www.chinaforeignrelations.net/node/164>.

consent. As such, the nationality of the Chinese living in Vietnam was not a problem for China or Vietnam before the end of colonial Vietnam.

In 1955, Vietnam became independent from France, splitting into socialist North Vietnam and capitalist South Vietnam. Meanwhile, in 1949 the Chinese Socialist Government took over Mainland China, and the Government of the Republic of China retreated to Taiwan. The Chinese Socialist Government announced abandonment of all laws of the Republic of China, but did not pass a nationality law until 1980. As a result, there was no law governing nationality in China from 1949 to 1979.

Both capitalist South Vietnam and socialist North Vietnam took steps to assimilate local Chinese residents. South Vietnam promulgated a decree imposing Vietnamese nationality on Vietnamese-born Chinese in 1956.[59] The enforcement of the decree provoked strong protest from the Chinese community in South Vietnam and the Republic of China in Taiwan, which then sent airplanes to evacuate a few thousand Chinese residents out of South Vietnam.[60] Beijing, on the other hand, hardly responded to the crisis.[61]

In 1955, North Vietnam and China reached an agreement that Chinese residents in North Vietnam would be *administered* by Vietnam.[62] The two countries also agreed that, on the condition that they enjoyed the same rights as the Vietnamese, Chinese residents in North Vietnam might adopt Vietnamese nationality step by step after being given "sustained and patient persuasion and ideological education".[63]

The 1955 agreement did not spell out the time needed for the process of naturalisation or whether the Chinese residents administered by Vietnam should be considered as Chinese nationals or fully fledged Vietnamese citizens during the interim period.[64] Nor did the 1955 agreement specify whether the Chinese residents in South Vietnam should be subject to the same principle of integration after the unification of North and South Vietnam.[65] In 1961, North Vietnam and China reached another agreement which allowed North Vietnam to issue travel

---

[59] Godley, above n 50, at 46; Ky, above n 57, at 155.
[60] Godley, above n 50, at 47; Ky, above n 57, at 156.
[61] Godley, above n 50, at 48.
[62] Chang, above n 50, at 196; Han, above n 51, at 10.
[63] *Renmin Ribao* commentator "Lies Cannot Cover up Facts" *Beijing Review* (Beijing, 16 June 1978) at 17.
[64] Chang, above n 50, at 196.
[65] At 196.

documents to the Chinese returning to China for short visits, but North Vietnam was still not authorised to issue passports to them.[66]

North and South Vietnam unified in 1975 and in the late 1970s Chinese–Vietnamese relations began to deteriorate quickly. At the time of the exodus in 1978, Chinese residents in Vietnam enjoyed all the rights and privileges of Vietnamese citizenship, but were exempted from military service and had more freedom in terms of travel and trade than Vietnamese citizens.[67] The Vietnamese Government argued that it treated the Chinese residents in Vietnam well because they were regarded as Vietnamese citizens instead of foreigners.[68] However, as Han argued, "in offering various privileges to the Chinese, the Vietnamese Government had preserved a tradition ... maintained by some Vietnamese dynasties as well as the French colonial government" of treating the Chinese residents as privileged foreign nationals.[69]

Despite the complexity surrounding the precise status of the Chinese residents in Vietnam, it is clear that, up to late 1978, the Chinese Government unequivocally claimed that they were Chinese nationals. This claim was well documented by scholarly writings and media reports in the late 1970s and early 1980s.[70] For example, between April 1978 and December 1978, Chinese state-run media, such as the *People's Daily* and the *Beijing Review*, published numerous articles condemning Vietnam for victimising Chinese nationals.[71]

---

[66] Hoàng Nguyên "Cong Jinbian dao Beijing" in *Zai Yuenan de huaren* (Foreign Languages Press, Hanoi, 1978) 11 (translation: "From Phnom Penh to Beijing" in *The Chinese in Vietnam*), cited in Han, above n 51, at 12; Vietnamese Ministry of Foreign Affairs *Tuyên Bô´ của bô´ ngoa᾿i giao nuo᾿c cô᾿ng hòa xã hô᾿i chủ nghiã Viê᾿t Nam vê᾿ vâ᾿n đê᾿ nguo᾿i Hoa ở Viê᾿t Nam* (Department of Culture and Information, Hanoi, 1978) (translation: *Declaration on the Issue of the Hoa People in Vietnam Issued by the Spokesperson of the Ministry of Foreign Affairs of the Socialist Republic of Vietnam*), cited in Han, above n 41, at 12; Chang, above n 50, at 197.

[67] Han, above n 41, at 14; Lee, above n 57, at 486; Chang, above n 55, at 9.

[68] Han, above n 41, at 14. For more discussion on the nationality of the Chinese in Vietnam at the time of the exodus, see Lee, above n 57, at 486; Chang, above n 55, at 9.

[69] Han, above n 41, at 15.

[70] See eg Godley, above n 50; Chang, above n 55.

[71] See eg "Statement by Spokesman of Consular Department of Chinese Foreign Ministry" *Beijing Review* (Beijing, 30 June 1978) at 20; "Who Is to Blame? – Why ships sent by China to bring back persecuted Chinese residents in Viet Nam are lying at anchor off its territorial sea" *Beijing Review* (Beijing, 7 July 1978) at 30; "China Compelled to Terminate Economic and Technical Aid to Viet Nam" *Beijing Review* (Beijing, 14 July 1978) at 27; "Sino-Vietnamese Negotiations at Vice-Ministerial Level" *Beijing Review* (Beijing, 4 August 1978) at 4; "Viet Nam Slams Door on Negotiations" *Beijing Review* (Beijing, 6 October 1978) at 33.

China's readiness to claim the Chinese residents in Vietnam as Chinese nationals in 1978 was underpinned by its policy towards overseas Chinese in general at that time. For decades after the establishment of the People's Republic of China, the Chinese Government valued the overseas Chinese community as a source of financial and political support and had long professed itself to be the protector of overseas Chinese.[72] From the 1950s through to the 1960s, in the absence of a Chinese nationality law and concrete political solution for the dual nationality issues concerning overseas Chinese in Southeast Asia, the Chinese Government in practice treated large numbers of overseas Chinese who returned to China as Chinese nationals. In the early 1950s, Malaya deported about 19,000 Malayan Chinese who were deemed communists; they were well received, and settled in China.[73] China established ad hoc committees at national and local levels to oversee and facilitate the reception and settlement of these Malayan Chinese; OCFs were established for the first time to settle them.[74] In 1959, 1966 and 1967, China sent ships to Indonesia to bring back about 136,000 ethnic Chinese expelled by Indonesia;[75] additional OCFs were opened to absorb these returnees. Ships were also sent to India in 1963 to pick up ethnic Chinese marginalised by India; ad hoc offices for reception and resettlement of Indian Chinese were established; most returnees were again settled on OCFs.[76] China regarded all of these ethnic Chinese who returned from overseas as Chinese nationals.[77] It should also be mentioned that from the 1940s through the 1970s, the ethnic Chinese living in Vietnam had frequently crossed into Guangxi, China from Vietnam due to wars in Vietnam.[78]

---

[72] See eg Stephen Fitzgerald *China and the Overseas Chinese: A Study of Peking's Changing Policy, 1949–1970* (Cambridge University Press, Cambridge, 1972).

[73] Shichao Deng and Lichang Huang "zhongguo yuenan guiguo nanqiao de anzhi yu shengchan shenghuo xianzhuang tanxi: yi Guangdong yangcun huaqiao ganjuchang weili" (2010) 58 *Ritsumeikan University Journal of Economics* 87 at 88 (translation: "Analysis on Reception of Overseas Chinese in Difficulty Returning from Vietnam and Their Present Work and Life Conditions: A Case Study of Guangdong Yang Village Overseas Chinese Mandarin Farm").

[74] Fitzgerald, above n 72, at 98.

[75] Deng and Huang, above n 74, at 88.

[76] Guangxi Zhuang Autonomous Region Local Chronicle Commission "guangxi tongzhi: qiaowuzhi" (online ed, Guangxi People's Press, 1996), s 5 ch 1 pt 2 <www.gxdqw.com/bin/mse.exe?seachword=&K=a&A=55&run=12> (translation: "Guangxi Chronicle: Overseas Chinese Affairs Chronicle").

[77] Section 5 ch 1 pt 2.

[78] Section 3 ch 1 pt 2. From 1940 to 1945, several thousand ethnic Chinese arrived in Guangxi from Vietnam to flee Japanese bombing. In 1947, upon the return of the French

They were all treated as returning Chinese nationals by the Chinese Government and were settled locally.[79]

Just months before the exodus, in February 1978, then Chairman of China, Hua Guofeng, emphasised that China opposed any attempt to compel overseas Chinese to change their citizenship and was duty-bound to protect those who decided to keep their Chinese citizenship.[80] China's response to the influxes of displaced persons from Vietnam clearly followed the pattern of its response to these earlier waves of overseas Chinese returnees. A network of the Office of Reception and Settlement of Indochinese Refugees was established at the national and provincial levels to oversee and facilitate the reception and settlement of displaced Chinese from Vietnam. The majority of the displaced Chinese from Vietnam were also settled on OCFs. China even sent two ships to Ho Chi Minh City and Haiphong on 15 June 1978 to bring back "victimised Chinese nationals persecuted by the Vietnamese authorities",[81] as had been done in 1959, 1967 and 1968 for the ethnic Chinese expelled by Indonesia.[82] Indeed, an officer from the Chinese MCA, who was involved in receiving the refugees from Vietnam, recalled that the Chinese Government treated the displaced persons from Vietnam as Chinese nationals based merely on the fact that the overwhelming majority of them were of Chinese ethnicity.[83] A refugee who fled Vietnam between 1978 and 1982 also confirmed that there was little verification of their nationality when they arrived at China:[84]

to Vietnam, more than 2,000 Chinese crossed into Guangxi, and the Kuomintang Government sent many planes to Hanoi to repatriate more Chinese; large numbers of Chinese fled to Guangxi as the French bombed northern Vietnam in the following two years. The flow continued well into the 1950s. In 1967, twenty-five Chinese sought asylum in Guangxi after the Chinese community in Vietnam protested and struck against the Vietnamese authorities, which had forced the Chinese to learn Vietnamese and to close down Chinese schools. During the Vietnam War, many Chinese again entered Guangxi for refuge between 1968 and 1972. Before and after the bombing of Haiphong in North Vietnam, more than 1,000 Chinese arrived each day at the tiny town of Fangcheng in Guangxi.

[79] Section 3 ch 1 pt 2.
[80] Chang, above n 55, at 26.
[81] "Who Is to Blame?", above n 71. Vietnam refused to let the Chinese ships dock, and the two Chinese ships returned to China empty at the end of July 1978.
[82] Deng and Huang, above n 73, at 88.
[83] Zhang, above n 51, at 58.
[84] Interview conducted by the author (Guangxi, August 2013). The interviewee insisted he/she, like many others who fled to China, was a Chinese national when he/she crossed into China and tearfully recounted the Vietnamese Chinese communities' demonstration

> Once we crossed the border, [officers from overseas Chinese organisa-
> tions] were waiting for us ... We registered. Collectively. We told them
> where we came from ... They asked some people [questions], not every-
> one. They did not have enough time to ask every person. The local
> residents in Dongxing vouched for many of us [who had relatives or
> acquaintances in Dongxing].

From April to July 1978, more than 160,000 persons fled to China from
Vietnam.[85] By the end of 1978, more than 200,000 displaced persons had
entered China from Vietnam.[86] They were promptly transferred to
OCFs, factories and fishing villages in six provinces and autonomous
regions in south and southwest China. As late as October 1978, China
clearly continued to claim that the displaced persons from Vietnam were
Chinese nationals.[87] As such, the majority of the 280,000 refugees from
Vietnam hosted by China were initially admitted and settled locally as
Chinese nationals.

Since they were considered Chinese nationals by the Chinese authority
at that time, it is natural that they were granted the same rights as other
Chinese nationals, such as access to the Chinese household registration
(*hukou*) system and a Chinese identity card, as well as a job and accommodation provided by the Chinese Government. This gives rise to the
following question: how did these Chinese nationals become refugees
in China?

4.2.4 Why Did China Recognise the Displaced Persons
from Vietnam as Refugees?

In late November and early December 1978, the *People's Daily* and the
Beijing Review published articles about international condemnation of
Vietnam's role in the Indochinese refugee crisis.[88] As Zheng rightly
noted, this shift was a signal of China's interest in adjusting its position

---

against forced naturalisation by Vietnam, but also mentioned that his/her Chinese
passport had expired when he/she arrived in China.

[85] Deng and Huang, above n 73, at 88; Lee, above n 57, at 487.

[86] Sara E Davies *Legitimising Rejection: International Refugee Law in Southeast Asia* (Martinus Nijhoff, Leiden, 2008) at 102; Ramses Amer "Vietnam's Policies and the Ethnic
Chinese since 1975" (1996) 11 *Sojourn: Journal of Social Issues in Southeast Asia* 76 at 83.

[87] "Viet Nam Slams Door on Negotiations", above n 71.

[88] "yuenan dangju canwu rendao de lesuo" *People's Daily* (Beijing, 30 November 1978) at 6
(translation: "The Vietnamese Authorities' Inhumane Extortion"); "Cargo Ships and
'Refugees': Vietnamese Authorities Export 'Refugees' in a Planned Way" *Beijing Review*
(Beijing, 22 December 1978) at 18.

on the status of the displaced Chinese from Vietnam.[89] From early 1979, China began to acknowledge that the displaced persons from Vietnam were a mixed group comprising not only Chinese nationals but also Vietnamese nationals of Chinese and Vietnamese descent.[90] In January 1979, for example, then Chinese Vice-Premier Deng Xiaoping, in his conversation with then US President Jimmy Carter during his historic first visit to the US, said: "[t]he Foreign Minister said it is also a question of nationality. Many of these people are Vietnamese citizens".[91]

On 4 August 1979, the 1979 Meeting declared that "[a]ll the [displaced] people [from Indochina] to be settled down should be collectively called refugees".[92] As Lee noted, the Chinese Government's recognition of the displaced persons as refugees was more a matter of policy than law.[93] Because China had no nationality law to fall back on as a point of reference in 1979, there was no legal barrier to the Chinese Government changing its position on the nationality of the displaced persons from Vietnam. The policy considerations underlying China's decision to recognise the displaced persons from Vietnam as refugees are discussed below.

In late 1978, Deng Xiaoping became the new leader in China. In December 1978, the 3rd Plenum of the 11th Central Committee of the Chinese Communist Party endorsed Deng's economic reform and open-door policy. The Chinese Government began to prioritise economic development over ideological tussles, and sought integration into the international community. These historic changes in China's leadership, political climate and economic policy in late 1978 led to the reshaping of China's foreign policy and overseas Chinese policy, which in turn made changes in China's policy towards the displaced persons from Vietnam not only possible but also necessary.

---

[89] Zheng, above n 38.

[90] See eg "qianglie kangyi yuenan buduan ba yuenan jumin qugan dao woguo jingnei" *People's Daily* (Beijing, 6 January 1979) at 4 (translation: "Strong Opposition to Vietnam Expelling Vietnamese Residents into China"); "zhizhi yuenan dangju yilingweihe de fandong zhengce" *People's Daily* (Beijing, 20 January 1979) at 5 (translation: "Stop Vietnam's Policy").

[91] Adam M Howard (ed) *Foreign Relations of the United States, 1977–1980: Volume 13 – China* (Department of State, Washington, DC, 1983) at 779.

[92] Han, above n 41, at 46, cited in Zheng, above n 38, at 98; see also Liang, above n 19, at 274.

[93] Lee, above n 57.

As revealed by then Chinese Vice-Premier Deng Xiaoping's conversation with US President Jimmy Carter in January 1979, the possible impact of China's policy shift towards the displaced from Vietnam on China's relationships with Southeast Asian countries was an important consideration in the minds of Chinese leaders. Carter asked Deng whether there was "any possibility of China accepting more refugees who are leaving Vietnam who are Chinese". Deng replied: "[t]his is a complicated question because the numbers are too great . . . *This question not only concerns Vietnam*; in Southeast Asia as a whole, we have ten million people of Chinese descent" (emphasis added).[94]

In late 1978, improving China's relations with Southeast Asian countries was high on the foreign policy agenda of Deng Xiaoping's Government.[95] The Chinese leadership identified three main issues to be addressed for a better Chinese–Southeast Asian relation, one of them being the long-standing dual nationality problem concerning large numbers of persons of Chinese descent in Southeast Asian countries.[96] Southeast Asian countries had long worried that China might mobilise overseas Chinese to "export revolution" to Southeast Asia, a policy pursued by the Chinese Government in the 1960s and early 1970s. Deng's Government declared three policies to address the dual nationality issue: first, to encourage and support Chinese residents in Southeast Asian countries to take up local nationality; second, to declare China's rejection of dual nationality; and third, to abandon the policy of trying to mobilise overseas Chinese for political purposes.[97] These policies were originally proposed by former Chinese Premier Zhou Enlai in the 1950s, but had not been effectively implemented. Giving up its claim over the 280,000 displaced persons from Vietnam as Chinese nationals allowed China to send a clear, positive message to Southeast Asian countries that the Chinese Government now was effectively implementing its policies to solve the dual nationality issue.

---

[94] Howard, above n 91, at 779.

[95] See Lee Lai To "Deng Xiaoping's ASEAN Tour: A Perspective on Sino-Southeast Asian Relations" (1981) 3(1) *Contemporary Southeast Asia* 58; Yanan Li "1978: chongxin renshi dongnanya" (issue 3, 2014) *Beijing Journal of Social Science* 121 (translation: "1978: Understanding of Southeast Asia Again").

[96] Zhenrui Dong "gaige kaifang yu dengxiaoping de waijiao zhanlue" (issue 1, 2012) *Journal of the China Youth University of Political Studies* 84 at 86 (translation: "Reform and Open-Up and Deng Xiaoping's Foreign Policy Strategies").

[97] Li, above n 95.

Indeed, at the 1979 Meeting, which officially declared China's recognition of the displaced from Vietnam as refugees, then Chairman of China and director of the Overseas Chinese Affairs Office Li Xiannian clearly indicated that China's desire to address Southeast Asian countries' concerns about overseas Chinese was one of the reasons why China no longer wanted to refer to the displaced from Vietnam as Chinese nationals:[98]

> In the past [China] used to claim that there were 20 million overseas Chinese, as if the more, the better. Thailand, Malaysia, Singapore, the Philippines, and Indonesia in Southeast Asia ... are very concerned about two things: our support for local communist parties and the overseas Chinese issue ... If [China] claims all [the displaced persons from Vietnam] as Chinese nationals, [other countries] will say [they] are your own responsibility. Too many overseas Chinese nationals is exactly what foreigners are afraid of.

Since a person must be outside his or her country of nationality (or in the case of a stateless person his or her country of habitual residence) to qualify for refugee status, it is implicit in China's recognition of the displaced persons from Vietnam as refugees that the Chinese Government no longer considered them Chinese nationals.

Additionally, as Li indicated in his speech above, recognising the displaced persons from Vietnam as refugees gave China the moral high ground, because China was no longer taking in its own nationals but generously offering asylum and humanitarian assistance to persecuted foreign nationals. Soon after the influx from Vietnam started, it became clear that the scale and the pace of the influx was overwhelming for China, which was still a poor country in the late 1970s, and that the majority of the displaced persons from Vietnam brought neither economic resources nor skills. As Deng Xiaoping put it in his conversation with President Carter:[99]

> [a]nd for us it is quite a heavy burden ... A lot of these refugees are really the bad elements in Vietnam – those who do not work or even hooligans – and those who really do honest work are left behind. And those refugees who escape or are driven out come with practically no property whatsoever – just the clothes on their back and maybe one shirt.

---

[98] State Council Office of Overseas Chinese Affairs *Party and State Leaders on Overseas Chinese Affairs* (1992) at 71, cited in Zheng, above n 38, at 100.

[99] Howard, above n 91, at 779.

As early as in mid-1978, China requested Vietnam to stop forcing out ethnic Chinese residents in Vietnam during several rounds of negotiations, to no effect.[100] China also sought, in vain, to pressure Vietnam by cutting economic aid to Vietnam and withdrawing technical assistance, claiming that aid was being diverted to settle the displaced persons expelled by Vietnam.[101] In July 1978, China temporarily closed the China–Vietnam land border.[102] But the influx from Vietnam continued. In February 1979, the Sino-Vietnamese War broke out. The two countries were now no longer comrades and brothers but enemies. By this time, it would have become clear to China that it was unlikely to be able to persuade or pressure Vietnam to stop persecuting and expelling ethnic Chinese residents in Vietnam. As the professed protector of overseas Chinese, China had not only borne the economic burden of hosting the displaced Chinese, but had also suffered the humiliation of failing to stop Vietnam from persecuting those whom China claimed as its own nationals.[103] Recognising the displaced persons from Vietnam as refugees allowed China to at least seize the moral high ground.

Recognising the displaced persons from Vietnam as refugees also gave China a good reason to accept international aid to alleviate the economic burden incurred by hosting them. In late 1978, the Chinese Government had just abandoned its long-term policy of refusing all UN aid.[104] According to Liang, Han and Zhang, UNHCR played an important role in China's recognition of the displaced persons from Vietnam as refugees.[105] In March 1979, Alexander Casella, who would later become UNHCR's director for Asia and Oceania, unofficially met with a Chinese delegate in Geneva and expressed UNHCR's willingness to assist the displaced persons from Vietnam.[106] He also explained that the new UN High Commissioner for Refugees, Poul Hartling, wanted to improve the

---

[100] Spokesman of the Overseas Chinese Affairs Office of the State Council, above n 53, at 16.

[101] Godley, above n 50, at 52.

[102] Jay Mathews "Refugees Worry South China: Thousands of Refugees from Vietnam Produce Uneasiness in South China" *The Washington Post* (Washington, 16 July 1978) at A18.

[103] Chang, above n 55, at 47.

[104] Hong Zhou, Jun Zhang and Min Zhang *Foreign Aid in China* (Springer, Heidelberg, 2015) at 162; Allen Carlson and Ren Xiao, *New Frontiers in China's Foreign Relations* (Lexington Books, Lanham (Maryland), 2011) at 72.

[105] Liang, above n 19, at 253; Song Han *yangguang jiayuan: rendao anzhi zai guangdong* (Lingnan Arts Publishing, Guangzhou, 1999) at 11 (translation: *A Sunshine Home: Humanitarian Settlement in Guangdong*); Zhang, above n 51, at 58.

[106] Alexander Casella *Breaking the Rules* (Editions du Tricorne, Geneva, 2011) at 176.

relationship between China and UNHCR.[107] In early 1979, a group of Chinese officials visited refugee camps in Thailand and "saw the impact of international financial assistance".[108] Hartling visited China in March 1979.[109] He advised the Chinese Government that the displaced Chinese from Vietnam qualified for refugee status under international law and that China should avail itself of UNHCR aid for refugees. The Chinese Government welcomed Hartling's advice.[110]

In July 1979, the Chinese delegation to the Geneva Meeting on Refugees and Displaced Persons in South-East Asia indicated that UNHCR aid would be welcomed by China.[111] Two weeks later, China recognised the displaced persons from Vietnam as refugees at the 1979 Meeting. Shortly after the 1979 Meeting, Casella and another UNHCR representative arrived in China to conduct research for the proposed assistance programme.[112] In September 1979, the UNHCR ExCom approved a five-year assistance programme of USD 50 million to aid the refugees from Vietnam in China.[113] The program became one of the first UN aid programmes to operate in China.

4.2.5   Why Does China Treat the Vietnamese Refugees More Favourably Than Other Refugees in China?

The Vietnamese refugees have generally enjoyed the same socio-economic rights as Chinese nationals in the past four decades. This is in stark contrast to the situation of the UNHCR refugees, who have no right to work and none of whom has been allowed to settle locally in China. Why has China treated the Vietnamese refugees more favourably?

---

[107] China had previously criticised UNHCR for its assistance to Tibetan refugees and Chinese refugees in Hong Kong and Macao; see Jerome Alan Cohen and Hungdah Chiu *People's China and International Law: A Documentary Study* (Princeton University Press, Princeton, 1974) vol 2 at 1386.

[108] Zhang, above n 51, at 62.

[109] *UNHCR Fonds 13 Records of the High Commissioner: Sub-fonds 2 Poul Hartling 1968–1987 (predominant 1977–1985)* (2 September 2009) <www.unhcr.org/4b2610be9.pdf>.

[110] Liang, above n 19, at 253; Han, above n 105, at 11; Zhang, above n 51, at 58.

[111] United Nations General Assembly *Meeting on Refugees and Displaced Persons in South-East Asia, convened by the Secretary-General of the United Nations at Geneva, on 20 and 21 July 1979 and subsequent developments: Report of the Secretary-General* UN Doc A/34/627 (7 November 1979) at Annex 1 [12].

[112] Casella, above n 106, at 200.

[113] Letter of Intent between the Government of the People's Republic of China and the Office of the United Nations High Commissioner for Refugees (8 May 1985).

As Zheng rightly pointed out, China's policy towards the Vietnamese refugees has been not a "pure" refugee policy but a mix of refugee policy and overseas Chinese policy.[114] He further noted that China's policy towards the Vietnamese refugees was "special and complicated",[115] and that the Chinese authority mainly regarded the matter of Vietnamese refugees as a historic matter to be isolated from other refugee matters in general.[116] The wording used by the 1979 Meeting was ambiguous. The recognition of the Vietnamese refugees' status came under the fourth principle established by the 1979 Meeting, which concerned enhancement of publicity and reporting of China's assistance to the displaced person from Vietnam, Laos and Cambodia.[117] It was required that "All the people to be settled down should be collectively called refugees. *Overseas Chinese refugees were parts of the refugees in general*" (emphasis added).[118] In his speech at the 1979 Meeting, then Chairman of China and director of the Overseas Chinese Affairs Office Li Xiannian said: "Among the refugees, who are *huaqiao*? Who are not *huaqiao*? They have entered into our country . . . [we] should settle them well, regardless of whether they are *huaqiao*, non-*huaqiao*, or [ethnic] Vietnamese".[119]

It is not uncommon that Vietnamese refugees in China are still referred to by Government officials, Chinese state media and scholars as overseas Chinese nationals in distress (*nanqiao*) or overseas Chinese nationals who returned to China (*guiqiao*).[120] A 2006 article written by the deputy director of the Guangxi Provincial Office for the Reception and Settlement of Indochinese Refugees, summarised the Chinese Government's equivocal position on the Vietnamese refugees:[121]

---

[114] Zheng, above n 38, at 104.
[115] At 104.
[116] At 108.
[117] Liang, above n 19, at 274.
[118] Han, above n 105, at 46.
[119] State Council Office of Overseas Chinese Affairs, above n 100, at 71.
[120] See eg Deng and Huang, above n 73; Han, above n 105, at 38; Huaquan Chen "cong nanmin dao guomin: chongxin Shenshi yuenan guiqiao jianit tequ 30nian" (20 August 2012) <http://zh.cnr.cn/2100zhfw/syyw/201208/t20120820_510637382_1 .shtml> (translation: "From Refugees to Nationals: Rethinking the Participation of Returned Overseas Chinese from Vietnamese in Developing the Special Zone in the Past 30 Years").
[121] Guohua Zeng "Guangxi nanqiao peixun gongzuo de lanshang xianzhuang he tiaozhan" (2006) 2 *bagui qiaokan* 47 at 47 (translation: "Status Quo of and Challenges for Training of Nanqiao in Guangxi" *Overseas Chinese Journal of Bagui*).

> In the international context, we refer to this group as refugees, because this group fits in the UN definition of refugees ... In the domestic context, we refer to them as *nanqiao*, they are *huaqiao* who returned to the motherland because of persecution.

In Guangxi, the Vietnamese refugees are usually considered by the local Chinese residents as overseas Chinese nationals who returned to China (*guiqiao*) or simply as overseas Chinese nationals (*huaqiao*), instead of as refugees. Despite the fact that they have not been naturalised, a number of Vietnamese refugees in Guangxi were allowed to hold government positions,[122] although Chinese law requires public servants to hold Chinese nationality.[123] A Vietnamese refugee I interviewed in 2013, who had fled to Guangxi in 1978, referred to himself as an overseas Chinese national (*huaqiao*) for most of the forty-five-minute interview.[124] This interviewee said repeatedly that "tens of thousands" of people with whom he had fled had Chinese nationality, and he emphasised, with strong emotions and tears in his eyes, that he would never take up Vietnamese nationality. When asked why they were called Indochinese refugees nowadays, the interviewee paused, looking confused, and said hesitantly: "Indochinese? It [Vietnam] was French Indochina. Then it is us, the *huaqiao*. I think so. But I only know, [pause] there was no such a name at that time".

In Yunnan, the Vietnamese refugees were actually divided into two groups locally. Only those who arrived during or after the war were known as refugees (*nanmin*), whereas those who arrived before the Sino-Vietnamese War in February 1979 were locally known as overseas Chinese nationals in distress (*nanqiao*).[125] Ironically, the *nanqiao* were mainly settled on OCFs and have been given household registration and Chinese identity cards in a timely manner, whereas the refugees were mainly accommodated in border villages and ordinary farms and were

---

[122] Guangxi Zhuang Autonomous Region Local Chronicle Commission, above n 76, at ch 1.4.
[123] Law of the People's Republic of China on Public Servants 2005 (China), art 11 <www.npc.gov.cn/englishnpc/Law/2007-12/13/content_1384101.htm>.
[124] Interview conducted by the author (China, 2013).
[125] Buzhi Ding, Zhen Xu and Jialin Liang "yige yi cunzai 30 nian de chenmo qunti: 30 wan nanmin zai zhongguo" (2009) *Nanfang zhoumo* (online ed, Guangzhou, 15 October 2009) (translation: "A Silent Community That Has Existed for 30 Years: 300 Thousand Refugees in China" *Southern Weekly*).

unable to obtain Chinese identity cards or household registration until 2009, despite their repeated requests.[126]

In retrospect, at the time of the 1979 Meeting, the majority of the Vietnamese refugees in China, who had been accepted and settled locally as returning overseas Chinese nationals, already enjoyed more or less the same treatment as local Chinese residents. It is questionable whether China's recognition of their refugee status was overall a decision in *their* favour. Refugee status barely gave them any additional protection from the Chinese authority compared to their previous status as returning overseas Chinese. Instead, as refugees, they have to live with the risk of being asked to leave. At a UNHCR meeting in 1996, speaking of the refugees from Vietnam who had locally settled in China, a Chinese representative stated that "the repatriation of the Vietnamese refugees in China had become a matter of urgency".[127] Although both the first-generation Vietnamese refugees and their descendants are eligible for Chinese nationality under the 1980 Nationality Law of the People's Republic of China,[128] and UNHCR has been advocating for their naturalisation for more than ten years,[129] China has not naturalised them. It is perhaps somewhat ironic that UNHCR, which encouraged China to recognise the displaced Chinese from Vietnam – who would otherwise have been Chinese nationals – as refugees, now advocates for their naturalisation as Chinese nationals.

4.3   North Korean Escapees

4.3.1   North Korean Escapees in China

In the mid-1990s, when a severe famine hit North Korea, large numbers of North Koreans fled into China in search of food. The famine eased in

---

[126] Yunnan Provinicial Bureau of Civil Affairs "duiwai hezuo chu 2009 nian gongzuo zongjie he 2010 nian gongzuo jihua" (8 March 2010) <http://yunnan.mca.gov.cn/art icle/ztzl/mzgzh/cszj/201003/20100300060711.shtml> (translation: "Office of External Cooperation 2009 Work Report and 2010 Work Plan").

[127] Executive Committee of the Programme of the United Nations High Commissioner for Refugees *Forty-seventh session: Summary Record of the 509th Meeting* UN Doc A/AC.96/ SR.509 (8 January 1997).

[128] Shuying Liang "Refugee Protection in China: The Issue of Citizenship and Potential Solutions" in Angus Francis and Rowena Maguire (ed) *Protection of Refugees and Displaced Persons in the Asia Pacific Region* (Ashgate, Farnham (UK), 2013) 67.

[129] Reuters "Indochinese refugees may get Chinese citizenship" (1 June 2007) <www.reuters .com/article/us-china-indochina-idUSPEK9279520070601>.

the late 1990s, but the exodus continued.[130] Since then, many of the escapees have stayed in China for longer periods or transited to a third country with the help of South Korean Christian churches or international NGOs operating underground in China. There are no official statistics for the number of North Korean escapees in China. Estimates vary from 5,000 to 300,000 people, at different points in time.[131]

The Chinese Government has insisted that North Korean escapees in China are illegal economic migrants, not refugees, although UN agencies, scholars and human rights groups have considered that most of them qualify for refugee status.[132] The Chinese Government has also repeatedly declined UNHCR's requests to access North Korean escapees in China. As a result, North Korean escapees in China generally have no access to RSD procedures.

Deprived of the opportunity to apply for recognition of refugee status, North Korean escapees live in China without legal status and, if caught by the Chinese authority, often face detention and then deportation to North Korea, where they normally face penalties, which vary from a few days of imprisonment to execution,[133] for committing the criminal offence of unauthorised departure under art 117 of the North Korean

---

[130] For discussion on North Koreans' motivations to leave North Korea, see eg Stephan Haggard and Marcus Noland *Witness to Transformation: Refugee Insights into North Korea* (Peterson Institute for International Economics, Washington DC, 2011) at 29; Human Rights Watch (HRW) *The Invisible Exodus: North Koreans in the People's Republic of China* (vol 14, no 8(C), November 2002) <www.hrw.org/reports/2002/north korea/> at 9; Rhoda Margesson, Emma Chanlett-Avery and Andorra Bruno *North Korean Refugees in China and Human Rights Issues: International Response and US Policy Options* (Congressional Research Service, Order Code RL34189, 26 September 2007) <www.fas.org/sgp/crs/row/RL34189.pdf> at 6.

[131] James D Seymour *China: Background Paper on the Situation of North Koreans in China* (January 2005) <www.refworld.org/docid/4231d11d4.html> at 15; Haggard and Noland, above n 130, at 2. See also eg Congressional-Executive Commission on China *2013 Annual Report* (10 October 2013) <www.cecc.gov/publications/annual-reports/2013-annual-report> at 118.

[132] For legal analysis on the status of North Korean escapees, see eg Roberta Cohen "Legal Grounds for Protection of North Korean Refugees" (13 September 2010) <www.brookings.edu/research/opinions/2010/09/north-korea-human-rights-cohen>; Elim Chan and Andreas Schloenhardt "North Korean Refugees and International Refugee Law" (2007) 19 *International Journal of Refugee Law* 215; Benjamin Neaderland "Quandary on the Yalu: International Law, Politics, and China's North Korean Refugee Crisis" (2004) 40 *Stanford Journal of International Law* 143.

[133] The severity of the penalisation depends on a number of elements, eg whether the escapee was in contact with South Korean missionaries and whether the escapee has previously committed unauthorised departure.

Criminal Code.[134] China's deportation of North Korean escapees has attracted wide criticism from the international community, including the UN Commission of Inquiry on Human Rights in the Democratic People's Republic of Korea, which stated in a 2014 report:[135]

> many such nationals of the Democratic People's Republic of Korea should be recognised as refugees fleeing persecution or refugees sur place ... In forcibly returning nationals of the Democratic People's Republic of Korea, China also violates its obligation to respect the principle of non-refoulement under international refugee and human rights law.

Neither China nor North Korea has published information about the number of repatriated North Koreans or the frequency of forced repatriation. The number of North Koreans reportedly repatriated has varied over the decades.[136] For example, a 1999 United States Committee for Refugees and Immigrants report noted that "Chinese authorities have informally tolerated the presence of North Koreans, even providing them assistance" before they began to expel large numbers of North Korean escapees in January 1999.[137] *The New York Times* estimated that about 7,200 escapees were repatriated to North Korea in 1999, about 10 per cent of new arrivals.[138] The Defense Forum Foundation based in the United States, in cooperation with NGOs working to rescue North Korean escapees, recorded 169 cases of repatriated North Korean escapees between 2007 and 2010, although it claimed that "[t]here were, of course, thousands and thousands" undocumented cases of repatriation of North Korean escapees.[139] Human Rights Watch recorded

---

[134] Seymour, above n 131, at 26.

[135] Commission of Inquiry on Human Rights in the Democratic People's Republic of Korea (CIHRDPRK) *Report of the commission of inquiry on human rights in the Democratic People's Republic of Korea* UN Doc A/HRC/25/63 (7 February 2014) at [43].

[136] See eg "List of North Korean Refugees and Humanitarian Workers Seized by Chinese Authorities" <www.seoultrain.com/content/resources/the_list.htm>.

[137] United States Committee for Refugees and Immigrants *US Committee for Refugees World Refugee Survey 1999 – China, (including Hong Kong and Tibet)* (1 January 1999) <www.refworld.org/docid/3ae6a8a61f.html>.

[138] Elisabeth Rosenthal "China in Campaign to Expel Koreans Who Enter Illegally" *The New York Times* (online ed, New York, 31 May 2000).

[139] *Escaping North Korea: The Plight of Defectors: Hearing before the Tom Lantos Human Rights Commission House of Representatives – One Hundred and Eleventh Congress – Second Session* (23 September 2010) at Appendix C <www.defenseforumfoundation .org/pdf/nkhearing_09232010.pdf>; see also "List of North Korean Refugees and Humanitarian Workers Seized by Chinese Authorities", above n 136; *The Plight of North Koreans in China: A Current Assessment: Roundtable before the Congressional-Executive Commission on China – One Hundred Eighth Congress – Second Session* (19 April 2004)

forty-nine cases of detention of North Korean escapees by the Chinese authorities between July and September 2017,[140] during which period China's crackdown on North Korean escapees was considered by Human Rights Watch to have intensified.[141] The number was a "steep increase" from the fifty-one North Korean escapees recorded by Human Rights Watch as having been detained over the entire previous twelve months.[142]

These numbers are of course incomplete.[143] However, they could be indicative of the fact that, on average, the number of reported repatriation cases may be relatively small in proportion to the estimated total number of North Korean escapees in China. A 2010 Brookings Institution report, for example, noted that "[i]n practice, however, China has allowed large numbers of North Koreans to reside illegally in its country although they have no rights and are vulnerable to exploitation and trafficking as well as to forced returns".[144] Another report issued by the United States Congressional Research Service in 2007 also noted that China tolerated inflows of North Korean escapees and the activities of foreign NGOs provided that such activities were carried out quietly.[145] On balance, it seems fair to say that China gives some – albeit obviously inadequate – humanitarian consideration to North Korean escapees.

at 43 <www.cecc.gov/sites/chinacommission.house.gov/files/documents/roundtables/2004/CECC%20Roundtable%20-%20The%20Plight%20of%20North%20Korean%20Migrants%20in%20China%20A%20Current%20Assessment%20-%204.19.04.pdf>.

[140] David Campanale and Joel Gunter "North Korean man begs China not to deport wife and young son" (11 November 2017) <www.bbc.co.uk/news/world-asia-41952298>.

[141] HRW "China: Redoubling Crackdowns on Fleeing North Koreans: Human Rights Watch Documented 41 North Koreans Detained by China in Summer 2017" (3 September 2017) <www.hrw.org/news/2017/09/03/china-redoubling-crackdowns-fleeing-north-koreans>.

[142] HRW, above n 141.

[143] See Chinese Vice Minister of Public Security Huanning Yang *State Council's Report on Administration of Exit and Entry, Residence, and Employment of Foreigners at the 26 Meeting of the National People's Congress 11th Standing Committee on 25 April 2012* <www.npc.gov.cn/wxzl/gongbao/2012-08/21/content_1736409.htm>. According to this report, the number of illegal immigrants handled by the Chinese public security authority reached over 10,000 for the first time in 1995 and continued to increase every year until 2007, after which the number slightly decreased. In 2011, the Chinese public security authority handled slightly over 20,000 illegal immigrants.

[144] Cohen, above n 132.

[145] Margesson, Chanlett-Avery and Bruno, above n 130, at 11.

4.3.2   Legal Status of North Korean Escapees in China

The Chinese Government refuses to recognise North Korean escapees as refugees and labels them illegal economic migrants.[146] They often face deportation to North Korea if caught by Chinese authorities. China's deportation of North Korean escapees has attracted criticism from the international community. China routinely claims that it has handled North Korean escapees in accordance with domestic law, international law and the spirit of humanity,[147] without elaborating the legal grounds for its decisions or providing details of its treatment of North Korean escapees. For example, the 2012 Chinese state report on the implementation of the Convention of the Rights of the Child stated:[148]

> The "children from the Democratic People's Republic of Korea", referred to in the Committee's concluding remarks, have illegally entered China's borders for economic reasons, and are not refugees. The Chinese government has always dealt properly with cases concerning illegal entrants from the DPRK, in accordance with domestic law, international law and a humanitarian spirit, and giving full consideration to the actual circumstances of the persons involved.

Similarly, the Chinese state report on the Implementation of the Convention on the Elimination of All Forms of Discrimination against Women stated:[149]

---

[146] See eg *Report of the Commission of Inquiry on Human Rights in the Democratic People's Republic of Korea*, above n 135; Embassy of the People's Republic of China in the Hellenic Republic "Foreign Ministry Spokesperson's Press Conference on January 16, 2003" (3 August 2004) <http://gr.china-embassy.org/eng/xwdt/xw2003/xw200301/t145873.htm>; Embassy of the People's Republic of China in the Commonwealth of Dominica "Foreign Ministry Spokesperson Qin Gang's Regular Press Conference on December 25, 2007" <http://dm.china-embassy.org/eng/zt/wjbfyrth/t393265.htm>; MFA press conference, Beijing, 22 January 2008, 22 February 2012, 28 February 2012, on file with the author.

[147] MFA press conferences, Beijing, 19 Mar 2002, 16 January 2003, 17 February 2004, 11 October 2005, 7 December 2006, 23 January 2007, 22 February 2008, 22 February 2012, on file with the author.

[148] Committee on the Rights of the Child *Consideration of reports submitted by States parties under article 44 of the Convention: Third and fourth periodic reports of States parties due in 2009 – China* UN Doc CRC/C/CHN/3-4 (6 June 2012), at [187].

[149] Committee on the Elimination of Discrimination against Women *Consideration of Reports Submitted by States Parties under Article 18 of the Convention on the Elimination of All Forms of Discrimination against Women: Combined Seventh and Eighth Periodic Report of States Parties – China* UN Doc CEDAW/C/CHN/7-8 (17 January 2013), at [225].

Illegal immigrants from North Korea who come to China for economic reasons are not refugees. China has been handling individual cases in this regard in accordance with its domestic law, international law and in the spirit of humanitarianism, fully taking into account the actual situation of the persons involved. The dignity and rights of North Koreans who enter China by illegal means and for economic reasons are respected and they are treated in the spirit of humanitarianism, by providing them with necessities of life.

The Chinese Government reportedly relied upon a Chinese–North Korean bilateral treaty to justify its repatriation of North Korean escapees.[150] Article 5 of the 1998 Agreement on Cooperation in the Work of Maintaining National Security and Social Orders at Border Areas between China and North Korea does require the parties to hand over to the other party criminal suspects from that party.[151] However, if a North Korean escapee qualifies as a refugee under the Refugee Convention and Protocol and is therefore entitled to protection against *refoulement*, China's obligation of *non-refoulement* will supersede its obligation to hand over North Korean criminal suspects under the 1998 bilateral agreement.

The UN, scholars and NGOs have considered North Korean escapees into China as refugees within the meaning of the Refugee Convention and Protocol.[152] One of the most influential theories advanced with regard to the legal status of North Korean escapees is that they qualify as refugees *sur place*. Article 1(2)A of the Refugee Convention, when read with its 1967 Protocol, defines a refugee as any person who:

> owing to well-founded fear of being persecuted for reasons of race, religion, nationality, membership of a particular social group or political opinion, is outside the country of his nationality and is unable or, owing to such fear, is unwilling to avail himself of the protection of that country; or who, not having a nationality and being outside the country of his former habitual residence as a result of such events, is unable or, owing to such fear, is unwilling to return to it.

---

[150] Margesson, Chanlett-Avery and Bruno, above n 130, at 11; Seymour, above n 131, at 4; HRW, above n 141, at 29.

[151] 1998 Agreement on Cooperation in the Work of Maintaining National Security and Social Orders at Border Areas between China and North Korea (signed 8 July 1998, entered into force 28 August 1998). The Chinese version of the bilateral protocol is available at <http://policy.mofcom.gov.cn/PDFView?id=TYCX000076&libcode=gjty>.

[152] See eg CIHRDPRK, above n 135, at [43]; Chan and Schloenhardt, above n 132; Neaderland, above n 132.

It is well recognised that the Convention refugee definition does not require the fear of being persecuted to have arisen before refugees leave their home country. A refugee *sur place* is a person who was not a refugee when he or she left their country of origin but becomes a refugee at a later date. Unauthorised departure from the home country may form the basis of a refugee status claim *sur place*.[153] If the sanction for illicit travel abroad is severe enough to effectively undermine the fundamental human right to leave and to return to one's country enshrined in art 12 of the International Covenant on Civil and Political Rights (ICCPR) and the country of origin treats unauthorised departure as an implied political opinion of disloyalty or defiance, the criteria of the Convention refugee definition are met.[154]

In light of the above, the key tests of whether North Korean escapees qualify as refugees *sur place* are:

(1) whether the punishment for unauthorised departure from North Korea effectively undermines the fundamental human right of North Koreans to leave and to return to their country; and

(2) whether North Korea treats unauthorised departure from the country as implied political opinion of disloyalty or defiance.

According to the Commission of Inquiry on Human Rights in the Democratic People's Republic of Korea (CIHRDPRK), North Korea strictly limits international travel of its citizens to such an extent that the travel restriction amounts to a total travel ban for ordinary North Koreans.[155] The North Korean authority "systematically uses violence and punishment to deter its citizens from exercising their human right to leave the country". North Korean escapees repatriated from China were commonly subjected to torture, arbitrary detention, summary execution, forced abortion and other forms of sexual violence.[156]

---

[153] James Hathaway and Michelle Foster *The Law of Refugee Status* (2nd ed, Cambridge University Press, Cambridge, 2014) at 77; Andreas Zimmermann and Claudia Mahlet "Article 1 A, para 2 1951 Convention" in Andreas Zimmermann (ed) *The 1951 Convention Relating to the Status of Refugees and Its 1967 Protocol: A Commentary* (Oxford University Press, Oxford, 2011) 281 at 330.

[154] At 77.

[155] CIHRDPRK *Report of the detailed findings of the Commission of Inquiry on Human Rights in the Democratic People's Republic of Korea*, A/HRC/25/CRP.1 (7 February 2014) at [380].

[156] At [380].

The North Korean authority considered unauthorised departure from North Korea as an act of treason, which is a crime punishable by a minimum of five-year "reform through labour" under art 62 of the North Korean Criminal Code.[157] Although it has been noted that the severity of punishments for unauthorised departure varied considerably over time,[158] given the substantial numbers of testified cases of torture, arbitrary detention and summary execution, it is reasonable to conclude that North Koreans who leave North Korea without authorisation are likely to have a well-founded fear of persecution for the reason of real or imputed political opinion.

Another issue that has been raised in relation to the status of North Korean escapees under the Refugee Convention is that of dual nationality.[159] A person with dual or multiple nationality would be considered as a refugee only if they are unable or legitimately unwilling to avail themselves of the protection of the government of either or any of their nationalities.[160] However, nationality may be deemed ineffective if it does not provide the protection normally granted to nationals.[161] For example, when the person is unable to travel to or enter the territory where the rights associated with nationality are in principle available, the benefits of nationality, while theoretically available, cannot in practice be accessed by the person concerned.

It is commonly understood that,[162] in accordance with art 3 of the South Korean Constitution and art 2 of the South Korean Nationality

---

[157] CIHRDPRK, above n 155, at [383]; Jianyi Piao and Zhipei Li "chaoxian 'tuobeizhe' wenti de guojihua yanbian jiqi yingxiang" (13 August 2012) <http://iaps.cass.cn/news/523644 .htm> (translation: "The Internationalisation of the Issue of North Korean 'Escapees' and Its Influence"); HRW, above n 141, at 2.

[158] Andrew Wolman "North Korean Asylum Seekers and Dual Nationality" (2013) 24 *International Journal of Refugee Law* 793 at 793, with further references; Eric Yong-Joogn Lee "National and International Legal Concerns regarding Recent North Korean Escapee" (2001) 13 *International Journal of Refugee Law* 142 at 143, with further references.

[159] See eg *KK (Nationality: North Korea) Korea CG* [2011] UKUT 92 (IAC) at [49]; *GP (South Korean citizenship) North Korea CG* [2014] UKUT 391 (IAC).

[160] Hathaway and Foster, above n 153, at 56; UNHCR *Handbook on Procedures and Criteria for Determining Refugee Status and Guidelines on International Protection under the 1951 Convention and the 1967 Protocol Relating to the Status of Refugee* (HCR/1P/4/ENG/REV. 4, reissued February 2019) at [106].

[161] UNHCR, above n 161, at [107].

[162] See Wolman, above n 159, at 798; Lee, above n 159, at 146; *KK*, above n 160; *GP*, above n 160.

Act,[163] North Koreans are South Korean nationals from birth in the eyes of South Korean law. The South Korean Supreme Court seems to have confirmed this position in the *Young Soon Lee* case.[164] The key question here is: are the benefit and rights associated with South Korean nationality available to North Korean escapees in China?

In 1997, South Korea passed the Protection of North Korean Residents and Support of Their Settlement Act (the Protection Act), which is designed to provide protection and support to North Koreans defecting from North Korea (art 1).[165] According to art 7 of the Protection Act, South Korean embassies and consulates overseas are responsible for receiving North Korean defectors who desire to seek South Korea's protection. The 2005 White Paper on Korean Unification issued by the South Korean Ministry of Unification also stated that:[166]

> In the case of North Korean refugees residing in a third country who file an application for protection, the South Korean Government will provide temporary protection through its consulate in the third country and assist them in entering South Korea. Upon entry into South Korea, the Government will decide on his/her protection based on the results of a joint investigation by relevant government agencies.

---

[163] The full text of the South Korean Constitution is available at <http://english.ccourt.go.kr/cckhome/images/eng/main/Constitution_of_the_Republic_of_Korea.pdf>; the full text of the South Korean Nationality Act is available at <http://elaw.klri.re.kr/eng_mobile/viewer.do?hseq=18840&type=part&key=7>. There are a few exceptions to this rule; see Wolman, above n 159, at 811; *GP*, above n 160, at [43]; *KK*, above n 160, at [50].

[164] In this case, the Court confirmed that the plaintiff, a North Korean national with a Chinese Foreign Resident Card, was a South Korean citizen (*Young Soon Lee* SC 96 Nu 1221, 12 November 1996, cited in Vitit Muntarbhorn *Question of the Violation of Human Rights and Fundamental Freedoms in Any Part of the World: Report of the Special Rapporteur on the Situation of Human Rights in the Democratic People's Republic of Korea* UN Doc E/CN.4/2006/35 (23 January 2006) at [61]); see also Jeewon Min "Surrogate Protection in Canada and Potential Nationality in South Korea: Does a North Korean Asylum-Seeker have a 'genuine link' to South Korea?" (paper submitted to the CARFMS Graduate Student Essay Contest, University of British Columbia, 2013) at 11 <http://carfms.org/wp-content/uploads/2014/11/North-Korean-Refugee-Status-In-Canada-2013-Essay-Contest-CARFMS-web.pdf>.

[165] Law number 6474, Partial revision on 24 May 2001, available at <www.refworld.org/docid/3ae6b4ef28.html>.

[166] Republic of Korea ministry of unification *Peace and Prosperity: White Paper on Korean Unification 2005* (2005), as cited in Muntarbhorn, above n 165; and United Nations Human Rights Committee *Concluding Observations and Recommendations of the Human Rights Committee: Democratic People's Republic of Korea* UN Doc CCPR/CO/72/PRC (2001) at [62].

According to a mid-level official at the South Korean Ministry of Unification, South Korean diplomatic missions had discretion in considering relations with the host country.[167] If the host country strongly opposed South Korean diplomatic assistance to North Korean defectors in that country, South Korean embassies and consulates would not assist them.[168]

The Chinese Government has shown strong opposition to diplomatic assistance, be it from South Korea or other countries, to North Korean escapees.[169] In the early 2000s, there were a series of incidents of North Koreans entering into foreign embassies and consulates in China, including the South Korean Embassy in Beijing, and international schools. The Chinese Government quickly tightened security around diplomatic compounds, seized and repatriated North Koreans who had attempted to seek asylum in foreign embassies/consulates in China, and arrested and jailed humanitarian workers assisting North Koreans in entering foreign embassies/consulates.[170] Although the South Korean Government has avidly advocated against China's repatriation of North Korean escapees,[171] as Lankov and Wolman rightly noted, with few exceptions, the South Korean Embassy and consulates in China clearly did not assist North Korean escapees in travelling to South Korea or provide them with South Korean citizenship papers.[172] Therefore, North Korean escapees in China generally do not have access to the protection associated with South Korean nationality and should not be denied refugee status merely because in theory they have South Korean nationality.

---

[167] HRW, above n 130, at 31.

[168] At 31.

[169] Elisabeth Rosenthal "9 More North Koreans Seek Asylum in Seoul Embassy in Beijing" *The New York Times* (online ed, New York, 12 June 2002).

[170] See eg Richard Spencer "Refugees sent back by China to face horror" *The Telegraph* (online ed, London, 10 November 2004) <www.telegraph.co.uk/news/worldnews/asia/china/1476321/Refugees-sent-back-by-China-to-face-horror.html>; Michael A Lev "China aggressively pursues asylum-seeking N. Koreans" (28 October 2004) *Chicago Tribune* <http://articles.chicagotribune.com/2004-10-28/news/0410280226_1_north-koreans-south-korean-consulate-refugee-crisis>; Ian Jeffries *North Korea: A guide to economic and political developments* (Routledge, London, 2006) at 99, with further references.

[171] Daming Li and others "zhonghan yin 'tuobeizhe' gekong duizhi" (23 February 2012) <http://news.xinhuanet.com/world/2012-02/23/c_122744929.htm> (translation: "Tension between China and South Korea Due to 'North Korean Escapees'").

[172] Andrei Lankov "North Korean Refugees in Northeast China" (2004) 44 *Asian Survey* 856 at 863; Wolman, above n 159, at 801 fn 41.

In light of the above, unless otherwise excluded by the Refugee Convention and Protocol, North Korean escapees in China who flee for fear of persecution because of their political opinion, race, nationality, religion or membership of a particular social group are refugees within the meaning of the Refugee Convention and Protocol; even those who left North Korea purely for economic reasons prima facie qualify as refugees *sur place*.

4.3.3   Policy Considerations Underlying China's Treatment of North Korean Escapees

Despite international pressure, the Chinese Government has demonstrated little willingness to give North Korean escapees refugee status or a humanitarian status that allows them to stay legally in China or transit through China to a third country. For example, in a 2014 reply to the United Nations CIHRDPRK, the Chinese Government stated: "China firmly opposes any attempt to make this issue [North Korean escapees in China] a refugee one and to internationalise and politicise the issue".[173]

Scholars have noted that the Chinese Government fears that allowing North Korean escapees to enter into or transit through China legally may encourage more North Koreans to flee from North Korea and that the exodus of North Korean citizens could destabilise the North Korean regime and lead to its collapse.[174] The collapse of North Korea could cause political instability in the East Asian region and create larger refugee flows into China and neighbouring countries. More importantly, China considers North Korea as a buffer zone between China and the United States military force in South Korea,[175] which hosts the largest US military base outside the United States. If North Korea collapses, China risks being directly exposed to the United States military force posted in South Korea.

Second, China's close relationship with North Korea probably also contributes to China's reluctance to protect North Korean escapees. According to art 2 of the 1961 Chinese–North Korean Treaty on Friendship and Mutual Assistance,[176] China is a formal ally of North Korea.

---

[173] CIHRDPRK, above n 135, at Annex II.

[174] Margesson, Chanlett-Avery and Bruno, above n 130, at 12; Seymour, above n 131, at 16.

[175] Eleanor Albert "The China–North Korea Relationship" (June 25, 2019) <www.cfr.org/backgrounder/china-north-korea-relationship>.

[176] Chinese-North Korean Treaty on Friendship and Mutual Assistance (10 September 1961). The full text of the Treaty is available at <http://news.china.com/domestic/945/20160712/23035234_all.html>. The Treaty was renewed in 1981 and again in 2001 for twenty years.

Under the 1998 Chinese–North Korean treaty on cooperation in maintaining security and social order in border areas, China is obliged to hand over North Korean criminals to North Korea.[177] Since North Korean escapees who leave North Korea without authorisation would be criminals under the North Korean Criminal Code,[178] granting asylum to them may strain Chinese–North Korean relations. It is also worth noting that, in the nineteenth and early twentieth centuries, Koreans in exile constantly used China as a base for carrying out revolutionary activities against Korean rulers and the Japanese colonial government.[179] Given North Korea's strategic location and its ability to destabilise the region through military provocation, China probably does not want to antagonise North Korea. In 2009, China temporarily suspended repatriation of North Korean escapees after North Korea launched a missile without giving prior notification to Beijing.[180] This seems to suggest that the Chinese–North Korean relationship does play a significant role in China's treatment of North Korean escapees.

Third, given the economic, political and ideological differences between North Korea and China, the presence of large numbers of North Koreans in China could destabilise Chinese society and domestic social stability. Maintaining domestic social stability is a top priority for the Chinese Government. The Chinese authority considers social stability crucial not only to the success of China's economic agenda but also to political stability and ultimately the survival of the Chinese Communist Party. Therefore, the Chinese Government desires to deter North Koreans from entering into China.

Fourth, China's overall policy towards North Korean escapees is probably influenced by China's own experience during the exodus of

---

[177] The Ministry of Public Security of the People's Republic China and the Ministry of National Security of the Democratic People's Republic of Korea Protocol on Cooperation in the Work of Maintaining National Security and Social Order at Border Areas, above n 151.

[178] Criminal Code (Democratic People's Republic of Korea), art 117, as cited in Seymour, above n 131, at 26.

[179] Meng Wang "1919–1945 dahan minguo linshi zhengfu zai zhongguo: ceng 'jie' Chongqing zuo shoudu" (3 July 2014) <www.guancha.cn/KanLiShi/2014_07_03_243305.shtml> (translation: "1919–1945 Korean Exile Government in China: Borrowing of Chongqing as Its Capital").

[180] Lan Lin "Beijing zanting qianfan chaoxian nanmin" (18 April 2012) <www.chinese.rfi .fr/%E4%B8%AD%E5%9B%BD/20120418-%E5%8C%97%E4%BA%AC%E6%9A%82% E5%81%9C%E9%81%A3%E8%BF%94%E6%9C%9D%E9%B2%9C%E9%9A%BE%E6% B0%91> (translation: "Beijing Suspended Repatriation of North Korean Refugees").

Chinese nationals to Hong Kong from 1949 to the mid-1980s. Following the founding of the People's Republic of China in October 1949, more than 700,000 Mainland Chinese citizens escaped to Hong Kong, then a British colony. The Chinese Government viewed the action of leaving China for Hong Kong equivalent to betrayal of China and as against the Chinese Government, and considered the Hong Kong Government's tolerant Touch Base policy towards Mainland Chinese escapees as "indirectly encouraging" the exodus to Hong Kong.[181] The Chinese Government sent soldiers to the China–Hong Kong frontier to stop people from leaving. The exodus, however, continued well into the 1970s.

Like North Korean escapees today, the Chinese escapees then were fleeing a strict, poor communist regime (as China was before its reform and opening-up in late 1970s). As will be discussed in Section 5.1, both China and Hong Kong at that time argued that the Chinese escapees were not refugees. The exodus, which continued for more than three decades, ended after China's economic reform.

Further, China has consistently emphasised addressing root causes through economic development in the country of origin, rather than protection of the displaced, and has often highlighted that poverty and underdevelopment were among the root causes.[182] Such emphasis on addressing root causes through economic development, coupled with political and security concerns, may have reduced China's willingness to protect North Korean escapees in China as refugees.

Lastly, one should not ignore the fact that the Chinese Criminal Law punishes unauthorised departure from China as a criminal offence,[183] and that until 2003 China heavily restricted ordinary Chinese nationals from obtaining a Chinese passport to travel internationally.[184] This

---

[181] Hongxiong Liu "zhengdong zhongyang de 'dataogang' fengchao" (1 August 2010) <www.people.com.cn/GB/198221/198819/198857/12308776.html> (translation: "The 'Great Escape to Hong Kong' that Shook the Central Government"). For discussion about the Touch Base policy, see Section 5.2.

[182] See Section 3.2.2.

[183] The official English translation is available at <www.fmprc.gov.cn/ce/cgvienna/eng/dbtyw/jdwt/crimelaw/t209043.htm>. Article 322 provides: "Whoever violates the laws and regulations controlling secret crossing of the national boundary (border), and when the circumstances are serious, shall be sentenced to not more than one year of fixed-term imprisonment and criminal detention or control".

[184] China News "gaige kaifang 30 nian: huzhao cong cengceng shenpi dao anxu shenling" (4 November 2008) <www.chinanews.com/gn/news/2008/11-04/1436222.shtml> (translation: "Thirty Years of Reform and Open-up: Obtaining a Passport as You Need No More Strict Approval Procedures").

possibly makes the Chinese Government reluctant to view North Korea's punishment of North Korean escapees for unauthorised departure as persecution.

In December 2017, an allegedly leaked internal document of China Telecommunications Corporation shows that China was building camps along the China–North Korea border in response to the tension in the Korean peninsula.[185] If the leaked document is genuine,[186] it signals China's willingness to provide at least temporary shelter to displaced North Koreans if the North Korean regime collapses.

4.3.4 Towards Improvement of the Situation of North Korean Escapees in China

It is undeniable that there is a pressing need to improve the situation of North Korean escapees in China. In the past twenty years, the international community has been trying to address that need mainly by pressurising the Chinese Government to recognise North Korean escapees as refugees, but has had limited success. This illustrates the challenges of enforcing the Refugee Convention and Protocol in regimes where adequate respect for the rule of law is lacking. A few lessons can be learned from past experience. First, naming and shaming could be combined with strategic pragmatism and good diplomacy. As Sceats and Breslin rightly noted in their report on China and the international human rights system, the Chinese Government traditionally opposed "naming and shaming" approaches with regard to human rights matters.[187] This is not to suggest that the international community should not continue to pressure China to improve its treatment of North Korean escapees through open criticism, but such criticism *alone* has proved to yield limited impact on China's policy towards North Korean escapees in the last twenty years. For example, in the early 2000s, a number of North Korean escapees in China, sometimes with the help

---

[185] Jane Perlez "Fearing the Worst, China Plans Refugee Camps on North Korean Border" *The New York Times* (online ed, New York, 11 December 2017) <www.nytimes.com/2017/12/11/world/asia/china-north-korea-border.html>.

[186] The Chinese authorities have yet to confirm or deny the authenticity of the allegedly leaked document.

[187] Sonya Sceats and Shaun Breslin *China and the International Human Rights System* (Chatham House, October 2012) <www.chathamhouse.org/sites/default/files/public/Research/International%20Law/r1012_sceatsbreslin.pdf> at 6.

of international NGOs and humanitarian workers who had arranged international media to document the action, made their way into the UNHCR office, foreign embassies and consulates, and international schools in China to seek asylum, attracting significant international attention and criticism of China's policy towards North Korean escapees. The Chinese Government reacted by tightening security around diplomatic buildings, launching crackdowns on North Korean escapees, and arresting and jailing humanitarian workers.[188] On the other hand, the Chinese Government held negotiations with the respective embassies and was willing to involve UNHCR in such negotiations; sometimes, as UNHCR noted, such negotiations reached "speedy" conclusions.[189] China eventually allowed the North Koreans who had made their way into the UNHCR office, diplomatic compounds or international schools to leave China (mostly for South Korea via a third country) for humanitarian reasons,[190] although it emphasised repeatedly that those cases were dealt with on an ad hoc and case-by-case basis and that China never recognised them as refugees.

Second, the Chinese Government, at least at local levels, seems to have been more tolerant of certain groups of North Korean escapees. In a report by the United States-based Committee for Human Rights in North Korea, which was informed by interviews with North Korean women in China conducted by Korean human rights activist Haeyoung Lee, noted:[191]

> local authorities are providing documents for married North Korean women and their children, in some cases even promising their safety and voluntarily issuing *hukou* [household registration] for their children born in China . . .

Others noted that some local Chinese authorities allowed female North Korean escapees who were married to Chinese men and had children,[192] as well as those who had lived in China for a long period without causing

---

[188] Seymour, above n 131.

[189] UNHCR UK "North Koreans leave China" (15 March 2002) <www.unhcr.org/uk/news/briefing/2002/3/3c91d7ba15/north-koreans-leave-china.html>.

[190] See eg UNHCR "Seven North Korean asylum seekers arrive in Seoul" (30 June 2001) <www.unhcr.org/3b4049cb1.html>.

[191] Committee for Human Rights in North Korea *Lives for Sale: Personal Accounts of Women Fleeing North Korea to China* (2009) at 60 <www.hrnk.org/uploads/pdfs/Lives_for_Sale.pdf>.

[192] Cohen, above n 132.

problems, to stay and even issued them with temporary residence permits or identity cards.[193] Incidentally, in November 2012 the Chinese Government began to allow children of UNHCR refugees to access public education in primary schools on the same conditions as local children.[194] This suggests that refugee women and children are a potential "soft spot" for China's refugee policy. From a pragmatic point of view, in the short term, it may be helpful to develop advocacy strategies specifically for women and/or children of North Korean escapees. It may also be helpful to consider persuading the Chinese Government to begin pilot projects of issuing identity documents to North Korean escapee women who are married to Chinese men for an extended period and/or children born to a Chinese national and a North Korean escapee at selected regions and gradually push for the inclusion of more regions and/or other groups of North Korean escapees.

Third, whereas international refugee law is undoubtedly a very powerful tool for protecting North Korean escapees in China, it is important to explore all possible tools that may help meet their protection needs. The example of Vietnamese refugees in China discussed above illustrates that refugee status may not be the only solution for displaced persons who are eligible for refugee status – had the Vietnamese refugees not been given refugee status, they would have been treated as Chinese nationals. Casella, a former UNHCR officer who was involved in establishing UNHCR's office in Beijing, noted that:[195]

> China is currently bordered by areas of potential instability with ongoing cross-border movements. Given the serious foreign policy implications, these should be at best addressed outside the scope of the convention.

From a pragmatic point of view, more attention could be paid to Chinese domestic law and relevant policy reforms in China. For example, children born to a Chinese parent and a North Korean escapee parent in China,

---

[193] Guofu Liu *Chinese Immigration Law* (Ashgate, Farnham, 2011) at 91; School of Asian Pacific Study of Sun Yat-Sen University "2012 nian zhongshan daxue moni lianheguo dahui nanmin anzhi yu nanmin quanli baozhang beijing wenjian" (19 April 2012) <http://saps.sysu.edu.cn/xsyd/zsdxmnlhg/96477.htm> (translation: "2012 Sun Yat-Sun University Moot UN Meeting on Refugee Settlement and Rights Protection Background Document").

[194] UNHCR *Regional Representation for China and Mongolia: Fact Sheet* (September 2014) on file with author.

[195] Alexander Casella "Time for China to make legal preparations for acceptance of refugees" *Global Times* (28 May 2013) <www.globaltimes.cn/content/785010.shtml#.U1tSpSgoyZY>.

who are commonly believed to have been excluded from Chinese nation-ality,[196] are entitled to Chinese nationality under the current Chinese Nationality Law, art 4 of which provides:[197]

> Any person born in China whose parents are both Chinese nationals and one of whose parents is a Chinese national shall have Chinese nationality.

Article 4 of the Chinese Nationality Law, like two other articles governing acquisition of Chinese nationality by birth,[198] seems to give the Chinese authorities no discretion to deny Chinese nationality to persons who meet the criteria set forth by these articles. Furthermore, no other provision in the Chinese Nationality Law requires acquisition of Chinese nationality by birth to be subject to the discretion of the Chinese Government. In contrast, arts 7 and 16 unequivocally require acquisition of Chinese nationality through naturalisation to be subject to the examination and approval by the relevant Chinese authorities.[199] Therefore, as a matter of law, any person who meets the criteria contained in art 4 of the Chinese Nationality Law is entitled to Chinese nationality and such entitlement is not subject to the discretion of the Chinese Government.[200] Children born in China to one parent who is a Chinese national and one North

---

[196] In China, a person needs to have been registered in the household registration system to access public education and social welfare.

[197] The official English translation is available at <www.china.org.cn/english/Livingin China/184710.htm>.

[198] Article 5 provides: "Any person born abroad whose parents are both Chinese nationals and one of whose parents is a Chinese national shall have Chinese nationality. But a person whose parents are both Chinese nationals and have both settled abroad, or one of whose parents is a Chinese national and has settled abroad, and who has acquired foreign nationality at birth shall not have Chinese nationality". Article 6 provides: "Any person born in China whose parents are stateless or of uncertain nationality and have settled in China shall have Chinese nationality".

[199] Article 7 provides: "Foreign nationals or stateless persons who are willing to abide by China's Constitution and other laws and who meet one of the following conditions may be naturalized upon approval of their applications"; Article 16 provides: "Applications for naturalization as Chinese nationals and for renunciation or restoration of Chinese nationality is subject to examination and approval by the Ministry of Public Security of the People's Republic of China".

[200] Acquisition of Chinese nationality in accordance with art 4 is, however, subject to the completion of formalities of application under art 14 of the Nationality Law: "Persons who wish to acquire, renounce or restore Chinese nationality, with the exception of the cases provided for in Article 9, shall go through the *formalities* of application. Applications of persons under the age of 18 may be filed on their behalf by their parents or other legal representatives" (emphasis added). Article 9 provides: "Any Chinese national who has settled abroad and who has been naturalized as a foreign national or has acquired foreign nationality of his own free will shall automatically lose Chinese nationality".

Korean escapee parent should be able to claim Chinese nationality by birth in accordance with art 4 of the Chinese Nationality Law.

At the policy level, in December 2015, the meeting of the Central Leading Group for Deepening Overall Reform, chaired by Chinese President Xi Jinping, promised that all Chinese nationals could lawfully register for *hukou*, noting that *hukou* is crucial for Chinese nationals to access public services in China.[201] In January 2016, the Chinese Central Government issued the Opinion on Resolving Issues of *Hukou* Registration for Persons with no *Hukou*. The Opinion listed eight categories of people who had generally not been able to register for *hukou* and should be allowed to do so, including children born outside marriage to a Chinese national and a foreign national or a stateless person.[202] Many provinces in China, including Jilin province, where the majority of the North Korean escapees in China live, have since issued their own provincial-level implementation opinion on the basis of the Central Government opinion.[203] The Jilin provincial opinion, issued in April 2016, also includes a similar category of children born outside marriage to a Chinese national and a foreign national or stateless person. Children born to a Chinese national and a North Korean escapee would fit perfectly into this category. The Jilin provincial opinion further states that, in the absence of a birth certificate, children born to a Chinese national and a foreign national or a stateless person can still register for *hukou* as long as the relation between the child and the Chinese parent is verified by the local police or, where such relation cannot be verified by the local police, by way of a DNA paternity test certificate issued by a qualified institute.[204] Thus it is possible to register the child for *hukou* without necessarily revealing the identity of the mother. At the time of writing, there has been little information as to whether children born to Chinese nationals and North Korean escapees have actually benefited from this recent policy reform. If they have not, it would seem to be a good time for relevant stakeholders to approach the

---

[201] Xinhua "Reform meeting tables healthcare, environmental, hukou proposals" (10 December 2015) <www.scio.gov.cn/m/32618/Document/1458841/1458841.htm>.

[202] General Office of the State Council *Opinion on Resolving Issues of Hukou Registration for Persons with no Hukou* (guofaban [2015] No 96, 14 January 2016) <www.gov.cn/zhengce/content/2016-01/14/content_10595.htm>.

[203] China News "jilinsheng gong'an jiguan qieshi jiejue wuhukou renyuan luohu wenti" (11 August 2017) <www.jl.chinanews.com/hyhc/2017-08-11/24565.html> (translation: "Jilin Provincial Public Security Authorities Dutifully Solve the Issue of *Hukou* Registration for People without *Hukou*").

[204] China News, above n 204.

Chinese Government to advocate for inclusion of children born to Chinese nationals and North Korean escapees in the Chinese *hukou* system to allow them access to public education and other social welfare.

4.4   Displaced Ethnic Kokangs from Myanmar

4.4.1   Influxes of Displaced Ethnic Kokangs

On 8 August 2009, approximately 37,000 civilians flooded into Nansan town in Yunnan province, China from Laukkai, the capital town of the Kokang Special Region in Shan State, Myanmar, as a result of a military standoff and clashes between the Tatmadaw and the MNDAA, an ethnic Kokang military group that had exercised actual control of the Kokang Special Region for decades.[205] The Chinese Government quickly opened seven camps to accommodate more than 10,000 displaced Kokangs, setting up more than 1,000 tents and providing RMB 10 million (about USD 1.6 million) worth of food, blankets, drinking water, medicine and even a small daily allowance in cash.[206] Displaced Kokangs were allowed to move around freely within Nansan town, but were not allowed to travel beyond its boundaries.[207] Journalists from Chinese and foreign media appear to have been allowed to visit Nansan to cover the situation of the displaced Kokangs. As the conflict in the Kokang Special Region eased in early September 2009, displaced Kokangs returned to Myanmar voluntarily and the camps in Nansan were promptly removed.[208]

---

[205] State Council Information Office of the People's Republic of China (SCIO) "Yunnan Sheng zhengfu jiu dangqian zhongmian bianjing jushi juxing xinwen fabuhui" (31 August 2009) <www.scio.gov.cn/xwfbh/gssxwfbh/xwfbh/yunnan/Document/398584/398584.htm> (translation: "Yunnan Provincial Government Holds Press Conference on the Situation on China–Myanmar Border"). The figure includes both Myanmar nationals of Kokang ethnicity and Chinese nationals returning home due to the conflict.

[206] SCIO, above n 206; Shan Herald Agency for News "Kokang Capital Falls: 'Not Shoot First' Policy under Fire" (26 August 2009) <https://democracyforburma.wordpress .com/2009/08/26/kokang-capital-falls-"not-shoot-first"-policy-under-fire/>.

[207] Xiong Zhang, "tanfang zhongmian bianjing: guogan taonan duiwu mianyan jiugongli" (8 September 2009) <http://news.sina.com.cn/w/sd/2009-09-09/181518615604.shtml> (translation: "A Visit to the China–Myanmar Border: A Nine-Kilometer Long Line of Fleeing Kokangs").

[208] Jun Liu "30,000 ming guogan nanmin tashang miandian guitu" *China Weekly* (16 September 2009) <www.chinaweekly.cn/bencandy.php?fid=60&id=4491> (translation: "30,000 Kokang Refugees on Their Way Home"); Shan Nan "Beijing chaichu yingdi qianfan guogan nanmin" (1 September 2009) <www.asianews.it/news-zh/%E5%8C% 97%E4%BA%AC%E6%8B%86%E9%99%A4%E8%90%A5%E5%9C%B0%E9%81%A3% E8%BF%94%E6%9E%9C%E6%95%A2%E9%9A%BE%E6%B0%91-16205.html> (translation: "Beijing Removed Camps and Repatriated Kokang Refugees").

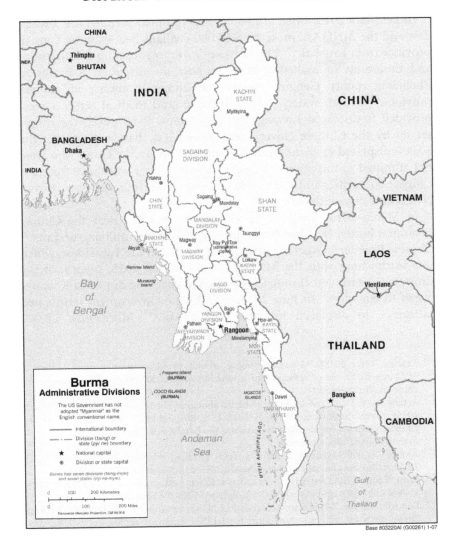

Figure 4.1 Map of Myanmar

Source: The United States Central Intelligence Agency <https://www.cia.gov/library/publications/resources/cia-maps-publications/map-downloads/Burma_Admin.pdf>

In February 2015, when armed conflict resumed between the Tatmadaw and the MNDAA, more than 60,000 civilians fled again to Yunnan province from Laukkai.[209] The Chinese Government set up fifteen camps and thousands of makeshift tents to host the displaced Kokangs in Zhenkang county, Gengma county and Cangyuan county in Yunnan province.[210] Food, water, clothes, blankets and medical services were provided to displaced Kokangs in these camps.[211] However, the camps set up by the Chinese Government hosted less than a quarter of the 60,000 displaced civilians from Kokang in Yunnan.[212] Those who were not admitted to the camps generally did not receive assistance from the Chinese authorities and had to rely on their own resources, support from NGOs and private donations.[213]

In March 2015, five Chinese villagers were killed near the China–Myanmar border by a bomb dropped by a Myanmar military aircraft.[214] Chinese Premier Li Keqiang blamed the deaths on the Tatmadaw, which was skirmishing with the MNDAA.[215] In March 2015, reports of the Chinese Government closing the camps and expelling displaced Kokangs began to emerge.[216] In June 2015, the Chinese Government terminated assistance to displaced Kokangs in Yunnan.[217] More than 20,000

[209] Xinhua "Over 60,000 Myanmar refugee arrivals in China since conflict outbreak" (7 March 2015) <https://reliefweb.int/report/china/over-60000-myanmar-refugee-arrivals-china-conflict-outbreak>.

[210] *Beijing Youth Daily* "paodan luoru 10 tianlai zhongguo zhengfu ruhe yingdui" (23 March 2015) <http://news.ifeng.com/a/20150323/43393886_0.shtml> (translation: "How the Chinese Government Has Responded since the Bombs Fell Ten Days Ago").

[211] *Beijing Youth Daily*, above n 211.

[212] Xinhua "14,000 Myanmar Border Residents Flocking to China Relocated" (3 March 2015) <http://usa.chinadaily.com.cn/world/2015-03/03/content_19701937.htm>.

[213] Nang Noom "China restricts border access as Kokang exodus continues" (2 March 2015) <www.unhcr.org/cgi-bin/texis/vtx/refdaily?pass=52fc6fbd5&id=54f56b385>.

[214] Lun Min Maung "Myanmar apologises to China over cross-border bombing" (3 April 2015) <www.mmtimes.com/national-news/13884-myanmar-apologises-to-china-over-cross-border-bombing.html>.

[215] Hannah Beech "China Accuses Burmese Military of Fatal Bombing Across Border" (16 March 2015) <http://time.com/3745604/china-burma-kokang-myanmar/>.

[216] Long Qiao "Guogan laojie zaifa wuzhuang chongtu yunnan guanbi nansan zhen nanminying" (7 March 2015) <www.rfa.org/mandarin/yataibaodao/junshiwaijiao/ql2-03072015122210.html> (translation: "Fresh Armed Conflict in Laukkai in the Kokang Region, Yunnan Closing Refugee Camps in Nansan Town"); Khin Oo Tha "China Reportedly Urging Kokang Refugees to Return" (9 March 2015) <www.irrawaddy.com/news/burma/china-reportedly-urging-kokang-refugees-to-return.html>.

[217] Ann Wang "The forgotten refugees of Kokang" (8 March 2016) <https://frontiermyanmar.net/en/the-forgotten-refugees-kokang>.

displaced Kokangs were still in Yunnan as of April 2016,[218] with little attention or assistance from China or the international community.[219] Displaced Kokangs interviewed by Wang in April 2016 said that local Chinese authorities had previously requested them to leave but had since acquiesced to their presence.[220]

In March 2017, fighting between the Tatmadaw and the MNDAA flared up again, driving more than 20,000 displaced Kokangs into Yunnan.[221] They stayed in private volunteer-run camps, temples, rented rooms or with relatives.[222] There is no evidence that the Chinese Government opened official camps to host displaced Kokangs this time. The Chinese Government has turned a blind eye to private donations and assistance to displaced Kokangs most of the time. But there is no evidence that a cogent policy towards the displaced Kokangs has been enforced on the ground by local authorities in Yunnan. For example, whereas Zhenkang county continues to tolerate the operation of private volunteer-run refugee camps and schools, neighbouring Gengma county has imposed a harder line, expelling displaced Kokangs and interfering in Chinese volunteer-run refugee schools in April and May 2016 and again in April and May 2017.[223] Some of the displaced Kokangs expelled by Gengma county moved to camps in Zhenkang county.[224]

---

[218] Sally Kantar "Ghost Villages Await the Return of Kokang Refugees" (12 May 2016) <www.newsdeeply.com/refugees/articles/2016/05/12/ghost-villages-await-the-return-of-kokang-refugees>; see also Yi Tu "shipai mianbei zhanhuopang de zhongguo xiaozhen: zhaoyang chifan shuijiao" (25 November 2016) <http://view.inews.qq.com/a/20161125A00YBH00> (translation: "Scenes from a Chinese Little Town Close to War: Eating and Sleeping As Usual").

[219] Kantar, above n 219.

[220] Wang, above n 218.

[221] James Pomfret "Relief camp in China swells as thousands flee conflict in Myanmar" (13 March 2017) <www.reuters.com/article/us-myanmar-insurgency-china-refugees/relief-camp-in-china-swells-as-thousands-flee-conflict-in-myanmar-idUSKBN16K0JW>.

[222] Zhijun Xu "guogan, qiangsheng weishei er'ming" (15 April 2017) <www.ifengweekly.com/detil.php?id=3803> (translation: "Kokang, Gunfire for Whom?").

[223] Huagang Li "liuluo de guogan – 2018 zhongmian bianjing guogan nanmin shengcun kunjing" (26 August 2018) <www.kokang123.com/thread-37177-1-1.html> (translation: "Kokang in Exile – Difficult Life of Kokang Refugees on the China–Myanmar Border in 2018"); Huan Wu "zhongmian bianjing nanmin er'tong jiuxue zaiyu dizhi" (1 April 2017) <http://news.dwnews.com/china/news/2017-04-01/59808561.html> (translation: "Refugee Children on the China–Myanmar Border Face Difficulty Going to School Again").

[224] Li, above n 224.

As of late 2018, more than 10,000 displaced Kokangs remained in Yunnan.[225] Despite the desperate needs of the displaced Kokangs in Yunnan, UNHCR and other mainstream international organisations have been blocked by the Chinese Government from accessing the displaced Kokangs in Yunnan.[226]

4.4.2   Refugees or Border Residents? Legal Status of Displaced Ethnic Kokangs in China

In 2009 and from 2015 to the present, the Chinese Government has referred to the displaced Kokangs in Yunnan as "border residents" (*bianmin*) and denied that they were refugees.[227] Displaced Kokangs in Yunnan are Myanmar nationals; they therefore meet the requirement of being outside their country of nationality in the Convention definition of a refugee. As for "well-founded fear of being persecuted", there is no definition of "persecution" in the Refugee Convention and Protocol or any other international instrument.[228] However, it is well accepted that severe violations of basic human rights amount to persecution.[229] Severe

---

[225] Miluyuzijiang "mainbei zhanluo guogan nanmin taodao zhongguo nansan zai nanminying jianku duri" (23 October 2018) <https://mbd.baidu.com/newspage/data/landing share?context=%7B%22nid%22%3A%22news_9058935335342101040%22%2C%22sour ceFrom%22%3A%22bjh%22%7D&type=gallery> (translation: "War in Northern Myanmar Drove Kokang Refugees into China's Nansan Having a Difficult Time in Refugee Camps").

[226] UNHCR "China: UNHCR Calls for Access to Myanmar Refugees" (4 September 2009) <www.unhcr.org/4aa108159.html>; Ann Wang "Myanmar refugees in China caught between political fault lines" (16 March 2016) <www.thenewhumanitarian.org/feature/ 2016/03/16/myanmar-refugees-china-caught-between-political-fault-lines>.

[227] Consulate-General of the People's Republic of China in Edinburgh "2009 nian 9 yue 1 ri waijioabu fayanren Jiang Yu juxing lixing jizhehui" <www.fmprc.gov.cn/ce/cgedb/chn/ wjbfyrth/t581720.htm> (translation: "Ministry of Foreign Affairs Spokesperson Jiang Yu Held Regular Press Conference"); Chinese Ministry of Foreign Affais "2017 nian 3 yue 7 ri waijiaobu fayanren Geng Shuang juxing lixing jizhehui" (7 March 2017) <www.fmprc.gov.cn/web/fyrbt_673021/jzhsl_673025/t1443750.shtml> (translation: "Ministry of Foreign Affairs Spokesperson Geng Shuang Held Regular Press Conference"); SCIO, above n 206; Xinhua, above n 213.

[228] Guy S Goodwin-Gill and Jane McAdam *The Refugee in International Law* (3rd ed, Oxford University Press, Oxford, 2007) at 90.

[229] See eg Directive 2011/95/EU of the European Parliament and of the Council of 13 December 2011 on standards for the qualification of third-country nationals or stateless persons as beneficiaries of international protection, for a uniform status for refugees or for persons eligible for subsidiary protection, and for the content of the protection granted (recast) [2011] OJ L337/9 art 9; Hathaway and Foster, above n 153, at

human rights abuses against ethnic minorities in northern Shan State, where the Kokang Special Region is located, during armed conflict, as well as peaceful times, are well recorded in many reports produced by a good variety of organisations.[230] For example, UNHCR noted that rape and sexual slavery were particularly prevalent in conflict-affected areas in Myanmar, such as Shan State.[231] Other documented widespread human rights abuses against ethnic Kokang civilians include fatal shootings, beheadings, torture, forced labour and home invasions.[232] Such measures of deprivation of life and liberty (fatal shooting, beheading and forced labour), torture and inhumane and degrading treatment (rape and sexual slavery),[233] and harassment of one's private life (home invasion) would seem sufficient to constitute persecution under the Refugee Convention.[234] In light of the prevalence of severe violations of basic human rights, it is reasonable to believe that displaced Kokangs in Yunnan would face a real risk of suffering such human rights abuses amounting to persecution upon return to Myanmar, hence their fear of persecution would be well-founded.

193–208; Goodwin-Gill and Jane McAdam, above n 229, at 90–93; UNHCR, above n 161, at [51].

[230] See eg Special Rapporteur on the situation of human rights in Myanmar *Situation of human rights in Myanmar* UN Doc A/70/412 (6 October 2015) at [50]; Amnesty International *Myanmar: Investigate alleged rape and killing of two Kachin women* (ASA 16/006/2015, 22 January 2015) <www.amnesty.org/en/documents/asa16/0006/2015/en/>; Hanna Hindstrom "Burma's Transition to Civilian Rule Hasn't Stopped the Abuses of Its Ethnic Wars" (1 April 2016) <http://time.com/4277328/burma-myan mar-suu-kyi-ethnic-wars/>; Shan Human Rights Foundation "Killing, beheading and disappearance of villagers instill fear of return among Kokang refugees" (11 May 2015) <www.shanhumanrights.org/index.php/news-updates/212-killing-beheading-and-disap pearance-of-villagers-instill-fear-of-return-among-kokang-refugees>.

[231] UN High Commissioner for Human Rights *Situation of human rights of Rohingya Muslims and other minorities in Myanmar* UN Doc A/HRC/32/18 (29 June 2016) at [60].

[232] HRW "'Untold Miseries': Wartime Abuses and Forced Displacement in Burma's Kachin State" (March 2012) <www.hrw.org/report/2012/03/20/untold-miseries/wartime-abuses-and-forced-displacement-burmas-kachin-state>; Shan Human Rights Foundation, above n 231; UN High Commissioner for Human Rights, above n 232, at [60].

[233] Peter Danchin "Article 5" Columbia Center for Teaching and Learning <http://ccnmtl.columbia.edu/projects/mmt/udhr/article_5/development_2.html>.

[234] As noted by Hathaway and Foster, in assessment of fear for persecution, the number of people affected is irrelevant; the issues at stake are the seriousness of the harm and its causal connection to the Convention grounds (Hathaway and Foster, above n 153, at 177).

The Convention definition further requires that the persecution feared must be "for reasons of race, religion, nationality, membership of a particular social group or political opinion". As Goodwin-Gill and McAdam noted, although decision-makers too often perceive the existence of civil conflicts as "giving rise to the situations of general insecurity that somehow exclude the possibility of persecution", close examination of the background to the conflict and the way it is fought will often establish a link to the five grounds provided in the Refugee Convention.[235]

It is well recognised that the armed conflicts displacing the Kokangs and the severe human rights abuses against the Kokangs are rooted in Myanmar's systemic discrimination and marginalisation of ethnic minorities as well as the consequent tension between ethnic minorities and the majority Burmese.[236] There is therefore a linkage between the persecution feared and ethnicity.[237] Victims of gender-based abuses during the armed conflict may also establish a nexus between feared persecution and the Convention ground of membership of a particular social group.

In light of the above, displaced ethnic Kokangs in Yunnan meet the criteria for refugee status under the Refugee Convention. China claimed that displaced Kokangs in Yunnan were border residents, not refugees. The Chinese authority has not elaborated what kind of legal status "border residents" have, but a look at the 1997 Agreement on China–Myanmar Border Management and Cooperation between China and Myanmar (1997 China–Myanmar Agreement),[238] and the 1990 Yunnan

---

[235] Goodwin-Gill and McAdam, above n 229, at 126.

[236] UN High Commissioner for Human Rights, above n 232, at [65]; Matthew J Walton "Ethnicity, Conflict, and History in Burma: The Myths of Panglong" (2008) 48 *Asian Survey* 889; Project MAJE, Mekong Network "The North War: A Kachin Conflict Compilation Report" (2011) <www.projectmaje.org/kachin_2011.htm>; Mae Sot "Myanmar's ethnic problems" (29 March 2012) <www.thenewhumanitarian.org/report/95195/briefing-myanmar%E2%80%99s-ethnic-problems>; CS Kuppuswamy *Challenging the Reconciliation Process: Myanmar's Ethnic Divide and Conflicts* (Institute of Peace and Conflict Studies, Issue Brief # 221, June 2013) <www.ipcs.org/issue-brief/southeast-asia/challenging-the-reconciliation-process-myanmars-ethnic-divide-and-con flicts-221.html>; Burma Link "Patterns of State Abuse" <www.burmalink.org/back ground/burma/human-rights-violations/patterns-of-state-abuse/>.

[237] It is commonly accepted that the term 'race' in the Convention definition encompasses ethnicity. See eg Goodwin-Gill and Jane McAdam, above n 229, at 70; Hathaway and Foster, above n 153, at 394.

[238] Agreement on China–Myanmar Border Management and Cooperation between China and Myanmar (signed 25 March 1997, entered into force 29 September 1997) <www .lawinfochina.com/display.aspx?id=317&lib=tax&SearchKeyword=&SearchCKeyword=>.

Province Administrative Rules of Entry–Exit of External Border Residents in the China–Myanmar Border Areas (1990 Yunnan Rules) would shed light on the meaning of the term and the legal rights it entails.[239]

The 1997 China–Myanmar Agreement defines "border residents" as "persons with habitual residence (*changzhu*) in border areas of each party".[240] It also defines "border areas" as the Chinese counties and cities and Myanmar towns and regions listed in Appendix I to the Agreement (see Table 4.1).[241]

Most displaced Kokangs in Yunnan fled from Laukkai, which is listed as a border area in the 1997 China–Myanmar Agreement. Therefore, most displaced Kokangs in Yunnan would qualify as border residents under the Agreement. The majority of the displaced Kokangs fled to Nansan town in Zhenkang county, as well as Gengma county, and Cangyuan county, which are also listed as border areas in the Agreement.[242]

The 1997 China–Myanmar Agreement allows border residents to cross the border with an exit–entry pass (*churujing tongxingzheng*),[243] exempting them from the normal visa requirements.[244] China and Myanmar respectively issue the exit–entry pass to their own nationals who qualify as border residents.[245] The exit–entry pass enables the holder to cross the border and travel within the border areas defined in the 1997 Agreement.[246]

The initial term of the agreement was ten years. The agreement automatically renews for another ten years upon expiry unless one party notifies the other party in writing six months prior to expiry that it wishes to terminate the agreement. As of June 2019, neither China nor Myanmar has expressed in public intention to terminate the agreement.

[239] The People's Government of Yunnan Province Yunnan Province Administrative Rules of Entry–Exit of External Border Residents in the China–Myanmar Border Areas, promulgated on 13 July 1990 <www.chinalaw.vip/law/云南省中缅边境地区境外边民入境出境管理规定/>.

[240] Art 2, Agreement on China–Myanmar Border Management and Cooperation between China and Myanmar, above n 239.

[241] Art 1.

[242] SCIO, above n 206.

[243] Art 20(2), Agreement on China–Myanmar Border Management and Cooperation between China and Myanmar, above n 239.

[244] Normally, Myanmar nationals need a visa to enter China and vice versa. Myanmar holders of an exit–entry pass do not obtain normal visas; instead, their exit–entry pass will be stamped.

[245] Art 20(2)(iv), Agreement on China–Myanmar Border Management and Cooperation between China and Myanmar, above n 239.

[246] Art 20(2)(ii).

Table 4.1 *Border counties/cities/towns listed in Appendix I to the 1997 China–Myanmar Agreement*

	China	Myanmar
1	Chayu	Nagmung
2	Gongshan	Khawbude
3	Fugong	Sawlaw
4	Lushui	Chipwi
5	Tengchong	Waingmaw
6	Longling	Momauk
7	Yingjiang	Mansi
8	Longchuan	Namhkam
9	Wanding	Muse
10	Ruili	Konkyan
11	Luxi	Laukkai
12	Zhenkang	Kunlong
13	Gengma	Hopang
14	Cangyuan	Mongmao
15	Lancang	Pangwaum
16	Ximeng	Mampan
17	Menglian	Pangyang
18	Menghai	Mongyang
19	Jinghong	Kengtung
20	Mengla	Mongyaung

Article 20(1) of the Agreement states that the two parties allow border residents to cross the border to take part in religious activities, visit relatives and friends, seek medical treatment, engage in commercial trade and participate in traditional ethnic festivals and events.[247] There is no mention of using the exit–entry pass to cross the border for personal safety or to seek asylum, but there is also no expression in the 1997 China–Myanmar Agreement that such numerated reasons for crossing under art 20(1) are exhaustive examples. The Agreement does provide that the exit–entry pass should specify the holder's reason(s) for crossing the border.[248] But in practice this requirement was not enforced by the Myanmar authority or the Chinese authority.[249]

---

[247] Art 20(1).
[248] Art 20(2)(i).
[249] Interviews conducted by the author (April 2013).

The 1997 China–Myanmar Agreement does not specify how long the exit–entry pass allows the holder to stay in China or Myanmar, or whether they can engage in paid employment during their stay on the other side of the border. In this regard, the Agreement is complemented by the 1990 Yunnan Rules issued by the Yunnan provincial government. The 1990 Yunnan Rules allow Myanmar border residents to enter and stay in border areas in Yunnan without a Chinese visa for fifteen days per entry (art 6). Subject to approval by the local Chinese public security bureau, the stay can be extended to up to ninety days (art 6).[250] Neither the 1997 China–Myanmar Agreement nor the 1990 Yunnan Rules limit the frequency of border crossing by a border resident within a certain period of time, thus allowing a border resident to enter and re-enter into Yunnan for unlimited times within the validity of the exit–entry pass.[251]

To summarise, displaced Kokangs in Yunnan qualify for refugee status under the Refugee Convention and Protocol, and most of them also qualify for the status of border resident under the 1997 China–Myanmar Agreement and the 1990 Yunnan Rules. There is nothing in international or Chinese law that suggests that refugee status and border resident status are mutually exclusive. As such, displaced Kokangs in Yunnan who fulfil the criteria for both statuses should be entitled to the rights attached to each.

As mentioned above, displaced Kokangs in Yunnan were generally not allowed to travel beyond the boundaries of the Chinese border town they entered. This seems to be in accordance with the relevant provisions on travel restriction applicable to border residents under the 1997 China–Myanmar Agreement and the 1990 Yunnan Rules. However, art 26 of the Refugee Convention requires states to allow refugees lawfully present to move freely within the country, subject only to limitations applicable to aliens generally in the same circumstances.[252] As Goodwin-Gill and McAdam noted, lawful presence "implies admission in accordance with

---

[250] For more detailed discussion about provisions of the 1990 Yunnan Rules, see Lili Song "Refugees or Border Residents from Myanmar? The Status of Displaced Ethnic Kachins and Kokangs in Yunnan Province, China" (2017) 29 *International Journal of Refugee Law* 466 at 482.

[251] Interviews conducted by the author (April 2013). According to holders of exit-entry passes in Kachin State, the exit-entry pass was generally valid for one year.

[252] Art 26 of the Refugee Convention provides: 'Each Contracting State shall accord to refugees lawfully in its territory the right to choose their place of residence to move freely within its territory, subject to any regulations applicable to aliens generally in the same circumstances.'

the applicable immigration law, for a temporary purpose".[253] Therefore, displaced Kokangs who enter Yunnan on a valid exit–entry pass are lawfully present in China and should be allowed to travel freely within China on the same footing as other foreigners in China.

4.4.3   Ambiguous Welcome? Policy Considerations Underlying China's Response to Displaced Ethnic Kokangs

Recognition of displaced Kokangs in Yunnan as border residents provides a legal justification for China's admission of displaced Kokangs into Yunnan, but the status of border residents per se does not give rise to any legal obligation from the host country to provide humanitarian relief aid to border residents under the 1997 China–Myanmar Agreement or the 1990 Yunnan Rules. In fact, China has signed bilateral border management treaties with several other neighbours, including North Korea,[254] Vietnam,[255] Nepal,[256] Laos[257] and Mongolia,[258] that contain provisions relating to border residents. These treaties all contain favourable border crossing arrangements for qualified "border residents", mainly to facilitate cross-border economic and cultural activities.[259] It would suffice to say that, in the context of bilateral border management agreements between China and neighbouring countries, the status of "border resident" is not a humanitarian status.

---

[253] Goodwin-Gill and McAdam, above n 229, at 524.

[254] The Ministry of Public Security of the People's Republic of China and the Ministry of National Security of the Democratic People's Republic of Korea Protocol on Cooperation in the Work of Maintaining National Security and Social Orders at Border Areas (8 July 1998) <http://policy.mofcom.gov.cn/PDFView?id=TYCX000076&libcode=gjty>.

[255] Agreement between the Government of the People's Republic of China and Vietnam on Management of Land Borders (18 November 2009) <www.mfa.gov.cn/mfa_chn//ziliao_611306/tytj_611312/tyfg_611314/t812100.shtml>.

[256] Agreement between the Government of the People's Republic of China and the Government of Nepal on Border Ports and Their Management Systems (14 January 2012) <http://np.chineseembassy.org/chn/zngxs/zywj/t1059642.htm>.

[257] Treaty between the Government of the People's Republic of China and the Government of Lao People's Democratic Republic (3 December 1993) <www.npc.gov.cn/wxzl/gong bao/2001-01/02/content_5003197.htm>.

[258] Treaty between the Government of the People's Republic of China and the Government of Mongolia on Border Management Mechanism (1 June 2010) <www.mfa.gov.cn/chn//gxh/zlb/tyfg/t812099.htm>.

[259] See eg the China–Korea Treaty, above n 255, art 3(3); the 2009 China–Vietnam Treaty, above n 256, arts 1(9) and 22; the 2012 China–Nepal Treaty, above n 257, arts 1(3) and 3 (2); the 1993 China–Lao Treaty, above n 258, art 13; the 2010 China–Mongolia Treaty, above n 259, art 1(8).

The Chinese Government claimed it treated the displaced Kokangs in the spirit of humanitarianism. Since it also claimed that it treated North Korean escapees and displaced Kachins in the spirit of humanitarianism,[260] the fact that China actually treats these three groups quite differently suggests that humanitarian consideration may not have been the only, or main, consideration behind China's response to each of these groups.

What motivated China to provide humanitarian assistance to displaced Kokangs in Yunnan in 2009 and 2015? Like the Vietnamese refugees, the ethnic Kokang in Myanmar are of the same ethnicity as the majority of the Chinese population, namely Han Chinese.[261] The Kokang Special Region, which is now part of Myanmar, was recognised as part of China when frontiers were first demarcated in Southeast Asian history in March 1894, but later ceded to Britain according to an 1897 agreement between the British and the Chinese.[262] The Kokangs, however, have maintained remarkably strong cultural and economic ties with China. Many Kokangs married Chinese nationals in Yunnan and have relatives and friends in Yunnan. Chinese has been the primary spoken and written language in the Kokang Special Region and many Kokangs do not speak Burmese. Television, publications and school education in the Kokang Special Region were all in Mandarin Chinese prior to the 2009 clash.[263] The Chinese yuan, instead of the Burmese kyat, was the main trading currency in the Kokang region.[264]

---

[260] Embajada de la República Popular China en la República Oriental del Uruguay "Foreign Ministry Spokesperson Hong Lei's Regular Press Conference on June 16, 2011" (17 June 2011) <http://uy.china-embassy.org/eng/fyrth/t832130.htm>; Embassy of the People's Republic of China in the Republic of Zimbabwe "Foreign Ministry Spokesperson Hong Lei's Regular Press Conference on May 22, 2012" (23 May 2012) <http://zw.china-embassy.org/eng/fyrth/t935031.htm>.

[261] The Kokang regard themselves as the descendants of the Ming dynasty royal family and scholar-official who fled to the Kokang region some 350 years ago (Righteous Kokang "guogan gaikuang" <www.righteouskokang.com> (translation: "Basic Facts of Kokang")).

[262] Sai Kaham Mong *Kokang and Kachin in the Shan State* (Institute of Asian Studies, Bangkok, 2005) at 31.

[263] After the 2009 clash, the Burmese Central Government gained control of the region and made significant efforts to replace the Chinese language with the Burmese language in the daily life in the Kokang Region (Hongwei Ying "Guogan jiannan rongru miandian" *Time Weekly* (online ed, China, 17 January 2013) (translation: "Kokang Painfully Integrate into Myanmar")).

[264] The dominance of foreign currency in Myanmar's border towns is not uncommon. For example, in Tachilek on the Myanmar–Thailand border, the Thai baht instead of Burmese kyat is used as trading currency.

A 2015 news story published by one of China's popular news outlets illustrates that close family and community ties between the Kokangs and the Chinese in Yunnan were key to a Chinese village's decision to accept displaced Kokangs.[265] Dashuisangshu is a village in Yunnan on the China–Myanmar border. Several villagers in Dashuisangshu were killed and injured by a bomb dropped by a Tatmadaw aircraft in mid-March 2015. When displaced Kokangs began to arrive in February 2015, the villagers held a meeting to discuss whether to host them, and the decision was affirmative. Several families in the village have sons- or daughters-in-law from the Kokang Special Region. "Speaking of our feelings, it was impossible to not to accept [them]", the village's Communist Party Branch Secretary was quoted in the news story, "[they are] all relatives".[266] The village received 900 displaced Kokangs, four times the number of the village's population. Displaced Kokangs who had no close relatives in the village were given accommodation in the village's Communist Party branch meeting rooms and, when all rooms were full, in tents.

At the national level, strong public sympathy towards the Kokangs probably created pressure on the central Chinese Government to assist the displaced Kokangs. There was a surge of media reports on the exodus of the Kokangs, which was partly fuelled by the MNDAA leader Peng Jiasheng's open letter, published online and written in Chinese, urging the Chinese people to support their fellow Han Chinese from the Kokang Special Region especially at a time when China was reclaiming its status as a great power.[267] Chinese netizens reacted strongly and called upon the Chinese Government to do more to protect the Kokangs.[268] Many Chinese civilians not only donated food, medicine and clothes to displaced Kokangs in Yunnan, but also volunteered as teachers and helpers in the camps for displaced Kokangs.[269] It is worth noting that in 1998 the

---

[265] Xu Yang "bianmin: taoguo guojing quemei taoguo zhadan" (22 March 2015) <https://xw.qq.com/cmsid/2015032201508900> (translation: "Border Residents: Fleeing across Borders but Still Cannot Escape Bombs").

[266] Yang, above n 266.

[267] Enze Han "Geopolitics, Ethnic Conflicts along the Border, and Chinese Foreign Policy Changes toward Myanmar" (2017) 13 *Asian Security* 59 at 67 and 69.

[268] Han, above n 268 at 69; United States Institute of Peace, *China's Role in Myanmar's Internal Conflicts: USIP Senior Study Group Final Report* (No 1, September 2018) at 26.

[269] See eg Li, above n 224; Xin Lin (translated by Luisetta Mudie) "Myanmar Army Holds Three Chinese Nationals on Suspicion of Spying" (14 May 2015) <www.rfa.org/english/news/china/myanmar-china-05142015125627.html>.

Chinese public took to the streets to protest against Beijing's inaction during the violent riots against ethnic Chinese in Indonesia.[270] Thus Beijing probably gave some weight to the obvious public sympathy for displaced Kokangs.

It is worth mentioning that border crossing has traditionally been part of the daily life of many cross-border ethnic communities living along the China–Myanmar border.[271] The special arrangement for border residents in the 1997 China–Myanmar Agreement and the 1990 Yunnan Rules could well be seen as legal recognition of and approval for such cross-border ties. The long-established and well-accepted presence of Myanmar nationals in the border area probably mitigated the Chinese authority's concern over stability issues that the influxes of Kokangs might cause.

In response to the 2009 influx, Beijing sent the Minister of Public Security to Yunnan, indicating that the issue was mainly regarded as one of security and stability. In March 2015, it was the Chinese Foreign Minister Wang Yi who flew to Yunnan in the aftermath of the deadly bomb incident at Dashuisangshu village, which was hosting nearly a thousand displaced Kokangs. As *The New York Times* rightly noted, the Chinese Foreign Minister had rarely made official trips within China.[272] This indicates that for Beijing, the Kokang–Yunnan situation was not only a border security and stability concern but also had implications for China–Myanmar relations. Sending Wang to Yunnan was a strong signal that Beijing attached great importance to the latter. The message Wang carried was that Beijing wanted to safeguard not only border security and the safety of Chinese nationals but also its overall relation with Myanmar.[273]

In comparison with the situation in 2009, Myanmar's significance in Chinese foreign policy had increased notably in 2015, following the "One Belt One Road" initiative and periphery diplomacy adopted by the new Xi Jinping Government in 2013. This coincided with Myanmar's

---

[270] Elisabeth Rosenthal "Beijing Students and Women, Defying Ban, Protest Anti-Chinese Violence in Indonesia" *The New York Times* (online ed, New York, 18 August 1998).

[271] Gang Luo "Yunnan bianjing minzu diqu renkou feifa liudong fazhi duice yanjiu" (2011) 9 Hebei Law Science 184 at 185 (translation: "A Study on Legal Strategies for Regulating Illegal Border Crossing in Yunnan Border Areas Inhabited by Ethnic Groups").

[272] Jane Perlez "Myanmar's Fight With Rebels Creates Refugees and Ill Will With China" *The New York Times* (online ed, New York, 21 March 2015).

[273] Xinhua "Chinese FM discusses Myanmar in border province after bombing" *The People's Daily* (online ed, Beijing, 17 March 2015).

opening-up after the National League for Democracy (NLD), led by Aung San Suu Kyi, won the Myanmar election in November 2013. As Yhome rightly noted, China began to view Myanmar's ethnic conflicts from a geostrategic perspective in 2013.[274] China has a long-standing and complicated relation with several Myanmar-based armed ethnic groups that exercised or still exercise actual control of areas along the Myanmar–China border. These groups, including the MNDAA, were formerly part of the Burma Communist Party, which received financial support as well as political advice from China during the 1960s and 1970s.[275] Although China completely terminated its support to the Burma Communist Party in 1984 and the Party fell apart in 1989, these groups maintained close, but largely informal, contact with the Yunnan provincial authority.[276]

In February 2015, the Myanmar Government accused local authorities in Yunnan of providing arms, food and medical care to MNDAA fighters and of allowing the MNDAA to use Chinese territory to outflank the Tatmadaw.[277] Although Myanmar's accusation did not explicitly refer to displaced Kokangs, China's assistance to the displaced Kokangs in Yunnan could easily be seen by a wary Myanmar as a convenient disguise for China to channel aid to the MNDAA. Indeed, a Tatmadaw representative explicitly criticised China for turning a blind eye to ethnic Kachin fighters (another ethnic group fighting the Tatmadaw) seeking shelter and medical treatment under the disguise of refugees.[278] The Chinese MFA, when asked to respond to Myanmar's accusation on 25 February 2015, denied assisting the MNDAA and stated that it had provided and would continue to provide to displaced Kokangs in Yunnan "necessary

[274] K Yhome *Understanding China's Response to Ethnic Conflicts in Myanmar* (Observer Research Foundation, Occasional Paper 188, April 2019).

[275] Yan Xu "jiemi: miandian gongchandang xingwang shimo yu jiaoxun" (2 December 2012) <http://dangshi.people.com.cn/GB/85039/13375304.html> (translation: "Secret Revealed: The Rise and Fall of the Burma Communist Party and Its Lessons").

[276] Myanmar Peace Monitor "International Response to Myanmar's Ethnic Conflict" <www.mmpeacemonitor.org/1504>.

[277] Khin Ei "Myanmar Says Kokang Rebels Getting Help from China's Side of Border" (26 February 2015) <www.rfa.org/english/news/myanmar/ye-htut-kokang-0226201516 2400.html>; Philip Wen "Myanmar's Kokang refugees caught between army, aged warlord and a pipeline to China" *The Sydney Morning Herald* (online ed, Sydney, 27 March 2015).

[278] Yang "beijing fengsuo bianjing nanmin zhong jingxian daliang junren" (14 January 2017) <http://news.dwnews.com/global/news/2017-01-14/59794169.html> (translation: "Beijing Closed Borders; Many Soldiers amongst Refugees").

assistance and proper settlement following the humanitarian spirit".[279] On 8, 12 and 13 March 2015, shells and bombs from Myanmar military forces "accidentally" hit villages in Yunnan, killing four Chinese villagers and injuring eight more, as well as one Kokang refugee.[280]

In March 2015, the Chinese Government began to close the camps and expel displaced Kokangs.[281] In June 2015, the Chinese Government closed all official camps and terminated assistance to displaced Kokangs in Yunnan.[282] It was in the same month that the leader of the NLD, Aung San Suu Kyi, arrived for her first official visit to China. When a new wave of displaced Kokangs crossed into Yunnan because of intensified fighting in February 2017, unlike in 2009 or 2015, the Chinese Government did not open any official camps to accommodate them.

Avoiding official assistance but allowing private aid may have been the Chinese Government's deliberate compromise balancing its domestic demand for action to help fellow Han Chinese in need against its security and foreign policy interests.

4.5   Displaced Ethnic Kachins from Myanmar

4.5.1   Influxes of Displaced Ethnic Kachins

Influxes of Kachin civilians displaced by armed conflicts into China's Yunnan province are not a new phenomenon. In 1992, thousands of ethnic Kachin escaped to Yunnan to flee "abuses at the hands of the Burmese military, including execution, rape, torture, destruction of villages and crops, and forced porterage".[283] By 1997, the Yunnan

---

[279] Chinese Ministry of Foreign Affairs "Foreign Ministry Spokesperson Hong Lei's Regular Press Conference on February 25, 2015" <www.fmprc.gov.cn/mfa_eng/xwfw_665399/s2510_665401/2511_665403/t1240548.shtml>.

[280] "Myanmar apologises for bombs that killed five in China's Yunnan province" *South China Morning Post* (online ed, Hong Kong, 3 April 2015); Lin Xin and Yuqing Wen "Myanmar Government Bombs Fall in China's Yunnan, Sparking Forest Fires" (12 March 2015) <www.rfa.org/english/news/china/bombs-03122015112650.html>.

[281] Long Qiao "Guogan laojie zaifa wuzhuang chongtu yunnan guanbi nansan zhen nanminying" (7 March 2015) <www.rfa.org/mandarin/yataibaodao/junshiwaijiao/ql2-03072015122210.html> (translation: "Fresh Armed Conflict in Laukkai in the Kokang Region, Yunnan Closing Refugee Camps in Nansan Town"); Khin Oo Tha "China Reportedly Urging Kokang Refugees to Return" (9 March 2015) <www.irrawaddy.com/news/burma/china-reportedly-urging-kokang-refugees-to-return.html>.

[282] Wang, above n 218.

[283] United States Committee for Refugees and Immigrants *World Refugee Survey 1997 – China* (1 January 1997) <www.unhcr.org/refworld/docid/3ae6a8af8.html>.

authorities were still assisting the estimated 7,000 remaining Kachins according to the United States Committee for Refugees World Refugee Survey.[284] But the situation attracted little media attention, and little information is available as to what assistance was provided.

In 1994, the Myanmar Central Government and the KIA, the biggest Kachin armed group and one of the strongest armed ethnic groups in Myanmar, reached a ceasefire which allowed the KIA to retain its armed forces and to exercise actual control of many areas in Kachin State, especially along the Myanmar–China border.[285] In the lead-up to the 2010 elections, the Myanmar Central Government demanded that the KIA transform into border guard units under the partial control of the Tatmadaw, but the KIA refused to do so.[286] The Myanmar Central Government later declared the ceasefire void.[287]

On 9 June 2011, armed conflict resumed between the Tatmadaw and the KIA, forcing tens of thousands of ethnic Kachins to flee towards the Myanmar–China border.[288] Many of the displaced Kachins crossed into neighbouring Yunnan province. The Chinese authority denied that the displaced Kachins in Yunnan were refugees, asserting that they were border residents who had come to China to live with their friends and relatives temporarily.[289] In mid-June 2011, about 1,000 displaced Kachins attempted to enter China, but only about 200, mostly elderly people and women with children, were allowed in by the Chinese border security forces.[290] Later, the Chinese authority generally allowed

---

[284] United States Committee for Refugees and Immigrants, above n 284.

[285] Euro-Burma Office *The Kokang Clashes – What Next?* (EBO Analysis Paper No 1, September 2009) <https://euroburmaoffice.s3.amazonaws.com/filer_public/b5/e5/b5e5f9ca-6754-4d38-b52b-94c1a1a05c56/ebo_analysis_no_1_kokang.pdf>.

[286] The New Humanitarian "Myanmar: Border guard plan could fuel ethnic conflict" (29 November 2010) <https://reliefweb.int/report/myanmar/myanmar-border-guard-plan-could-fuel-ethnic-conflict>.

[287] International Crisis Group *A Tentative Peace in Myanmar's Kachin Conflict* (Asia Briefing Number 140, 12 June 2013) <www.crisisgroup.org/asia/south-east-asia/myanmar/tentative-peace-myanmar-s-kachin-conflict>.

[288] Kachin News "Kachin IDPs Reach over 40,000 due to Civil War in Northern Burma" (2 September 2011) <www.kachinnews.com/news/2040-kachin-idps-reach-over-40000-due-to-civil-war-in-northern-burma.html>.

[289] Consulate-General of the People's Republic of China in Istanbul Turkey "2011 nian 6 yue 16 ri waijiaobiu fayanren Hong Lei juxing lixing jizhehui" (16 June 2011) <www.fmprc.gov.cn/ce/cgtur/chn/wjbfyrth/t831378.htm> (translation: "Ministry of Foreign Affairs Spokesperson Hong Lei Held Regular Press Conference on 16 June 2011").

[290] Saw Yan Naing "Kachin Conflict Sparks Refugee Situation" (15 June 2011) <www2.irrawaddy.org/article.php?art_id=21495>; China News "Miandian keqin wuzhuan zan

displaced Kachins to enter Yunnan,[291] although small-scale forced repatriations were also reported.[292] By late June 2012, about 10,000 displaced Kachins had entered Yunnan.[293]

The majority of displaced Kachins in Yunnan stayed in self-established camps, where they lived in empty warehouses or makeshift huts built with plastic sheets and bamboo; others lived in relatives' homes or rented rooms.[294] They were not allowed to travel outside the boundaries of the Chinese border towns they were staying in.[295] Although the Chinese authority claimed that they provided "necessary assistance in conformity with common practices on the basis of humanitarianism",[296] various reports confirmed that they provided almost no humanitarian assistance to the displaced Kachins in Yunnan.[297] The displaced Kachins in self-

bu pohuai zhongmian youqi guandao deng zhongguo huiying" (6 June 2011) <www .chinanews.com/gj/2011/06-16/3115812.shtml> (translation: "Burma's Kachin Army Has Not Ruined China–Myanmar Oil and Gas Pipes, Awaiting China's Response").

[291] HRW *Isolated in Yunnan: Kachin Refugees from Burma in China's Yunnan Province* (June 2012) <www.hrw.org/report/2012/06/25/isolated-yunnan/kachin-refugees-burma-chinas-yunnan-province> at 30.

[292] Naing, above n 291; Ba Kaung "Kachin State Refugees Face Uncertain Future" (1 July 2011) *The Irrawaddy* <www2.irrawaddy.org/article.php?art_id=21612>; Voice of America "Aid Groups Say China is Expelling Kachin Refugees" (23 June 2011) <http://blogs .voanews.com/breaking-news/2011/06/23/aid-groups-say-china-is-expelling-kachin-refu gees/>.

[293] The New Humanitarian "Kachin refugees in China in need" (27 June 2012) <www .thenewhumanitarian.org/news/2012/06/27kachin-refugees-china-need>. The figure was provided by the IDPs and Refugees Relief Committee based in Laiza. HRW estimated that 7,000–10,000 displaced Kachins had entered China's Yunnan province (HRW, above n 292, at 36). Others estimated that between 20,000 and 25,000 displaced Kachin fled to Yunnan (Chenggang Fan and Shiwei Shao "dao zhongguo qu: zhongmian bianjingxianshang de shiwan keqin nanmin" *Southern Weekly* (Guangzhou, 17 January 2013) <www.infzm.com/content/85250> (translation: "Go to China: The 100 Thousand Displaced Kachins on the China–Myanmar Border")).

[294] Interviews conducted by the author (April 2013 and December 2014); Kachin News Group "War Snowballs: Kachin Refugees Influx to China Border" (24 June 2011) <www.kachinnews.com/news/1955-war-snowballs-kachin-refugees-influx-to-china-border.html>.

[295] Interviews conducted by the author (April 2013 and December 2014). All of the displaced Kachins I interviewed stayed in self-established camps.

[296] Consulate-General of the People's Republic of China in Istanbul Turkey, above n 290.

[297] HRW, above n 292, at 6; The New Humanitarian, above n 294; Chinese Christian Journalist Association "keqin nanmin jiuzhu: keqin chongtu lishi beijing fenxi" (9 April 2012) <www.chinaaid.net/2012/04/blog-post_9.html> (translation: "Assistance of Displaced Kachins: Historical Analysis of the Kachin Conflict").

established camps relied mainly on donations from local residents and a small number of non-governmental charity groups.[298]

In late August and early September 2012, the Chinese authority forcibly sent back about 5,000 displaced Kachins, mainly those who were staying in self-established camps.[299] Those who were staying in private houses were allowed to remain.[300] Despite the Chinese Government's claim that the displaced Kachins left voluntarily,[301] various reports have confirmed the opposite.[302] Most of the people I interviewed confirmed that the repatriation was forced. For example, a displaced Kachin I interviewed said:

> When we were pushed back, we left with our heart filled with sadness. During the process, at six in the morning, more than 100 border guards and police. Several trucks also came. Some people were cooking. There were children. The Chinese police tore down the [shelter] and drove us out . . .

The Kachins were put on Chinese trucks and sent to KIA controlled areas which were still heavily affected by armed conflict between the Tatmadaw and the KIA. Most of the repatriated Kachins ended up in camps for internally displaced persons administered by the KIA.

Since then, many displaced Kachins have continued to flee to and remain in Yunnan.[303] There have been mixed reports of denial of entry at

---

[298] HRW, above n 292, at 6; The New Humanitarian, above n 294. See also *The Economist* "The Kachin dilemma: Over the border, the Kachin conflict causes headaches for China" (2 February 2013) <www.economist.com/news/asia/21571189-over-border-kachin-con flict-causes-headaches-china-kachin-dilemma>.

[299] UNHCR "UNHCR reaches Kachins sent back from China" (7 September 2012) <www .unhcr.org/5049cdba9.html>.

[300] Interview conducted by the author (April 2013).

[301] Edward Wong "Chinese Deny Forcing Refugees to Myanmar" *The New York Times* (online ed, New York, 25 August 2012).

[302] See eg Edward Wong "China Forces Ethnic Kachin Refugees Back to a Conflict Zone in Myanmar's North" *The New York Times* (online ed, New York, 23 August 2012); Luisetta Mudie "Kachin Forced Back to Burma" (24 August 2014) <www.rfa.org/ english/news/china/kachin-08242012105036.html/>; HRW "China: Refugees Forcibly Returned to Burma – Thousands of Kachin at Risk From Conflict, Abuses, Aid Short- ages" (24 August 2012) <www.hrw.org/news/2012/08/24/china-refugees-forcibly- returned-burma>.

[303] See Lianhe Zaobao "weibi zhanhuo mianbei pingmin fentao yunnan" (14 January 2017) <www.zaobao.com.sg/news/sea/story20170114-713261> (translation: "Escaping War- fare: Civilians from Northern Myanmar Fled to Yunnan Province"); Radio Free Asia "mianbei zhanhuo chongran dapi nanmin taowang zhongguo" (21 November 2016) <www.rfa.org/cantonese/news/myanmar-civilwar-11212016083635.html> (translation:

the border, tolerance of entry and permitted extended stay.[304] For example, in April 2014 the Chinese authority suspended border crossing at the Bang Kham crossing near Nongdao town, Yunnan.[305] On the other hand, in December 2014, about 100 displaced Kachins had been taking shelter in a self-established camp near Nongdao town on the Chinese side of the Myanmar–China border river for a few months.[306] Chinese policemen visited their camp several times and gathered basic information, such as the total number of persons staying in the camp, but did not request that they leave.[307]

As of June 2019, the KIA and the Myanmar Government has not reached a new ceasefire, and large numbers of displaced Kachins remain in Yunnan. The Chinese authority reportedly offered as much as RMB 120,000 (about USD 20,000) to each displaced Kachin refugee family willing to return to Myanmar.[308] In the meantime, the Chinese authority has not allowed UNHCR or other mainstream international organisations to access the displaced Kachins in Yunnan,[309] and has acquiesced to only a few Kachin and Yunnanese relief groups accessing and assisting displaced Kachins in Yunnan.[310] However, during a recent meeting between Chinese officials and Kachin church representatives on 1 March 2019, Chinese officials threatened a blockade if the

---

"Armed Conflict Resumed in North Myanmar: Large Numbers of Refugees Fled to China"); Lawi Weng "Analysis: A Window Opens for China to Nudge Myanmar Army Forward on Peace Process" (23 November 2017) <www.irrawaddy.com/news/burma/analysis-window-opens-china-nudge-myanmar-army-forward-peace-process.html>.

[304] Elaine Lynn-Ee Ho "Interfaces and the Politics of Humanitarianism: Kachin Internal Displacement at the China–Myanmar Border" (2018) 31 *JRS* 407 at 416; Kachinland News "China Closes Border as Thousands Flee Ongoing War" (11 April 2014) <http://kachinlandnews.com/?p=24308>; Fortify Rights "China: Protect Ethnic Kachin Refugees Fleeing War in Northern Myanmar – Prevent forced returns, allow humanitarian agencies unfettered access to displaced communities" (news release, 13 January 2017) <www.fortifyrights.org/publication-20170113.html>.

[305] Kachinland News, above n 305.

[306] Interviews conducted by the author (December 2014). See also International Media Support *Conflict sensitive journalism: Handbook – Special Edition Myanmar*" (September 2014) <www.mediasupport.org/wp-content/uploads/2014/10/conflict-sensitive-journalism-myanmar-2014-ims.pdf>.

[307] Interviews conducted by the author (December 2014).

[308] Mizzima "China offers cash to Kachin refugees willing to return" (9 March 2019) <http://mizzima.com/article/china-offers-cash-kachin-refugees-willing-return>.

[309] Mizzima, above n 309.

[310] *The Economist* "The Han that rock the cradle" (12 March 2015) <www.economist.com/news/asia/21646248-kokang-conflict-causes-problems-china-too-han-rock-cradle>; HRW, above n 292, at 11.

KIA was to refuse to sign a peace deal with the Myanmar Central Government.[311]

4.5.2   Legal Status of Displaced Ethnic Kachins in China

Like displaced Kokangs in Yunnan, displaced Kachins in Yunnan are Myanmar nationals fleeing from areas where severe human rights abuses, such as rape and sexual slavery, against ethnic Kachins are well documented and prevalent.[312] It is also well recognised that such severe human rights abuse in Kachin State is rooted in Myanmar's problematic ethnic policy. The ethnic Kachins, who are predominantly Christian, have also faced restrictions in their freedom of religion or belief.[313] Therefore, displaced Kachins in Yunnan, like displaced Kokangs, have well-founded fear of persecution because of their ethnicity and religion, and therefore prima facie qualify as refugees under the Refugee Convention and Protocol.

Many displaced Kachins in Yunnan also qualify as border residents under the 1997 China–Myanmar Agreement and the 1990 Yunnan Rules. The list of border areas contained in the Appendix to the 1997 China–Myanmar Agreement includes six Myanmar towns affected by the Kachin conflict,[314] namely Mansi, Waingmaw, Momauk, Nam Kham, Konkyan and Muse. It also includes four counties/cities in Yunnan province that received large numbers of displaced Kachins,[315] namely Yingjiang county, Longchuan county, Ruili city and Tengchong city. Specifically, Yingjiang county borders Mansi, Tengchong city borders Waingmaw, Longchuan county borders Nam Kham, and Ruili

---

[311] Khin Ei and Kyaw Tun Naing "China Urges Kachins to Return to Myanmar and Join Peace Process" (8 March 2019) <www.rfa.org/english/news/myanmar/china-kachins-03082019173425.html>.

[312] For example, Special Rapporteur on the situation of human rights in Myanmar, above n 231, at [50]; Amnesty International, above n 231; Hanna Hindstrom "Burma's Transition to Civilian Rule Hasn't Stopped the Abuses of Its Ethnic Wars" (1 April 2016) <http://time.com/4277328/burma-myanmar- suu-kyi-ethnic-wars/>; Shan Human Rights Foundation, above n 231.

[313] United Nations High Commissioner for Human Rights *Situation of Human Rights of Rohingya Muslims and Other Minorities in Myanmar: Report of the United Nations High Commissioner for Human Rights* UN Doc A/HRC/32/18 (28 June 2016) at [63].

[314] Free Burma Rangers "Burma Army Offensive in Waingmaw Township Continues" (4 October 2016) <www.burmalink.org/burma-army-offensive-waingmaw-township-continues/>.

[315] Beijing Youth Daily, above n 211.

city borders Konkyan. In light of this, it is likely that a significant portion of the displaced Kachins in Yunnan were residents of Mansi, Waingmaw and Nam Kham, although no authoritative statistics on the places of origin of all or most of the displaced Kachins have been published;[316] those displaced Kachins who were residents of Mansi, Waingmaw and Nam Kham or other listed Myanmar border towns would qualify as border residents under the 1997 China–Myanmar Agreement.

4.5.3 Same Same but Different? Explaining Differences between China's Treatment of Displaced Ethnic Kachins and Displaced Ethnic Kokangs

At a glance, the situation of displaced Kachins in Yunnan was similar to that of displaced Kokangs in Yunnan. Both were referred to by the Chinese authority as "border residents". Both were displaced groups of ethnic minorities in Myanmar fleeing military standoff or armed conflicts between the Tatmadaw and local ethnic military forces. Both fled to medium to small border towns in Yunnan province. Both arrived in large numbers during a short period. In both cases, China declined UNHCR's requests to access the displaced minorities from Myanmar.

Yet the treatment they received in China was different in several significant ways. First, whereas displaced Kokangs generally had no difficulty in entering Yunnan, many displaced Kachins reported denial of entry at the border by Chinese border guards.[317] According to my interviewees, many of the displaced Kachins who fled to Yunnan held an exit–entry pass issued by Myanmar immigration offices near the border, but many others, mostly villagers from remote mountainous areas, did not. It was those without an exit–entry pass who were questioned and initially denied entry by Chinese guards at the border. Two displaced Kachins I interviewed said that they did not have an exit–entry pass. Along with several hundred mountain villagers without an exit–entry pass, they pushed their way into Yunnan in July 2011:

> The Chinese border guards asked us not to enter China. We desperately pushed our way across the border ... The Chinese border guards were not able to stop us.

---

[316] Many of the displaced Kachins who fled to Yingjiang county did have an exit–entry pass, which is issued to qualified border residents under the 1997 China–Myanmar Agreement (Interviews conducted by the author (April 2013 and December 2014)).

[317] Kachinland News, above n 305; Fortify Rights, above n 305.

They estimated that up to 3,000 villagers entered Yunnan in the same way in the months following the resumption of the conflict in June 2011. These two interviewees then went to Nongdao town without difficulties. According to individuals who worked with displaced Kachins in Yunnan, the leaders among displaced Kachins had held unofficial negotiations with and obtained consent from the local Chinese authorities; otherwise the displaced Kachins would not have been able to force their way into Yunnan against the armed Chinese border guards.[318]

Second, whereas the Chinese Government set up camps to provide shelter and other humanitarian assistance to displaced Kokangs in 2009 and 2015, they have provided almost no humanitarian assistance to displaced Kachins since the beginning of their arrival in June 2011. Although the Chinese Government claimed that they provided "necessary assistance in conformity with common practices on the basis of humanitarianism",[319] various reports confirmed that the Chinese authorities provided almost no humanitarian assistance to the displaced Kachins in Yunnan.[320]

The majority of the displaced Kachins in Yunnan stayed together in self-established camps where they lived in makeshift shelters built from bamboo and plastic sheets or in warehouses, relying mainly on donations from local residents and non-governmental charity groups. The rest stayed with relatives or friends or rented private rooms. All of the ten displaced Kachins I interviewed in 2013 and 2014 said that they stayed in self-established camps while in Yunnan. Most of them said that they or their family members received only occasional medical assistance (such as vaccinations or medical treatment for skin diseases) from medical teams dispatched to the camps by the local municipal-/county-level Chinese authorities, while others said they did not receive assistance from the Chinese authorities.[321]

---

[318] Interviews conducted by the author (April 2013).

[319] Consulate-General of the People's Republic of China in Istanbul Turkey, above n 290.

[320] HRW, above n 292, at 6; The New Humanitarian "Kachin refugees in China in need" (27 June 2012) <www.thenewhumanitarian.org/news/2012/06/27/kachin-refugees-china-need>; Chinese Christian Journalist Association "keqin nanmin jiuzhu: keqin chongtu lishi beijing fenxi" (9 April 2012) <www.chinaaid.net/2012/04/blog-post_9.html> (translation: "Assistance of Displaced Kachins: Historical Analysis of the Kachin Conflict").

[321] Interviews conducted by the author (April 2013 and December 2014).

Why did China treat displaced Kachins differently? As Cohen rightly noted,[322] the scale of the crises could have been a key factor. The Kachin State has a total population of more than 1,200,000 and more than 150,000 civilians have been uprooted since the resumption of the conflict in June 2011.[323] In comparison, the total population of the Kokang Special Region is less than 150,000, of whom 37,000 and 60,000 took refuge in China in 2009 and 2015 respectively. The population affected, or potentially affected, by the Kachin conflict is much larger than that in the Kokang conflict.

Second, the cultural and ethnic links between the ethnic Kachins and the Chinese are weaker than those between the ethnic Kokangs and the Chinese. The Kachins are of the same ethnicity as the ethnic Jingpos in China, who are one of China's fifty-six officially recognised ethnic minority groups. In this sense, the Kachins are similar to the North Koreans, who have their Chinese-Korean counterpart in China. As noted by Han, the Kachins did not attract enough interest or sympathy from the nationalist Chinese netizens.[324] In addition, the Kachins have a different language from the majority Han Chinese and are mostly Christian. These differences could have been seen by China as destabilising elements.

Third, China has different strategic and economic interests in Kachin State and the Kokang Special Region.[325] Whereas the economy in the Kokang Special Region mainly relies on gambling businesses and border trade, resource-rich Kachin State hosts several large projects heavily invested by Chinese state-owned enterprises, such as the Myitsone hydropower station and the Taiping hydropower station, which caused controversy in local communities because of environmental and other issues.[326] The Chinese investors had relied heavily on the Myanmar

---

[322] David Cohen "China's Myanmar Problem" (17 January 2013) <http://thediplomat.com/china-power/chinas-myanmar-problem/>.

[323] AsiaNews "Kachin, 405 villages destroyed and 150 thousand displaced in seven years of conflict" (6 December 2018) <www.asianews.it/news-en/Kachin,-405-villages-destroyed-and-150-thousand-displaced-in-seven-years-of-conflict-44147.html>.

[324] Han, above n 268, at 68.

[325] Cohen, above n 323.

[326] Myo Lwin "China hopes to resume Myitsone hydro dam" (9 March 2016) <www.mmtimes.com/index.php/business/19377-china-hopes-to-resume-myitsone-hydro-dam.html>; Sophie Song "China and Myanmar Activists Joust over Controversial Shwe Oil And Natural Gas Pipeline" (6 August 2013) <www.ibtimes.com/china-myanmar-activists-joust-over-controversial-shwe-oil-natural-gas-pipeline-1373579>; Aung Hla Tun and others "Myanmar to get more profit from controversial Chinese-backed mine"

Central Government to suppress local protests and activism against these Chinese projects.[327] In particular, the construction of the Myitsone hydropower station (about USD 3.6 billion), the biggest of the Chinese-invested projects in Myanmar, is located in Kachin State and was suspended by the Myanmar Central Government in September 2011, just a few months after the resumption of the Kachin conflict.[328] China has been trying to obtain consent from Naypyidaw for the resumption of the construction of the Myitsone hydropower station.[329] Therefore, China's reliance on Naypyidaw to protect Chinese investment interest in Kachin is far greater than in the Kokang situation, and that need has existed since the beginning of the Kachin influx.

Commentators have pointed out that assisting displaced Kachins could be seen by the Tatmadaw as supporting the KIA and thus could strain China–Myanmar relations.[330] Indeed, representatives of the Tatmadaw had accused China of tolerating the entry of Kachin soldiers disguised as refugees into Yunnan for shelter and medical treatment.[331] In particular, unlike the MNDAA, which was defeated by the Tatmadaw and lost its control of the Kokang Special Region, the KIA still exercises control of many areas along the China–Myanmar border in Kachin State and its administrative wing, the KIO, manages large camps that host about 60 per cent of internally displaced Kachins.[332] The Myanmar Central Government only allowed occasional delivery of international humanitarian assistance to these camps; as a result, internally displaced Kachins relied mainly on support from the KIA. If China assists displaced Kachins, who would otherwise be a strain on the KIA's finance

---

(2 October 2013) <http://uk.reuters.com/article/uk-myanmar-mine-idUKBRE99103M 20131002>.

[327] Xingjie Sun "zhongmian youqi guandao, zhongguo anggui de yike?" (11 July 2013) <http://cn.nytimes.com/china/20130711/cc11myanmar/> (translation: "China–Myanmar Oil and Gas Pipelines: An Expensive Lesson for China?").

[328] Thomas Fuller "Myanmar Suspends Construction of Myitsone Dam" *The New York Times* (online ed, New York, 30 September 2011).

[329] Myo Lwin, above n 327.

[330] Bertil Lintner "Myanmar in The Middle: China–Myanmar – Border war dilemma" (2 December 2011) <www.atimes.com/atimes/Southeast_Asia/ML02Ae01.html>; Chinese Christian Journalist Association, above n 321.

[331] Yang "Beijing fengsuo zhongmian bianjing nanminzhong jingxian daliang junren" (14 January 2017) <http://news.dwnews.com/global/news/2017-01-14/59794169.html> (translation: "Beijing Closes China–Myanmar border: Large Numbers of Soldiers among Refugees").

[332] The New Humanitarian, above n 321.

and resources, it could be seen by the Tatmadaw as indirectly supporting the KIA.

However, China does not want to be too hostile to the KIA either. The KIA still exercises actual control over many areas along the China–Myanmar border and had threatened to attack the Sino-Myanmar oil and gas pipelines that run through Kachin State.[333] In addition, like the MNDAA, the KIA also has connections with China. It received weapons indirectly from China via the Burma Communist Party, which China supported directly, in the 1960s and 1970s, and maintained informal contacts with Yunnan officials and intelligence agents after China officially terminated its support for foreign communist forces in the late 1970s. Commentators believed that China wanted to play a subtle game of balancing its relations with both sides of the conflict.[334] Such policy considerations probably explain why China provided little assistance but quietly allowed some displaced Kachins, including those who did not have border resident status, to enter and remain in Yunnan.

Since 2013, China has actively sought to increase its involvement in peace talks between the Myanmar Central Government and armed ethnic groups,[335] a move notably deviating from the principle of non-interference that has long been the cornerstone of Chinese foreign policy,[336] but seemingly reflecting China's preference of addressing root causes to solve refugee problems. In March 2013, China appointed a special envoy for Asian Affairs, with a focus on Myanmar, to serve as lead point of contact and formal observer to Myanmar's peace talks.[337] It also

---

[333] Stratfor "Myanmar, China: Border Insecurity Threatens Political Interests" (13 June 2012) <https://worldview.stratfor.com/article/myanmar-china-border-insecurity-threatens-political-interests>.

[334] Lintner, above n 339; The Economist, above n 307; Brent Crane "Kachin and China's Troubled Border: The Kachin conflict is a thorn in China's side as it tries to manage its relations with Myanmar" (14 January 2015) <http://thediplomat.com/2015/01/kachin-and-chinas-troubled-border/>.

[335] See Yun Sun *China and Myanmar's Peace Process* (United States Institute of Peace, Special Report 401, March 2017); Yuichi Nitta "China plays peace broker for Myanmar talks with ethnic groups" <https://asia.nikkei.com/Politics/International-relations/China-plays-peace-broker-for-Myanmar-talks-with-ethnic-groups>.

[336] Loreen Tsin *China and Myanmar: Beijing's Conflicting Role in the Kachin Peace Process* (merics: Mercator Institute for China Studies, China Monitor: Number 9, 6 June 2014) <www.merics.org/sites/default/files/2017-09/China_Monitor_9_Myanmar_EN.pdf> at 2; Joe Kumbun "Does China Want Peace in Myanmar?" (14 August 2017) <www.irrawaddy.com/opinion/guest-column/china-want-peace-myanmar.html>.

[337] Transnational Institute *China's Engagement in Myanmar: From Malacca Dilemma to Transition Dilemma* (Myanmar Policy Briefing 19, 19 July 2016) at 26.

hosted several rounds of talks between the Myanmar Central Government and the KIA,[338] and donated USD 300,000 to facilitate peace talks between those two parties.[339] Chinese delegations even met with Kachin Baptist church representatives to call for the support of the Kachin public for the national peace agreement proposed by the Myanmar Government, and threatened a blockade if the KIA was to refuse the peace agreement.[340] Whether these efforts will successfully lead to a durable solution to the situations of displaced Kokangs and Kachins in Yunnan remains to be seen.

[338] AsiaNews "China hosts a meeting between Myanmar government and rebels" (9 June 2018) <www.asianews.it/news-en/China-hosts-a-meeting-between-Myanmar-government-and-rebels-44864.html>; Tsin, above n 345.

[339] Doug Bock Clark and Corey Pattison "China Is Playing Peacemaker in Myanmar, but with an Ulterior Motive" (18 April 2017) <https://foreignpolicy.com/2017/04/18/china-is-playing-peacemaker-in-myanmar-but-with-an-ulterior-motive-myitsone-dam-energy/>.

[340] Ei and Naing, above n 312.

II

Hong Kong Special Administrative Region and
Macao Special Administrative Region

Refugee Law and Policy in Hong Kong

5.1 The Making and Unmaking of a Refugee City: Hong Kong's Experience

The Hong Kong Special Administrative Region of the People's Republic of China (Hong Kong) has a land area of about 1,107 square kilometres and a population of about seven million people as of 2017.[1] It is a major international trade and financial hub and one of the most economically prosperous regions in the world with a GDP per capita of USD 48,717 in 2018.[2]

Between 1842 and 1 July 1997, Hong Kong was a British colony as a result of a series of treaties between the Chinese Qing imperial Government and the United Kingdom. On 1 July 1997, the United Kingdom returned Hong Kong to China following the 1984 Joint Declaration of the Government of the United Kingdom of Great Britain and Northern Ireland and the Government of the People's Republic of China on the Question of Hong Kong (1984 Joint Declaration).[3] In accordance with the "one country, two systems" principle enshrined in the 1984 Joint Declaration and the subsequent 1990 Basic Law of Hong Kong (Hong Kong Basic Law),[4] which is Hong Kong's constitutional document, Hong Kong should have a high degree of autonomy except for foreign and defence affairs, which are the responsibility of the central Chinese Government. The Hong Kong Basic Law guarantees that Hong Kong's capitalist system and way of life should remain unchanged for fifty years

---

[1] Hong Kong Government "Hong Kong – the Facts" (February 2019) <www.gov.hk/en/about/abouthk/facts.htm>.

[2] World Bank "GDP per capita (current US$): Hong Kong SAR China" (2018) <https://data.worldbank.org/indicator/NY.GDP.PCAP.CD?locations=HK>.

[3] Joint Declaration of the Government of the United Kingdom of Great Britain and Northern Ireland and the Government of the People's Republic of China on the Question of Hong Kong (19 December 1984) <www.cmab.gov.hk/en/issues/jd2.htm>.

[4] Basic Law of the Hong Kong Special Administrative Region of the People's Republic of China 1990 (Hong Kong) <www.basiclaw.gov.hk/en/basiclawtext/index.html>.

after Hong Kong's return to China,[5] and that Hong Kong enjoys legislative, executive and independent judicial power, including that of final adjudication.[6] Hong Kong is generally perceived as a rule of law society that has separation of powers.[7] It remains a common law jurisdiction.

Hong Kong has been called a "refugees city", "a city built by refugees" and "a magnet for refugees".[8] During the Chinese Civil War (1945–1949) and following the establishment of the People's Republic of China in 1949, hundreds of thousands of Mainland Chinese fled to Hong Kong. In 1949 and 1950 alone, more than 700,000 Mainland Chinese citizens escaped to Hong Kong.[9] By 1953, four in every five of Hong Kong's two and a half million residents were those who had fled from China between 1945 and 1953.[10]

UNHCR, scholars and media have often referred to Mainland Chinese who fled to Hong Kong in the 1950s and 1960s as refugees;[11] however,

---

[5] Art 5.

[6] Art 2.

[7] See World Justice Project "Hong Kong SAR, China Ranked 16 out of 126 Countries on Rule of Law" (28 February 2019) <https://worldjusticeproject.org/sites/default/files/docu ments/Hong%20Kong%20SAR%2C%20China_0.pdf>; Anthony Mason "The rule of law in the Shadow of the Giant: The Hong Kong Experience" (2011) 33 *Sydney Law Review* 623; Daniel Fung "Foundation for the Survival of the Rule of Law in Hong Kong: The Resumption of Chinese Sovereignty" (1996) 1 *UCLA Journal of International Law & Foreign Affairs* 283; Albert Chen "Constitutional Crisis in Hong Kong: Congressional Supremacy and Judicial Review" (1999) 33 *The International Lawyer* 1025; Kemal Bokhary "The Rule of Law in Hong Kong Fifteen Years after the Handover" (2012–2013) 51 *Columbia Journal of Transnational Law* 287; Eric Ip "Mapping Parliamentary Law and Practice in Hong Kong" (2015) 3(1) *CJCL* 97; Ian Scott "The Disarticulation of Hong Kong's Post-Handover Political System" (2000) 43 *The China Journal* 29.

[8] Botao Zhen "nanmin: ziwo de fanying yu zheshe" (17 April 2017) <www.hk01 .com/周報/178358/難民-自我的反映與折射> (translation: "Refugee: Reflection and Refraction of Self"); Laurie Chen and Yujing Liu "Explainer: How Hong Kong Has for Decades been a Magnet for Refugees and Migrants" *South China Morning Post* (online ed, Hong Kong, 23 December 2017); Siulun Wong *Emigrant Entrepreneurs: Shanghai Industrialists in Hong Kong* (Oxford University Press, Hong Kong, 1988); Leticia Ho-Ling Tang "The Situation of Asylum Seekers and Torture Claimants in Hong Kong" (2009) 3 *Hong Kong Journal of Legal Studies* 9 at 9.

[9] Alexander Betts, Gil Loescher and James Milner *UNHCR: The Politics and Practice of Refugee Protection into the 21st Century* (2nd ed, Routledge, Abingdon, 2012) 25.

[10] Wantai Zheng and Siulun Wong "xianggang huaren de shenfen rentong: jiuqi qianhou de zhuanbian" (2002) 73 *Century Bi-Quarterly* 21, <www.cuhk.edu.hk/ics/21c/media/articles/ c073-200207038.pdf> (translation: "Hong Kong Chinese Identity: Changes around 1997").

[11] See UN General Assembly "Chinese refugees in Hong Kong 1167 (XII)" (26 November 1957) <www.unhcr.org/excom/bgares/3ae69ee618/chinese-refugees-hong-kong.html>; Chi Kwan Mark "The 'Problem of People': British colonials, Cold War Powers, and the Chinese Refugees in Hong Kong, 1949–62" (2007) 41(6) *Modern Asian Studies* 1145;

both the United Kingdom and China claimed that they were not refugees.[12] The United Kingdom argued that Chinese escapees in Hong Kong were "not all political refugees in the normal sense of the word" as they had a number of reasons, including the presence of close relatives in Hong Kong, for leaving the mainland and that the influx was one more "akin to a mass migration of disgruntled citizens than to a flight from actual oppression or economic disaster".[13]

Despite the United Kingdom's reluctance to recognise Chinese escapees to Hong Kong as refugees, from 1949 to October 1980 the Hong Kong Government's policy towards Chinese escapees was relatively tolerant. Officially, in the absence of relevant law governing refugee status in Hong Kong,[14] all Mainland Chinese who sought to enter Hong Kong were subject to an immigration quota system introduced by the Hong Kong Government in May 1950, under which Hong Kong would issue entry permits to a certain number of Mainland Chinese, who would also obtain an exit permit from the Chinese Government.[15] In practice, until November 1974 the Hong Kong Government exercised immigration discretion in allowing virtually all Chinese escapees who entered Hong Kong illegally to register and remain in Hong Kong, although it did police the China–Hong Kong frontier to reduce illegal entry.[16]

Betts, Loescher and Milner, above n 9, at 23. For discussion about the legal status of Chinese escapees in Hong Kong under international law, see Edvard Hambro *The Problem of Chinese Refugees in Hong Kong: Report Submitted to the United Nations High Commissioner for Refugees* (AW Sijthoff, Leiden, 1955); Glen Peterson "To Be or Not to Be a Refugee: The International Politics of the Hong Kong Refugee Crisis, 1949–55" (2008) 36(2) *The Journal of Imperial and Commonwealth History* 171.

[12] For discussion about China's view on Chinese escapees in Hong Kong, see Section 3.2.2; also Mark, above n 11, 1152.

[13] Public Records Office, London England, CO 1030/1312, May 15 and May 21, 1962, cited in Laura Madokoro "Borders Transformed: Sovereign Concerns, Population Movements and the Making of Territorial Frontiers in Hong Kong, 1949–1967" (2012) 25(3) *Journal of Refugee Studies* 407 at 419.

[14] Britain did not extend the Refugee Convention and Protocol to Hong Kong, see Section 5.2.1. Local Hong Kong law contained no provision governing refugee status; see Madokoro, above n 13; Chan Kwok Bun "Hong Kong's Response to the Vietnamese Refugees: A Study in Humanitarianism, Ambivalence and Hostility" (1990) 18(1) *Southeast Asian Journal of Social Science* 94.

[15] Madokoro, above n 13, at 412; Kamyee Law and Kimming Lee "Citizenship, economy and social exclusion of mainland Chinese immigrants in Hong Kong" (2006) 36(2) *Journal of Contemporary Asia* 217 at 220.

[16] Law and Lee, above n 15, at 220; John Burns "Immigration from China and the Future of Hong Kong" (1987) 27(6) *Asian Survey* 661 at 664.

In November 1974, Hong Kong introduced the more restrictive Touch Base policy, which Skeldon called "a very British, 'sporting' approach to a unique international problem".[17] Under the Touch Base policy, Chinese escapees intercepted in the rural areas in northern Hong Kong were regarded as "out" and immediately repatriated to China, whereas those who successfully evaded Hong Kong border security and reached urbanised areas of Hong Kong were considered "safe" and issued with Hong Kong identity cards.[18] From 1975 to 1978, about 30,500 Mainland Chinese who entered Hong Kong illegally were granted residence under the Touch Base policy, whereas in the same period 11,840 were repatriated.[19] Following China's adoption of a reform and open-up policy in late 1978 and early 1979, social and political controls at the local level in China started to relax, thus making population movement easier. In 1979 and 1980, a total of 325,300 Mainland Chinese crossed into Hong Kong illegally, of whom 152,600 were granted the right to stay.[20] It became clear to the Hong Kong Government that as China was undergoing profound reform, the Touch Base policy was no longer an effective policy for managing migration from China.[21] Hong Kong abandoned the policy on 23 October 1980. After that date, all Mainland Chinese who entered Hong Kong without a proper permit were classified as illegal immigrants and subject to repatriation.[22]

Hong Kong's relatively tolerant approach to Chinese escapees between 1949 and 1980 could be attributed to a number of factors. First, as Peterson noted, the mass movement of people from China to Hong Kong needs to be understood in the context of Hong Kong's historic relationship to China.[23] Prior to 1950, there was an open border between China and Hong Kong. The Hong Kong Government encouraged economic integration and cultural continuity. Socially, there were strong family and cultural ties between Hong Kong and

---

[17]   Ronald Skeldon "Hong Kong and its Hinterland: A Case of International Rural-to-Urban Migration?" (1986) 5(1) *Asian Geographer* 1 at 7.

[18]   At 7.

[19]   Burns, above n 16, at 664.

[20]   At 664.

[21]   At 664.

[22]   Jean-Francois Destexhe "Hong Kong and 1997: The Facts" in Werner Menski (ed) *Coping with 1997: the reaction of the Hong Kong people to the transfer of power* (Trentham Books, Staffordshire, 1995) 17 at 29; Kitchun Lam and Pakwai Liu *Immigration and the Economy of Hong Kong* (City University Press, Hong Kong, 1998) 15.

[23]   Peterson, above n 11, at 172.

the neighbouring Guangdong province; economically, trade with China was vital for the Hong Kong economy.[24] At the same time, the Hong Kong Government wanted to establish a sense of political distinction between Hong Kong and China, and thus was prepared for Hong Kong to take up the role of a refuge.[25] Second, as noted by both Peterson and Madokoro, an important consideration that guided the British approach to influxes of Chinese escapees into Hong Kong was to avoid unduly provoking China or allowing the issue to damage Britain's relations with China.[26] By avoiding references to refugees and emphasising its authority in border control, the Hong Kong authority avoided provoking the Chinese authority, while at the same time instilling confidence in the British governance amongst the residents of Hong Kong.[27] Third, the British Government believed that forcibly repatriating Chinese escapees would have greatly damaged Hong Kong and the United Kingdom's international image, particularly in light of the rampant anti-communist rhetoric in the West at that time.[28] Last but not least, from the 1950s through to the 1970s there was a serious shortage of unskilled labour in Hong Kong as a result of rapid labour-intensive industrialisation, and the Chinese escapees provided much-needed cheap labour for Hong Kong's economy take-off during that period.[29] Thus there were economic incentives for the Hong Kong Government to be lenient to illegal immigrants. As Destexhe rightly noted:[30]

> [i]n Hong Kong, the somewhat lenient approach to worker migration was not implemented, as in some European countries, through officially advertised sympathetic rules on political asylum . . . for those who wanted to escape from oppression and, in particular, cold-war communist rule. Rather, Hong Kong's model for discretionary immigration control resembles that of countries which do not officially admit that they take worker migrants, but do so in practice.

---

[24] See Madokoro, above n 13; Peterson, above n 11, at 172; Agnes Ku "Immigration Policies, Discourses and the Politics of Local Belonging in Hong Kong (1950–1980)" (2004) 30(3) *Modern China* 326 at 333.

[25] Ku, above n 24, at 333.

[26] Peterson, above n 11, at 176; Madokoro, above n 13, at 416.

[27] Madokoro, above n 13, at 416.

[28] At 416.

[29] Law and Lee, above n 15, at 220.

[30] Destexhe, above n 22, at 28.

During the Indochinese refugee crisis, Hong Kong received more than 200,000 Vietnamese refugees as a port of first asylum. Initially, all Vietnamese asylum seekers arriving in Hong Kong automatically received refugee status and qualified for resettlement to a third country.[31] The Vietnamese refugees were housed in open centres until resettlement and were allowed to work outside the centres.[32] As noted by Fan, then member of the Hong Kong Executive and Legislative Councils, from 1975 to 1980 Hong Kong coped with more than 80,000 Vietnamese refugees "cheerfully and uncomplainingly".[33] Public sympathy in Hong Kong lay overwhelmingly with the Vietnamese refugees, and Western countries fulfilled their resettlement promises relatively quickly.[34]

In 1979, Western countries became increasingly reluctant to provide resettlement for Vietnamese refugees from Hong Kong as "compassion fatigue" began to set in.[35] In 1982, with the intention of deterring new Vietnamese arrivals, Hong Kong began to house all Vietnamese refugees in closed camps on remote outlying islands and no longer allowed them to work outside the camps. From 1982 to 1987, the number of new Vietnamese arrivals was relatively low and the camps hosted just under 10,000 people.

In 1988, following Vietnam's termination of the orderly departure programme, there was a sharp increase in the number of Vietnamese asylum seekers in Asia, leading to the endorsement of the UN Comprehensive Plan of Action (CPA) in June 1989, according to which Vietnamese asylum seekers arriving at places of first asylum would no longer be automatically considered as refugees and would be subject to RSD processes. Hong Kong had already introduced a new policy in June 1988, under which all Vietnamese asylum seekers were treated as "illegal immigrants" unless they were recognised as refugees.[36] According to the 1988 Statement of Understanding between the Hong Kong Government and UNHCR, from 16 June 1988, the Hong Kong Government would assess Vietnamese boat people in accordance with the Refugee

---

[31] Roda Mushkat "Refuge in Hong Kong" (1989) 1(4) *International Journal of Refugee Law* 449 at 474.

[32] Bun, above n 14, at 95.

[33] Rita Fan "Hong Kong and the Vietnamese Boat People: A Hong Kong Perspective" (1990) 2 (special issue) *International Journal of Refugee Law* 144 at 145.

[34] At 145.

[35] Henry Litton "The Vietnamese boat people story: 1975–1999" (2001) 26(4) *Alternative Law Journal* 179 at 181.

[36] Mushkat, above n 31, at 474.

Convention and Protocol and the UNHCR Handbook for Procedures and Criteria for Determining Refugee Status, and UNHCR had a monitoring role in the screening process.[37]

Vietnamese asylum seekers who were screened out had access to judicial review in Hong Kong.[38] Of the five principal places of first asylum in Asia during the Indochinese refugee crisis, Hong Kong was the only one that allowed judicial review of RSD decisions.[39] However, it also had the lowest recognition rate. Whereas about 28 per cent of all Vietnamese asylum seekers who were screened under CPA procedures were granted refugee status, Hong Kong only recognised 18.8 per cent of the 60,275 Vietnamese asylum seekers it screened as refugees.[40]

In the mid-1990s, China repeatedly requested that the United Kingdom solve the problem of Vietnamese refugees and asylum seekers remaining in Hong Kong before the handover of Hong Kong in 1997.[41] In Beijing's view, the United Kingdom's decision to make Hong Kong a port of first asylum was a wrong one and that wrong policy created a heavy burden on the people of Hong Kong.[42] The Chinese MFA stated that the Chinese Government had no obligation in that matter and that the Chinese Government did not think Hong Kong should continue to host Vietnamese refugees and asylum seekers after 1997.[43] Chinese officials also stated that Beijing would not recognise the status of Vietnamese children born in Hong Kong before January 1983, even though they had the right of residence there according to Hong Kong immigration laws.[44] The last Vietnamese refugee camp in Hong Kong closed in 2000 and the

---

[37] At 474.

[38] See Arthur Helton "Judicial Review of the Refugee Status Determination Procedure for Vietnamese Asylum Seekers in Hong Kong" (1991) 17(1) *Brooklyn Journal of International Law* 263.

[39] UNHCR *The State of the World's Refugees 2012: In Search of Solidarity* (Oxford University Press, Oxford, 2000) 85.

[40] At 85.

[41] Qiushi Yuan *Xianggang huigui dashiji 1979–1997* (2nd ed, Joint publishing, Hong Kong, 2015) 217, 219, 298 and 352 (translation: *Historic Events Relating to Hong Kong's Return to China*).

[42] Office of the Commissioner of the Ministry of Foreign Affairs of the People's Republic of China in Hong Kong "gongshu fayanren jiu zhigang de yuenan chuanmin wenti da jizhewen" (17 June 1999) <www.fmprc.gov.cn/ce/cohk/chn/xwfb/gsxwg/2000/t40777.htm> (translation: "Office of the Commissioner Answers Journalists' Questions regarding Vietnamese Refugees in Hong Kong").

[43] Yuan, above n 41, at 219.

[44] Mushkat, above n 31, at 477.

last 1,400 Vietnamese refugees remaining in Hong Kong were eventually allowed to integrate into the local community.[45]

After the Indochinese refugee crisis, Hong Kong has not experienced mass influxes of refugees. In the early 2000s, UNHCR was assisting fewer than 5,000 refugees and asylum seekers in Hong Kong and their number was less than 0.1 per cent of Hong Kong's population of nearly seven million at that time.[46] Most of them came from Africa and South Asia. It is perhaps worth mentioning that in 2013 American whistle-blower Edward Snowden fled to Hong Kong and Hong Kong's asylum policy attracted considerable international attention.[47] It has never been confirmed whether Snowden applied for asylum in Hong Kong. However, it is clear that the Hong Kong Government now has a firm policy of not granting asylum. The Government explained its position to the Hong Kong Legislative Council in 2006:[48]

> Hong Kong is small in size and has a dense population. Our unique situation, set against the backdrop of our relative economic prosperity in the region and our liberal visa regime, makes us vulnerable to possible abuses if the 1951 UN Convention were to be extended to Hong Kong. We thus have a firm policy of not granting asylum and do not have any obligation to admit individuals seeking refugee status under the 1951 UN Convention.

5.2   Current Legal and Policy Framework

5.2.1   Hong Kong's Status under the Refugee Convention and Protocol

When Hong Kong was a British colony, the United Kingdom, which became a signatory to the Refugee Convention in 1954 and a party to the

---

[45] Jon Gordon "FYI: What happened to Hong Kong's Vietnamese refugee community?" *South China Morning Post* (online ed, 15 June 2008) <www.scmp.com/article/641644/fyi-what-happened-hong-kongs-vietnamese-refugee-community>.

[46] See eg UNHCR Global Trends 2003, 2004, 2005 and 2005 <www.unhcr.org/search?page=search&skip=9&docid=&cid=49aea93aba&comid=56b079c44&tags=globaltrends>; see also UNHCR online population database for statistics in other years <http://popstats.unhcr.org/en/time_series>.

[47] Hilary Whiteman "Scenarios for Snowden: Escape, arrest, asylum" (21 June 2013) <https://edition.cnn.com/2013/06/20/world/asia/snowden-scenarios-hong-kong/index.html>.

[48] Paper presented to the Legislative Council Panels on Security and Welfare Services, Situation of Refugees, Asylum Seekers and Torture Claimants in Hong Kong (18 July 2006) CB(2)2747/05-06(01), cited in Tang, above n 8, at 9.

Refugee Protocol in 1968, did not extend the Refugee Convention or the Refugee Protocol to Hong Kong. When the British Secretary of State for Foreign and Commonwealth Affairs was asked why the Refugee Convention and Protocol were not extended to Hong Kong during a sitting of the House of Commons on 6 March 1984, Mr Luce stated:[49]

> The 1951 convention relating to the status of refugees was not extended to Hong Kong because of the territory's small size and its geographical vulnerability to mass illegal immigration. The 1967 protocol was applied only to those territories to which the 1951 convention was extended.

According to art 153(1) of the Hong Kong Basic Law, the application to Hong Kong of international agreements to which China is a party or becomes a party shall be decided by the Chinese Gentral Government, in accordance with the circumstances and needs of Hong Kong and after seeking the views of the Hong Kong Government.

On 20 June 1997, the Chinese Government informed the UN Secretary-General about the status of Hong Kong in relation to treaties deposited with the UN Secretary-General by way of a notification (the 1997 Note). According to the 1997 Note, after Hong Kong's return to China, international treaties that would apply to Hong Kong fall within two broad categories:[50]

> I. The treaties listed in Annex I to this Note [herein under], to which the People's Republic of China is a party, will be applied to the Hong Kong Special Administrative Region with effect from 1 July 1997 as they:
>
> (i) are applied to Hong Kong before 1 July 1997; or
>
> (ii) fall within the category of foreign affairs or defence or, owing to their nature and provisions, must apply to the entire territory of a State; or
>
> (iii) are not applied to Hong Kong before 1 July 1997 but with respect to which it has been decided to apply them to Hong Kong with effect from that date (denoted by an asterisk in Annex I).
>
> II. The treaties listed in Annex II to this Note [herein under], to which the People's Republic of China is not yet a party and which apply to Hong Kong before 1 July 1997, will continue to apply to the Hong Kong Special Administrative Region with effect from 1 July 1997.

---

[49] Lord Trefgarne, Parliamentary Under-Secretary of State for Armed Forces, House of Lords Debates, 27 February 1985, cited in Roda Mushkat *One Country, Two International Legal Personalities: the Case of Hong Kong* (Hong Kong University Press, Hong Kong, 1997) 87 n 9.

[50] United Nations Treaty Section "Historical Information: China", n 2 <https://treaties.un.org/Pages/HistoricalInfo.aspx?clang=_en#China>.

As mentioned above, the Refugee Convention and Protocol, to which China had become a party in 1982, did not apply to Hong Kong before 1 July 1997. In retrospect, it was possible for China – in consultation with Hong Kong pursuant to art 153 of the Hong Kong Basic Law – to extend of these instruments to Hong Kong under category I(iii) of the 1997 Note. However, given the Chinese Government's attitude towards the Vietnamese refugees in Hong Kong and the Hong Kong Government's firm opposition to the application of the Refugee Convention and Protocol to Hong Kong,[51] it is perhaps not surprising that the Chinese and Hong Kong Governments did not take the opportunity to extend the Refugee Convention and Protocol to Hong Kong.[52] As the Refugee Convention and Protocol are not listed in the Annexes to the 1997 Note, their extension to Hong Kong is subject to section IV of the 1997 Note:

> IV. With respect to any other treaty not listed in the Annexes to this Note, to which the People's Republic of China is or will become a party, in the event that it is decided to apply such treaty to the Hong Kong Special Administrative Region, the Government of the People's Republic of China will carry out separately the formalities for such application. For the avoidance of doubt, no separate formalities will need to be carried out by the Government of the People's Republic of China with respect to treaties which fall within in the category of foreign affairs or defence or which, owing to their nature and provisions, must apply to the entire territory of a State.

As of June 2019, China has not carried out the formalities to extend the Refugee Convention or the Refugee Protocol to Hong Kong.

---

[51] Security Bureau "Torture Claim Screening Mechanism: Enhanced Mechanism and Way Forward" (November 2009) LC Paper No. CB(2)370/09-10(03) at [9]; Hong Kong Security Bureau, Immigration Department and Social Services Department "Response to the Motion of the LegCo Panel on Security on Asylum Seekers and Torture Claimants" (September 2006) LC Paper No. CB(2)2994/05-06(01) at [1] <www.legco.gov.hk/yr05-06/english/panels/se/papers/se0731cb2-2994-01-e.pdf>.

[52] For criticism of non-extension of the Refugee Convention and Protocol to Hong Kong, see Lawrence Cox "The Failure of the People's Republic of China to Extend the Refugee Convention to Hong Kong: the Contemporary Use of the 'Colonial Clause' by A Non-Colonial Power to Circumvent Human Rights Obligations" (2008) 4(2) *Journal of Migration and Refugee Issues* 80; Ada Lai and Kerry Kennedy "Refugees and civic stratification: The 'Asian Rejection' Hypothesis and Its Implications for Protection Claimants in Hong Kong" (2017) 26(2) *Asian and Pacific Migration Journal* 206.

5.2.2   Immigration and Human Rights Law

Hong Kong law, as it currently stands, gives no special status to asylum seekers and refugees.[53] They are subject to the provisions of the Hong Kong Immigration Ordinance (Cap 115), which only distinguishes legal and illegal immigrants.

According to art 154 of the Hong Kong Basic Law, the Hong Kong Government is authorised to "apply immigration controls on entry into, stay in and departure from the Region by persons from foreign states and regions".[54] Under the Hong Kong Immigration Ordinance, the power of immigration control in Hong Kong is conferred upon the director of immigration, who enjoys wide discretionary powers.[55] The director of immigration may grant or refuse permission to land or give permission to land subject to a limit of stay and impose conditions.[56] The director is also empowered by sec 13 to authorise illegal immigrants to remain in Hong Kong, subject to such conditions of stay as he thinks fit.[57] However, the Hong Kong Immigration Ordinance is silent on how the director of immigration's wide powers should be exercised.[58]

Hong Kong is a party to most of the core human rights treaties,[59] including the Convention against Torture (CAT), which contains an article on *non-refoulement*.[60] By way of the Immigration (Amendment) Ordinance 2012, Part VIIC Torture Claims was inserted into the Hong Kong Immigration Ordinance.[61] Part VIIC provides for a statutory procedure for making and processing claims for *non-refoulement*

---

[53] During the Indochinese Chinese refugee crisis, a "Part IIIA Vietnamese Refugees" was inserted in the Hong Kong Immigration Ordinance. That Part was effectively repealed with effect as of 9 January 1998. Mark Daly "Refugee law in Hong Kong: Building the legal infrastructure" (2009) 9 *Hong Kong Lawyer* 14.

[54] Hong Kong Basic Law, art 154 para 2.

[55] Hong Kong Immigration Ordinance 1971, s 5.

[56] Hong Kong Immigration Ordinance, s 11.

[57] Hong Kong Immigration Ordinance, s 13.

[58] *C and Others v Director Of Immigration And Another* [2013] HKCFA 21 at [18].

[59] See "List of Treaties in Force and Applicable to the Hong Kong Special Administrative Region" <www.doj.gov.hk/sc/laws/interlaw.html>.

[60] The CAT, art 3. For discussion on human rights law and refugee protection in Hong Kong, see Kelley Loper "Human Rights, *Non-refoulement* and the Protection of Refugees in Hong Kong" (2010) 22(3) *International Journal of Refugee Law* 404 at 406. Hong Kong Courts have demonstrated their willingness to engage with international standards generally and frequently refer to international and comparative human rights materials when interpreting constitutional rights

[61] Hong Kong Immigration (Amendment) Ordinance 2012 <www.legco.gov.hk/yr11-12/english/ord/ord023-12-e.pdf>.

protection on the ground of a torture risk.[62] Since March 2014, as a matter of policy, all *non-refoulement* claims, including those on the ground of a persecution risk (see below), have been processed following the procedure provided under Part VIIC.

5.2.3   Non-Refoulement *and the Unified Screening Mechanism*

Prior to 2014, UNHCR was the only venue in Hong Kong which conducted refugee status determination for asylum seekers who were not covered by the screening process established during the Indochinese refugee crisis, and the Hong Kong Government relied upon UNHCR decisions when determining whether potential deportees were entitled to *non-refoulement* protection. Despite its policy of not granting asylum, the Hong Kong Government did allow persons who were identified by UNHCR as refugees to stay in Hong Kong pending third-country resettlement. UNHCR decisions were not published and, because of UNHCR's immunity as a UN agency, were not subject to judicial review by Hong Kong courts.[63]

In response to a series of court cases between 2009 and 2014 (discussed below), the Hong Kong Government launched a policy regime known as the unified screening mechanism (USM) in 2014, under which the Hong Kong Government undertakes to determine claims for *non-refoulement* protection on grounds of, inter alia, risk of "persecution with reference to the *non-refoulement* principle under Article 33 of the 1951 Convention relating to the Status of Refugees".[64] The USM commenced operation on 3 March 2014;[65] at the same time, UNHCR ceased its RSD procedures in Hong Kong.[66]

There are three categories of applicable grounds for *non-refoulement* claims under the USM,[67] and risk of persecution is the only one that

---

[62] Hong Kong Legislative Committee "Updated background brief prepared by the Legislative Council Secretariat for the meeting on 6 June 2017" (27 March 2018) LC Paper No. CB(2)1533/16-17(04), <www.legco.gov.hk/yr16-17/english/hc/sub_com/hs54/papers/hs5420180327cb2-1110-1-e.pdf>.

[63] *Secretary For Security v Sakthevel Prabakar* [2004] HKCFA 43 at [46].

[64] Hong Kong Government "Commencement of Unified Screening Mechanism for Claims for *Non-refoulement* Protection" (7 February 2014) <www.info.gov.hk/gia/general/201402/07/P201402070307.htm>.

[65] Hong Kong Government, above n 64.

[66] UNHCR "Unified Screening Mechanism" (26 March 2014) <www.unhcr.org/hk/en/750-unified-screening-mechanism.html>.

[67] Applicable grounds under the USM include risk of (i) torture defined under s 37U of the Hong Kong Immigration Ordinance, (ii) absolute and non-derogable rights under the Hong Kong Bill of Rights Ordinance, Cap 383, and (iii) persecution with reference to the

currently lacks a statutory underpinning. The Hong Kong Government undertakes to assess *non-refoulement* claims grounded in persecution risk as a result of the 2012 Hong Kong Court of Final Appeal decision in *C* (see below). The criteria for establishing persecution risk under the USM are set out in paragraph 13 of the Notice to Persons Making a *Non-Refoulement* Claim (Notice to Claimants) issued by the Hong Kong Immigration Department to all *non-refoulement* claimants:[68]

> a person should be considered as having a persecution risk for the purpose of his *non-refoulement* claim if:
>
> (a) he, owing to well-founded fear of being persecuted on account of one or more of race, religion, nationality, membership of a particular social group or political opinion, is outside the country of his nationality and is unable or, owing to such fear, is unwilling to avail himself of the protection of that country; and
>
> (b) his life or freedom would be threatened on account of his race, religion, nationality, membership of a particular social group or political opinion should he be expelled or returned to the frontiers of a Risk State.

Whereas paragraph 13(a) is similar to art 1(A)(2) of the Refugee Convention, which provides a general definition of the term refugee, paragraph 13 (b) is similar to art 33(1) of the Refugee Convention, which provides on the obligation of *non-refoulement*. In a footnote in the Notice to Claimants, the Hong Kong Immigration Department stated that, drawing on the provision of article 33(1) of the Refugee Convention, the expression "life or freedom" in paragraph 13(b) "may be considered as a shorthand for the risks that are similar to those that give rise to refugee status under the terms of Article 1 of [the Refugee Convention]". Thus paragraph 13(b) is not intended to create additional requirements other than those of art 1 of the Refugee Convention.[69] Apart from the Notice to Claimants, Hong Kong statutory and policy documents provide little guidance as to the meaning of persecution, well-founded fear, race, religion, nationality, membership of a particular social group or political opinion.

---

non-refoulement principle under art 33 of the Refugee Convention. See Hong Kong Immigration Department "Notice to Persons Making a *Non-refoulement* Claim" (4 September 2017) <www.immd.gov.hk/pdf/notice_non-refoulement_claim_en.pdf> at 1; Hong Kong Legislative Council "Report of Subcommittee to Follow Up Issues Relating to the Unified Screening Mechanism for *Non-refoulement* Claims" (1 March 2019) LC Paper No. CB(2)874/18-19 at 2.

[68] Hong Kong Immigration Department, above n 67, 6.

[69] Kirsteen Lau et al, *Non-Refoulement Law in Hong Kong* (LexisNexis, Hong Kong, 2017) at 76.

The screening procedure of the USM follows that of the torture claim screening mechanism which has been used in Hong Kong since 2009 and which became a statutory mechanism by way of the Hong Kong Immigration (Amendment) Ordinance 2012. A *non-refoulement* claim in Hong Kong can only be lodged by a person who is liable to removal.[70] A person with a valid visa in Hong Kong cannot lodge a *non-refoulement* claim. Claimants for *non-refoulement* protection must first inform the Hong Kong Immigration Department of their claims. They will then have twenty-eight days to complete and return a *non-refoulement* claim form, stating alleged grounds of their *non-refoulement* claim and providing supporting evidence.[71] The claimant must attend screening interviews to make clarifications and answer questions relating to their claim. The Hong Kong Immigration Department will make a decision and inform the claimant, by a written notice of decision, of the reasons for accepting or rejecting their claim. The processing time of a *non-refoulement* claim was twenty-five weeks on average at the early implementation of the USM, and has been reduced to about ten weeks as of March 2019 after the Hong Kong Immigration Department created eighty-three new posts to handle *non-refoulement* claims.[72] Decisions on *non-refoulement* claims by the Hong Kong Immigration Department are not published.

Non-refoulement claimants who receive negative decisions from the Hong Kong Immigration Department may lodge an appeal within fourteen days after they are notified of such decision.[73] The appeal will be considered independently by the Torture Claims Appeal Board (TCAB), a statutory body established under sec 37ZQ of the Hong Kong Immigration Ordinance. As of March 2019, the TCAB consisted of ninety-seven members including former judges or magistrates, as well as overseas and local experts with relevant experiences.[74] Decisions by the TCAB include reasons for the decision and are provided to the claimant.[75] However, they are not published.

---

[70] Hong Kong Immigration Ordinance s 37W.
[71] Hong Kong Legislative Council, above n 67, at 2 and Appendix IV.
[72] At 9.
[73] Hong Kong Immigration Ordinance, s 37ZR and s 37ZS.
[74] Hong Kong Legislative Council, above n 67, at 9. For more details about appointment of TCAB members, see Hong Kong Immigration Ordinance Schedule 1A s 2.
[75] At 9.

5.3   The Role of the Judiciary

Hong Kong is one of the few Asian jurisdictions that allow judicial review of RSD decisions. Judicial review is available to *non-refoulement* claimants who receive negative decisions from the TCAB as a remedy.[76] They must apply to the Court of First Instance for a leave to apply for judicial review.[77] Once leave has been granted, judicial review applications can proceed to full hearing in court.

In *Khan*, Lam J explained the Courts' approach to judicial review of *non-refoulement* claims:[78]

> Judicial review is concerned with the reasonableness, lawfulness and fairness of the decisions and the process of reaching such decisions by the authorities.
>
> A *non-refoulement* claim involves 'life and limb'; any decision will bear significant consequences on an applicant. Therefore, high standards of fairness must be achieved. The court should look at an applicant's case under 'rigorous examination and anxious scrutiny'.

He continued, citing *Re Islam Rafiqul* with approval:[79]

> it is said in *Re Islam Rafiqul*:
> "The role of the Court in a judicial review is not to provide a further avenue of appeal. The primary decision-makers are the Director [of Immigration] and the [Torture Claim Appeal] Board. Though in *non-refoulement* cases the Court will adopt an enhanced standard in scrutinising the decision of the Board due to the seriousness of issue at hand, the Court should not usurp the role of the Board. Assessment of evidence and COI materials and risk of harm, state protection and viability of internal relocation are primarily within the province of the Board (and the Director). The Court will not intervene by way of judicial review unless there are errors of law or procedural unfairness or irrationality in the decision of the Board".

The judiciary has played an important role in shaping the procedures and standards for processing claims for *non-refoulement* protection in Hong

---

[76] See Hong Kong Legislative Council Secretariat "Judicial review and *non-refoulement* claims" (5 December 2018) ISSH11/18-19 <www.legco.gov.hk/research-publications/english/1819issh11-judicial-review-and-*non-refoulement*-claims-20181205-e.pdf>.

[77] Hong Kong High Court Ordinance 1997, s 21K; Hong Kong Rules of the High Court 1998, r 3(1). For more discussion about judicial review of TCAB decisions, see Lau et al, above n 69, ch 10.

[78] *Alam Khan V. Torture Claims Appeal Board / Non-refoulement Claims Petition Office* [2018] HKCFI 2138 at [32]–[33].

[79] *Khan*, above n 78, at [33].

Kong in the past fifteen years. As mentioned above, in 2004, UNHCR processed claims for refugee status in Hong Kong. Its decisions usually did not give reasons for rejection of refugee status, and failed asylum seekers could not appeal UNHCR decisions to Hong Kong Courts.[80] From 2004 to 2014, a period which Lau called "a time of genesis",[81] Hong Kong Courts decided a series of cases which ultimately transformed the way *non-refoulement* claims were handled in Hong Kong.

The first landmark case was *Prabakar* in 2004. Prabakar was an ethnic Tamil asylum seeker from Sri Lanka, who claimed that he was tortured in Sri Lanka. The Hong Kong Government, having relied on a UNHCR decision refusing refugee status to Prabakar, issued a deportation order against him. UNHCR later granted refugee status to Prabakar, but the Hong Kong Government refused to rescind the deportation order. Prabakar sought judicial review of the deportation order and of the refusal to rescind it.[82]

In *Prabakar*, the Hong Kong Court of Final Appeal recognised that a person not protected by the Refugee Convention might nevertheless be protected by the CAT and vice versa.[83] The CAT was extended to Hong Kong by the United Kingdom in 1992 and continues to bind Hong Kong after 1997. But the provision of art 3(1) of the CAT, which imposes an obligation of *non-refoulement* on state parties,[84] had not been incorporated into Hong Kong law at the time of the *Prabakar* hearing.[85] In practice, the Hong Kong Government had adopted the policy of not deporting a person to a country where that person would face a real risk of torture, and the policy was stated in the report submitted by the People's Republic of China to the Committee against Torture in 1999.[86] Prabakar's lawyers argued that the Hong Kong Government was under a legal duty of *non-refoulement* of torture claimants on one of the following bases: the Basic Law, the Bill of Rights, customary international law and

---

[80] *Prabakar*, above n 63, at [46].

[81] Lau et al, above n 69, at 3.

[82] *Prabakar*, above n 63, at [39].

[83] At [14].

[84] Art 3(1) of the CAT provides: 'No State Party shall expel, return ("refouler") or extradite a person to another State where there are substantial grounds for believing that he would be in danger of being subjected to torture.'

[85] For discussion about incorporation of international treaties into domestic law in Hong Kong, see Oliver Jones "Customary *non-refoulement* of refugees and automatic incorporation into the common law: A Hong Kong perspective" (2009) 58(2) *ICLQ* 443.

[86] *Prabakar*, above n 63, at [3].

legitimate expectation.[87] The Hong Kong Government argued that, as a matter of domestic law, it did not have a legal duty to do so.[88] The Court of Final Appeal found that it did not have to decide whether such a legal duty existed,[89] and that the existence of the Government's policy mentioned above provided a sufficient basis for classic judicial review.[90] The question for the Court was "the standards of fairness that must be observed by the [Government] in determining in accordance with the *policy* the potential deportee's [torture] claim" (emphasis added).[91] As the claimant's "life and limb are in jeopardy and his fundamental human right not to be subjected to torture is involved", high standards of fairness must apply when the Government determines torture claims.[92] The Court went on to conclude that the Government's mere reliance on UNHCR's unexplained rejection of refugee status to determine a potential deportee's torture claim "would fall well below the high standards of fairness required".[93]

As a result of *Prabakar*, the Hong Kong Government introduced an administrative mechanism for assessing torture claims independent to UNHCR's RSD procedure and introduced a new Part VII C to the Hong Kong Immigration Ordinance to deal with torture claimants.[94] In 2008, the Court of First Instance found in *FB* that the Government's blanket policy of denying legal representation to torture claimants was illegal and failed to meet the required high standards of fairness.[95] This led to the Government's decision to provide publicly funded legal assistance to torture claimants in 2009, and this assistance has been extended to all *non-refoulement* claimants following the commencement of the USM.[96]

---

[87] At [4].

[88] At [4].

[89] At [4] per Li CJ and at [67] per Bokhary PJ. For discussion about the Court's position on this, see Kelley Loper, above n 60, at 415; Jones, above n 85, at 449; Michael Ramsden "Using International Law in Hong Kong Courts: An Examination of Non-Refoulement Litigation" (2013) 42 *Common Law World Review* 351 at 367.

[90] At [67].

[91] At [43].

[92] At [44].

[93] At [48].

[94] *C*, above n 58, endnote 19.

[95] *FB v Director of Immigration* [2008] HKEC 2072.

[96] Legislative Council, above n 51, at 2; Hong Kong Security Bureau, Immigration Department and Social Welfare Department "Provision of Publicly-funded Legal Assistance and Humanitarian Assistance to *Non-refoulement* Claimants" (January 2019) LC Paper No. CB(2)581/18-19(01) at 1.

After the Hong Kong Government started to process torture claims in late 2004, UNHCR continued to process claims for refugee status for nearly ten years.[97] In the 2013 case of *C*, the Court of Final Appeal was asked to consider whether the Hong Kong Government must also independently assess refugee claims.[98] The applicants in *C* were asylum seekers from Africa and South Asia whose refugee claims were rejected by UNHCR. The Hong Kong Government, having relied solely on UNHCR decisions refusing refugee status to the applicants, issued deportation orders against them. The applicants applied for judicial review of the deportation orders. They put forward two arguments before the Court of Final Appeal. Their first argument was that the principle of *non-refoulement* enshrined in art 33(1) of the Refugee Convention had become a rule of customary international law as well as a peremptory norm, and as such, had become part of the common law of Hong Kong.[99] Thus the applicants argued that the Hong Kong Government should conduct its own RSD and must not deport any refugee claimant without appropriate enquiry into their *non-refoulement* claims.[100] Both the Court of First Instance and the Court of Appeal found that the principle of *non-refoulement* had become part of customary international law but not a peremptory norm, and both dismissed the applicants' appeal.[101] This was the first comprehensive recognition, by common law courts, of the *non-refoulement* principle as part of customary international law.[102] The Court of Final Appeal found that it was unnecessary to discuss this argument as it accepted the applicants' second argument.

The applicants' second argument relied on *Prabakar*. They argued that, although the Refugee Convention did not bind Hong Kong, the Government had a policy of not deporting refugees to a country where they would face real risk of persecution. Such a policy is evidenced by the agreement between the Hong Kong Government and UNHCR and the fact that the Hong Kong Government had not refouled any refugees. Thus the Government must observe high standards of fairness in determining whether to

---

[97] Loper, above n 60, at 412.

[98] *C*, above n 58.

[99] At [11].

[100] At [11].

[101] *C V. Director Of Immigration* [2008] HKCFI 109 at [194]; *C V. Director of Immigration and Another* [2011] HKCA 159 at [67].

[102] Jones, above n 85, at 443.

deport a refugee claimant, and reliance on UNHCR decisions would not meet the high standards of fairness required.

The Government argued that *Prabakar* should not apply because, firstly, the CAT applied to Hong Kong whereas the Refugee Convention did not and, secondly, the Government did not have a policy with respect to *non-refoulement* of refugees but only a practice. The Court of Final Appeal rejected both defences. It noted that *Prabakar* did not depend on the application of the CAT to Hong Kong; thus it made no difference in *C* that Hong Kong was not bound by the Refugee Convention.[103] It also noted that as the director of the Immigration Department must exercise the powers under the Immigration Ordinance in a principled manner, the exercise of such power was inevitably facilitated by a practice or policy; what label is used does not matter.[104]

In *C*, the Government also argued that a decision averse to the Government "might result in a flood of economic migrants" into Hong Kong and that to require the Government to conduct RSD would require much expense and expertise.[105] The Court of Final Appeal stated that it was not concerned with the granting of asylum, but with potential deportation of persons to a place where they have well-founded fear for persecution on the grounds mentioned in the Refugee Convention.[106] It pointed out that UNHCR, the Hong Kong Bar Association and the Hong Kong Law Society had advocated a unified screening system for all *non-refoulement* claims and said their suggestion merited careful consideration.[107] The Court did not accept the Government's "expense and expertise" argument, noting that the Hong Kong Government had been supplying, at its own cost, immigration officials to UNHCR to carry out RSD in the UNHCR procedure.[108] The Court said: "[i]n any event, the solution is not to reduce Hong Kong's human rights standard. The rule of law has real consequences and effect must be given to them".

In conclusion, the Court held that, when exercising the power to remove a refugee claimant, the Hong Kong Government must determine whether the refugee claim is well-founded and "such determination must satisfy the high standards of fairness required having regard to the gravity

---

[103] *C*, above n 58, at [33].
[104] At [38].
[105] At [47] and [52].
[106] At [49].
[107] At [50].
[108] At [53].

of the consequence of the determination".[109] As a result of *C*, the Hong Kong Government launched the USM in 2014 and UNHCR terminated its RSD procedure in Hong Kong.

It is perhaps worth noting that in *C* as well as in *Prabakar*, the Court did not order the Government to establish an independent assessment mechanism. As Jones noted, it appears that the Court of Final Appeal's judgement in *Prabakar* could have been "satisfied by the UNHCR providing reasons and supporting documentations for its conclusion" and that "an assessment by reference to such material, combined with an opportunity for further comment by the claimant, would surely fulfil the requirement" laid down in *Prabakar*.[110] However, the Hong Kong Government was more cautious and chose to assess torture claims independently. The same can be said about the Hong Kong Government's response to the Court of Final Appeal's judgement in *C*. It suffices to say that, if there was no general respect for the rule of law in Hong Kong society, the Court's decisions would have been less likely to have the impact they have had.

As Lau and Barbour rightly noted, the judiciary was instrumental in bringing about almost all recent positive changes in refugee protection in Hong Kong in recent years.[111] The Hong Kong judiciary's willingness to hear refugee and *non-refoulement* cases and to uphold human rights standards is particularly valuable and plausible given the fact that that the Refugee Convention and Protocol do not apply to Hong Kong and that the Hong Kong Government pursues a firm policy of not granting asylum. At the regional level, as Hong Kong is one of the few Asian jurisdictions that allow judicial review of RSD decisions, Hong Kong Courts' interpretation of refugee law will undoubtedly make valuable contributions to the discourse on refugee law and refugees in Asia.

5.4   The Role of Civil Society

Hong Kong has a vibrant civil society that has played a role in many aspects of social life.[112] In terms of refugee protection, members of Hong Kong civil society have made positive contributions.

---

[109] At [56].

[110] Jones, above n 85, at 449.

[111] Lau et al, above n 69, at 3; Brian Barbour "Protection in Practice: The Situation of Refugees in East Asia" (2012) 2 *Nanmin Kenkyu Journal* (translation: *Refugee Studies Journal*) 81 (Published in Japanese; English original available at <www.refugeestudies.jp/>).

[112] See Ma Ngok *Political Development in Hong Kong: State, Political Society, and Civil Society* (Hong Kong University Press, Hong Kong, 2007); M Sing "Economic development, civil society and democratization in Hong Kong" (1996) 26(4) *Journal of*

In comparison to China, Hong Kong has a good number of NGOs that actively support and advocate for refugees and asylum seekers. For example, the Justice Centre Hong Kong (formerly Hong Kong Refugee Advice Centre) provides free legal information and assistance to asylum seekers and advocates for better refugee protection through working with Government officials, Legislative Council members and media.[113] A support network formed by large churches provides rental assistance to refugees and asylum seekers and arranges for them to visit local schools, churches and community organisations as an effort to reduce negative media stereotyping.[114] The International Social Service Hong Kong Branch, a non-governmental organisation, has been working with the Hong Kong Government as its implementing service provider of counselling, food, accommodation and other basic needs to refugees and asylum seekers since 2006.[115] Other organisations, such as Christian Action Chungking Mansions Service Centre, Society for Community Organisation, Vision First, Branches of Hope, Refugee Union, Rebuild Unite Nurture and the Hong Kong Society for Asylum-Seekers and Refugees also provide a wide range of support including financial and material assistance, education support, psycho-social support and counselling, empowerment and recreation programmes, advocacy and outreach to local communities.[116]

The legal profession and academics in Hong Kong have shown strong support for refugee rights. Human rights lawyers in Hong Kong deserve a lot of credit for the positive changes in Hong Kong's refugee law and policy. Through step-by-step strategic litigation, human rights lawyers such as those at Daly & Associates (formerly Barns & Daly) have

Contemporary Asia 482; Christine Loh "Alive and well but frustrated: Hong Kong's civil society" 2007 (issue 2) *China Perspectives* 40; but see Elaine Chan and Joseph Chan "Hong Kong 2007–2017: a backlash in civil society" (2017) 39(2) *Asian Pacific Journal of Public Administration* 135; Alvin So "HONG KONG: Vibrant Civil Society undergoing National Unification" in Akihiro Ogawa (ed) *Routledge Handbook of Civil Society in Asia*, (Routledge, Abingdon, 2017) 66.

113 Justice Centre Hong Kong "Who We Help" <www.justicecentre.org.hk/who-we-help/>.

114 Roy Njuabe "The role of civil society in Hong Kong" *Forced Migration Review* (online ed, Oxford, February 2018) <www.fmreview.org/syria2018/njuabe>.

115 International Social Service Hong Kong Branch, "Provision of Assistance for *Non-refoulement* Claimants" <www.isshk.org/en-us/services/index/NRC>.

116 See eg Alison Mackay "Chungking Mansions Service Centre: Serving refugees and asylum seekers in Hong Kong" <www.law.hku.hk/hrportal/wp-content/uploads/file/Alison-Mackay.pdf>; KPMG "Society for Community Organization" <https://home.kpmg/cn/en/home/about/corporate-social-responsibility/key-partnerships/society-for-community-organization.html>; Vision First "About" <www.vfnow.org/about/at-a-glance/>.

successfully drawn upon human rights law and common law principles to push for better refugee protection in Hong Kong. They have also been vocal in the media.[117] The Hong Kong Bar Association and the Law Society of Hong Kong have also actively engaged in the discourse on refugee protection in Hong Kong, and joined forces in advocating for better protection for asylum seekers on several occasions.[118] Through their research and publications, many members of the Hong Kong academic community have not only advocated for rights of refugees and asylum seekers but have also given voice to refugees and asylum seekers.[119]

---

[117] Raquel Carvalho and Alvin Lum "Rights lawyers slam Hong Kong plans to tighten asylum procedures, calling proposals 'wholly unreasonable'" (7 July 2018) <www .scmp.com/news/hong-kong/hong-kong-law-and-crime/article/2154233/rights-lawyers-slam-hong-kong-plans-tighten>.

[118] Hong Kong Bar Association "Security Bureau's Proposals to Enhance the Unified Screening Mechanism: Submission of the Hong Kong Bar Association" (2015) <www .hkba.org/sites/default/files/Unified%20Screening%20Mechanism%20-%20Proposals% 20to%20enhance%20the%20Unified%20Screening%20Mechanism%20-%20Final%20% 282%29%20-%20%28webpage%29.pdf>; Law Society of Hong Kong "*Non-refoulement* Protection: the Government's Proposals to Amend the Immigration Ordinance – the Law Society's Submission" (February 2019) <www.hk-lawyer.org/content/*non-refoule ment*-protection-government's-proposals-amend-immigration-ordinance>; Law Society of Hong Kong and Hong Kong Bar Association "Joint Position Paper by the Law Society of Hong Kong and the Hong Kong Bar Association on the Framework for Convention against Torture ('CAT') Claimants and Asylum Seekers" (31 March 2009) <www.hkba .org/whatsnew/submission-position-papers/2009/20090331.pdf>; Law Society of Hong Kong and Hong Kong Bar Association "Joint submission of the Law Society of Hong Kong and the Hong Kong Bar Association to the Legislative Council Security Panel on framework for legal representation for torture claimant and asylum seekers" (July 2009) <www.hkba.org/sites/default/files/20090703.pdf>. See also Mark Daly "Refugee and *Non-refoulement* Law in Hong Kong: The Introduction of the Unified Screening Mechanism" (October 2014) <www.hk-lawyer.org/content/refugee-and-*non-refoulement*-law-hong-kong-introduction-unified-screening-mechanism>; Alvin Lum "Refugees appeal to Hong Kong government to end their 'long wait' and allow them to leave city" (6 March 2019) <www.scmp.com/news/hong-kong/society/article/2188914/refugees-appeal-hong-kong-government-end-their-long-wait-and>.

[119] See eg Kelley Loper "Toward Comprehensive Refugee Legislation in Hong Kong? Reflections on Reform of the 'Torture Screening' Procedures" (2009) 39 *Hong Kong Law Journal* 253; Jones, above n 85; Ramsden, above n 89; Puiyan Flora Lau and Iulia Gheorghiu "Vanishing Selves under Hong Kong's Unified Screening Mechanism, Cultural Diversity in China" (2018) 3(1) *Cultural Diversity in China* 21; James Rice "Hong Kong's policies relating to asylum-seekers: torture and the principle of non-refoulement" (2011) 28(2) *Pacific Basin Law Journal* 148; Terence Chuntat Shum *Asylum-Seeking Journeys in Asia: Refugees in Hong Kong and Bangkok* (Routledge, Abingdon, 2019); Francesco Vecchio *Asylum Seeking and the Global City* (Routledge, Abingdon, 2014); Isabella Ng, Sharice Choi and Alex Chan "Framing the Issue of Asylum Seekers and

5.5 Current Challenges and Opportunities

As of June 2019, the Refugee Convention and Protocol have not been extended to Hong Kong. As Loper rightly noted, although recent progresses in refugee law and policy in Hong Kong have proved the value of human rights standards and legal principles associated with procedural fairness and the rule of law, there are limits to the approach of relying solely on those tools.[120] In Hong Kong, persons who have been granted *non-refoulement* protection still do not have a legal status under Hong Kong law. Their status remains that of illegal immigrants and they have no right to work in Hong Kong. Lawyers and advocates continue to challenge this but have had limited success.[121]

The USM currently exists as a policy regime as of June 2019. The Hong Kong Bar Association and the Law Society of Hong Kong have called for the USM to be established by legislation.[122] The design and the operation of the USM have attracted considerable criticism, including low recognition rate, the lack of accountability and transparency of the TCAB, poor quality of decision-making by and inadequate training of both immigration officials and TCAB adjudicators, denial of liberty through prolonged detention, the short time limit for claimants to return the completed claim form, and the lack of disclosure of field reports carried out by the director of immigration to obtain the country of origin information.[123]

Refugees for Tougher Refugee Policy a Study of the Media's Portrayal in Post-colonial Hong Kong" (2019) 20 *Journal of International Migration and Integration* 593; Michael Ramsden and Luke Marsh "Refugees in Hong Kong: Developing the Legal Framework for Socio-Economic Rights Protection" (2014) 14 *Human Rights Law Review* 267.

[120] Kelley Loper "The Protection of Asylum Seekers in East Asian State Parties to the 1951 Convention Relating to the Status of Refugees and its 1967 Protocol" in Ademola Abass and Francesca Ippolito (ed) *Regional Approaches to the Protection of Asylum Seekers: An International Legal Perspective* (Ashgate, Farnham, 2014) 347 at 368.

[121] Ramsden and Marsh, above n 119.

[122] Daly, above n 118.

[123] See "Concluding observations on the fifth periodic report of China with respect to Hong Kong, China" (3 February 2016) CAT/C/CHN-HKG/5 at 2 <https://documents-dds-ny.un.org/doc/UNDOC/GEN/G16/017/38/PDF/G1601738.pdf?OpenElement>; Hong Kong Bar Association "Submissions of the Hong Kong Bar Association ("HKBA"): On Proposals to Amend the Immigration Ordinance (Cap 115) Pursuant to the Comprehensive Review on the Strategy of Handling *Non-refoulement* Claims" (2019) at 2 <www.hkba.org/sites/default/files/*Non-refoulement*%20Claims%20%20-%20HKBA%20Submission%20on%20propsoed%20amendments%20re%20USM%2020180813%20%283%29%20%28Webpage%29.pdf>; Hong Kong University Centre for Comparative and Public Law "Submission to the United Nations Committee on the Elimination of all Forms of Racial Discrimination" (July 2018) <https://tbinternet.ohchr.org/Treaties/

In 2016, the Hong Kong Government commenced a review of the USM,[124] and put forward a proposal for further amendments to the Hong Kong Immigration Ordinance in January 2019 with a view to improving the existing *non-refoulement* mechanism.[125] As of June 2019, no amendment bill relating to the proposed amendments has been passed by the Hong Kong legislature.

CERD/Shared%20Documents/HKG/INT_CERD_NGO_CHN_31900_E.pdf>;   Daly, above n 118; Karen Cheung "'Curt and unsympathetic': High Court judge slams adjudicator's attitude towards pregnant torture claimant during hearing" (15 March 2018) <www.hongkongfp.com/2018/03/15/curt-unsympathetic-high-court-judge-slams-adjudicators-attitude-towards-pregnant-torture-claimant-hearing/>; Allan Mackey and Maya Bozovik "Asian Perspectives and Realities in Asylum Protection and Associated Human Rights", Presented at the 11th World Conference of the IARLJ, Athens, Greece, 29 Nov–1 Dec 2017 at 29 <www.iarmj.org/images/_region-apc/docs/asian_perspectives_and_realities_in_asylum_protection_and_associated_human_rights.pdf>.

[124] Hong Kong Government "LCQ21: Comprehensive review of strategy of handling *non-refoulement* claims" (April 2019) <www.info.gov.hk/gia/general/201904/03/P2019040300531.htm>.

[125] Legislative Council Panel on Security "An Update on the Comprehensive Review of the Strategy of Handling *Non-refoulement* Claims: Proposals to Amend the Immigration Ordinance (Cap. 115)" (January 2019) LC Paper No CB(2)529/18-19(03) <www.legco.gov.hk/yr18-19/english/panels/se/papers/se20190108cb2-529-3-e.pdf>.

Refugee Law and Policy in Macao

6.1 Macao and Refugees

The Macao Special Administrative Region of the People's Republic of China (Macao) is about 32 square kilometres in land area and had a population of about 670,000 as of the first quarter of 2019.[1] Macao has the world's highest population density.[2] It also had a GDP per capita of USD 86,355 in 2018, one of the world's highest.[3]

Macao was under Portuguese administration from 1557 to 1999 and was returned to China on 20 December 1999. Like Hong Kong, Macao should have high autonomy according to the principle of "one country two systems" enshrined in the 1987 Joint Declaration of the Government of the Portuguese Republic and the Government of the People's Republic of China on the Question of Macao,[4] as well as the 1993 Basic Law of Macao (Macao Basic Law),[5] which is Macao's constitutional document. Macao should enjoy executive, legislative and independent judicial power, including that of final adjudication.[6] The Macao Basic Law provides that the capitalist system and way of life Macao had before

---

[1] Macao DSEC "Principal indicators" <www.dsec.gov.mo/home_enus.aspx>.

[2] Macau News "Macau records the highest population density per sq km" (11 May 2016) <https://macaunews.mo/macau-records-highest-population-density-per-sq-km/>.

[3] Niall Fraser "Macau poised to become richest place on the planet by 2020" (8 August 2018) <www.scmp.com/news/hong-kong/hong-kong-economy/article/2158708/macau-poised-become-richest-place-planet-2020>.

[4] Joint Declaration of the Government of the Portuguese Republic and the Government of the People's Republic of China on the Question of Macao (13 April 1987) <https://treaties.un.org/doc/Publication/UNTS/Volume%201498/volume-1498-I-25805-English.pdf>.

[5] The Basic Law of the Macao Special Administrative Region of the People's Republic of China 1993 (Macao). An unofficial English translation is available at <www.wipo.int/edocs/lexdocs/laws/en/mo/mo019en.pdf>.

[6] Macao Basic Law, art 2.

1999 should remain unchanged for fifty years.[7] Macao is a civil law jurisdiction.

Like Hong Kong, Macao traditionally provided refuge to displaced Mainland Chinese when there were wars or political upheavals in China.[8] During the Japanese occupation of China, Macao people raised funds for displaced Mainland Chinese.[9] After the Japanese army captured Guangzhou in October 1938 and Hong Kong in December 1941, large numbers of displaced people from these two cities fled to Macao. The Portuguese Macao Government provided refuge to the displaced. As O'Neill noted:[10]

> The refugees included women and children who owned only what they could carry, as well as wealthy foreigners and Chinese who moved to Macao as a safe haven, bringing their money, skills and connections. This meant good business for the city's hotels, restaurants, inns and casinos. The Bela Vista Hotel accepted overseas Portuguese who came from Shanghai; the government set up refugee camps on Taipa island.

In February 1942, as the price of daily necessities began to soar, the Portuguese Macao Government allowed the newcomers to grow food on allocated land in the urban area,[11] and used the revenue from gambling taxes to support the refugees and diverted resources to relief and charity organisations.[12]

Like Hong Kong, Macao experienced influxes of large numbers of Chinese escapees following the establishment of the People's Republic of China in 1949. In 1964, the situation of Chinese escapees in Macao was similar to that of those in Hong Kong.[13] However, in 1966 Portugal agreed to repatriate all new Chinese escapees, prompting Taiwan to send a note of protest to the UN.[14] Nevertheless, the number of Chinese

---

[7] Macao Basic Law, art 5.

[8] Bill Chou "State, Market Forces and Building National Identity in China's Hong Kong and Macao" in CX George Wei (ed) *Macao: The Formation of a Global City* (Routledge, Abingdon, 2014) 186 at 200.

[9] Mark O'Neill "Scourge of War" *Macao Quarterly* (July 2011) 43 at 44, <www.macao magazine.net/sites/default/files/MM8.pdf>.

[10] At 44.

[11] At 45.

[12] At 46.

[13] Ivor C Jackson *The Refugee Concept in Group Situations* (Kluwer Law International, The Hague, 1999) at 211.

[14] Jerome Alan Cohen and Hungdah Chiu *People's China and International Law Volume 1: A Documentary Study* (Princeton University Press, Princeton, 1974) at 194.

escapees hosted by Macao remained between 65,000 and 80,000 between 1964 and 1978 according to UNHCR statistics.[15]

During the Indochinese refugee crisis, Macao set up camps to host about 40,000 Vietnamese refugees and asylum seekers from 1978 to 1991.[16] Vietnamese refugees in Macao were allowed to work.[17] The Macao Government maintained that it was unable to allow refugees to settle locally because of Macao's size and problems such as water supply and accommodation.[18] All Vietnamese refugees in Macao eventually resettled to third countries, and the camps closed in 1991.[19]

In the past two decades, Macao has received few refugees and asylum seekers. From 2002 to early September 2011, Macao received fifteen applications for refugee status involving twenty-five claimants, of which ten were denied and one was cancelled.[20] After 2012, the number of asylum seekers in Macao has remained less than ten.[21] They mainly come from the Middle East, Africa and South Asia.[22]

6.2   Current Legal and Policy Framework

6.2.1   Macao's Status under the Refugee Convention and Protocol

On 27 April 1999, less than eight months before Macao's return to China on 20 December 1999, Portugal informed the UN Secretary-General that the Refugee Convention and Protocol would apply to Macao.[23] Portugal

---

[15] Source: UNHCR Population Statistics Database <http://popstats.unhcr.org/en/time_series>. The UNHCR database does not have statistics for Macao before 1964.

[16] Xianbing Liu and others, *Aomen Jinxi* (2nd ed, Joint Publishing, Hong Kong 2009) 125 (translation: *Macao Past and Present*).

[17] Sofia Jesus "A Safe Haven" (28 March 2016) <http://martmagazine.net/stories/a-safe-haven/>.

[18] Australian Senate Standing Committee on Foreign Affairs and Defence "Indochinese Refugee Resettlement: Australia's Involvement. Report from the Senate Standing Committee on Foreign Affairs and Defence" (1982) at 5 <www.aph.gov.au/Parliamentary_Business/Committees/Senate/Foreign_Affairs_Defence_and_Trade/Completed_inquiries/~/link.aspx?_id=7CFFA28C81444D9CA7E342525B7B72CA&_z=z>.

[19] Ye Jian "Yuenan nanmin yu aomen" (16 November 2018) <www.inmediahk.net/node/1060659> (translation: "Vietnamese Refugees and Macao").

[20] Macao Daily Times "No Refugee Status Ever Granted" (29 September 2014) <www.Macao dailytimes.com.mo/Macao/30055-no-refugee-status-ever-granted.html>.

[21] Source: UNHCR Population Statistics Database <http://popstats.unhcr.org/en/time_series>.

[22] Source: UNHCR Population Statistics Database <http://popstats.unhcr.org/en/time_series>.

[23] UN Treaty Section "Convention relating to the Status of Refugees", endnote 3, <https://treaties.un.org/Pages/ViewDetailsII.aspx?src=TREATY&mtdsg_no=V-2&chapter=5&Temp=mtdsg2&clang=_en#3>; UN Treaty Section "Protocol relating to the Status of

had acceded to the Refugee Convention and the Refugee Protocol in 1960 and 1976 respectively, but did not extend either instrument to Macao until 1999. China informed the Secretary-General of the status of Macao in relation to treaties deposited with the Secretary-General by way of a notification dated 13 December 1999 (the 1999 Note), which, in relevant part, reads as follows:[24]

> I. The treaties listed in Annex I to this Note [herein below], to which the People's Republic of China is a Party, will be applied to te [sic] Macao Special Administrative Region with effect from 20 December 1999 so long as they are one of the following categories: (i) Treaties that apply to Macao before 20 December 1999; (ii) Treaties that must apply to the entire territory of a state as they concern foreign affairs or defence or their nature or provision so require.
>
> II. The Treaties listed in Annex II to this Note, to which the People's Republic of China is not yet a Party and which apply to Macao before 20 December 1999, will continue to apply to the Macao Special Administrative Region with the effect from 20 December 1999.
>
> ...
>
> IV. With respect to other treaties that are not listed in the Annexes to this Note, to which the People's Republic of China is or will become a Party, the Government of the People's Republic of China will go through separately the necessary formalities for their application to the Macao Special Administrative Region if it so decided.

The list in Annex I to the Note includes the Refugee Convention and Protocol, which thus continue to apply to Macao after Macao's return to China. It is worth noting that with respect to treaties to which China is a party and which did not apply to the Special Administrative Regions before the date of their return to China and which do not require compulsory application to the entire territory of a state, the arrangement for Macao in the 1999 Note differs slightly from that for Hong Kong. Whereas the 1997 Note specifically mentions in section I(iii) that some such treaties would apply to Hong Kong without separate formalities,[25] the 1999 Note makes no specific mention of such treaties. Thus such treaties would not apply to Macao unless separate formalities are carried out by China. Had Portugal not extended the Refugee Convention and

Refugees", endnote 6, <https://treaties.un.org/Pages/ViewDetails.aspx?src=TREATY&mtdsg_no=V-5&chapter=5&clang=_en#6>.

[24] UN Treaty Section "Historical Information: China", note 3, <https://treaties.un.org/Pages/HistoricalInfo.aspx?clang=_en#China>.

[25] UN Treaty Section "Historical Information: China", note 2, <https://treaties.un.org/Pages/HistoricalInfo.aspx?clang=_en#China>.

Protocol to Macao before it returned to China, the Refugee Convention and Protocol would not have applied to Macao unless China carried out separate formalities to apply for such application.

6.2.2   Refugee Status Determination in Macao

To implement the Refugee Convention and Protocol, Macao adopted the Regime of the Recognition and Loss of Refugee Status (Refugee Status Regime) in 2004.[26] The Macao Government adopted several laws relating to immigration control in 2003 and 2004 with a view to making necessary adjustments following its return to China in 1999.[27] The Refugee Status Regime could be seen as part of this exercise. Macao further adopted a law on refugee identity documents in 2010.

The Refugee Status Regime establishes a mechanism for processing refugee status claims. The Regime defines a refugee as a person who (1) qualifies as a refugee under the terms of the Refugee Convention and Protocol or (2) is under the mandate of UNHCR pursuant to arts 6 and 7 of the UNHCR Statute.[28]

A Refugee Affairs Commission was set up in accordance with the Regime. The commission is responsible for assessing refugee status applications and making recommendations to the chief executive, namely the head of the Macao Government, who will make a decision on whether to grant the applicant refugee status.[29] Applicants for refugee protection must lodge their application at the Macao Immigration Department.[30] The application is to be immediately referred to the Refugee Affairs Commission, which is to make a recommendation on whether the application is admissible to the chief executive, who in turn is to decide on the admissibility of the application.[31] Under art 14, the

---

[26] Prior to the enactment of the Refugee Status Regime, applications for asylum in Macao were processed by UNHCR's sub-office in Hong Kong and the Macao Government relied upon UNHCR decisions to grant refugee status. See Macao Court of Second Instance, case 108/2003, <www.court.gov.mo/sentence/zh/9421>.

[27] Jianwei Luo and others *aomen falv xinlun (xia juan)* (Social Sciences Academic Press, Beijing, 2010) (translation: *New Essays on Macao Law, Volume II*).

[28] Refugee Status Regime 2004 (Macao), art 3. The official Chinese and Portuguese version is available at <https://images.io.gov.mo/bo/i/2004/08/lei-1-2004.pdf>; an unofficial English translation is available at <www.refworld.org/pdfid/571f2a80d.pdf>.

[29] Arts 5 & 6.

[30] Art 12(1).

[31] Art 15(1).

Regime provides for six circumstances under any of which an application for refugee status is inadmissible:[32]

(1) the applicant has committed any of the acts mentioned in art 1F of the Refugee Convention;

(2) the applicant's entry into the territory of the People's Republic of China has been prohibited pursuant to a decision of the Security Council of the UN;

(3) the applicant is already receiving protection or assistance from the organs or agencies of the UN other than UNHCR;

(4) the applicant has been granted refugee status elsewhere; and

(5) it is obvious the applicant does not satisfy the criteria for refugee status under the Refugee Convention, because his or her claims are groundless or clearly fraudulent, or because the application constitutes an abusive usage of the procedure for recognition of refugee status.

A decision on admissibility should be made within forty-eight hours of the date of application by the chief executive on the recommendation of the Commission.[33] Inadmissible applications will not be considered and applicants whose application is not admitted may appeal against the chief executive's decision to the Macao Court of Second Instance within fifteen days of the notification of the decision.[34]

Article 14 has the effect of excluding an applicant from refugee protection. Given the significant consequences that exclusion from refugee status may have on an applicant, high standards of fairness should apply to the relevant decision-making process. As the Refugee Status Regime provides that a decision on admissibility is to be made within only forty-eight hours, it raises the question of whether the decision could reasonably be made to a high standard of fairness within such a short time frame. Further, it is generally accepted that provisions of the Refugee Convention and Protocol on the loss and denial of refugee status are exhaustive and should be interpreted restrictively and applied with caution. Although arts 14(1) and 14(3) of the Refugee Status Regime respectively refer to and reflect the provisions of arts 1F and 1D of the Refugee Convention,[35] arts 14(2) and 14(5) have no basis in

---

[32] Art 14.

[33] Art 15(1).

[34] Art 15(5).

[35] With regard to art 14(4), see the discussion about exclusion of persons recognised as refugees by other countries and art 1E of the Refugee Convention in James Hathaway and

international refugee law. In particular, the expression "abusive usage of the procedure" in art 14(5) is not defined and could be interpreted broadly. When the Refugee Status Regime was submitted to the Macao Legislative Assembly for deliberation, the Assembly rightly cautioned that art 14(5) should be examined carefully to avoid erroneous denial of refugee status application.[36]

If an application is admitted, the Refugee Affairs Commission shall conduct the first interview with the applicant within five days of the submission of the application.[37] UNHCR as well as the applicant's representative are allowed to attend the interview.[38] The Refugee Affairs Commission shall complete fact-finding within thirty days of the date of the first interview.[39] In cases where there are difficulties in obtaining the information necessary to the fact-finding phase of the proceedings, it could be extended up to one year.[40] Within ten days of the end of the fact-finding phase, the Commission shall make a recommendation to the chief executive on whether to grant refugee status and should give reasons for its recommendation.[41] The chief executive will then make a decision, which will be served to the applicant.[42] An applicant who receives a negative decision on their application can appeal against the chief executive's decision to the Court of Second Instance within fifteen days of the notification of the decision.[43]

Any person who is recognised as a refugee in Macao is entitled to an identity card and a travel document of Macao.[44] They have the right to work and will receive equal treatment with those who are legally residing in Macao.[45] Applicants awaiting a decision on their application are eligible for government support, including food, accommodation and

Michelle Foster *The Law of Refugee Status* (2nd ed, Cambridge University Press, Cambridge, 2014) at 506–509; Guy Goodwin-Gill and Jane McAdam *The Refugee in International Law* (3rd ed, Oxford University Press, Oxford, 2007) at 161–162.

[36] Macao Legislative Assembly First Permanent Committee, Opinion 1/II/2004, 16 January 2004, <www.al.gov.mo/file/colect/col_lei-01/cn/08/1-4.htm>.

[37] Refugee Status Regime, art 16(1).

[38] Art 17.

[39] Art 18.

[40] Art 18.

[41] Art 19.

[42] Art 20.

[43] Art 22.

[44] Art 23.

[45] UN Committee on the Elimination of Racial Discrimination *Consideration of reports submitted by States parties under article 9 of the Convention: International Convention on the Elimination of All Forms of Racial Discrimination: 14th to 17th periodic reports of*

monthly economic assistance, referral of medical services and admission of minors to schools.[46] Since 1 April 2013, refugees and asylum seekers in Macao have access to legal aid, according to the Macao Legal Aid General Regime,[47] which amended previous legal aid regulations to extend legal aid to both residents and non-residents.[48] As of April 2017, the Macao Legal Aid Commission had not received any applications for legal aid from refugees or asylum seekers.[49]

Article 24 provides on the loss of refugee status:

> Besides the reasons referred to in Section C Article 1 of the Convention, causes for the loss of refugee status are:
> (1) The express waiver;
> (2) The falsely alleged grounds for the recognition of the status of refugee;
> (3) The existence of facts which, had they been known at the time of recognition of refugee status, would have implied a negative decision;
> (4) The reasons which justified the recognition of refugee status have ceased to exist;
> (5) A conviction from a trial court in the MSAR of a felonious crime punishable with three years or more of imprisonment;
> (6) The abandonment of MSAR, the applicant has already settled outside the territory.

Persons who lose their refugee status in accordance with arts 24(2), (3) or (5) must be expelled from Macao.[50] The Legislative Assembly raised concerns about the provision of art 24(5) and the consequential expulsion, noting that only very serious offences justify expulsion.[51] The Macao Government responded that it had compared this provision with the law of other countries, and that a three-year sentence is very serious and the offence had to be intentional.[52] The Legislative Assembly

---

States parties due in 2015: Macao, China (3 April 2017) CERD/C/CHN-MAC/14-17 at [35] <https://digitallibrary.un.org/record/1310920>.

[46] US Department of State "2016 Human Rights Reports: China (includes Tibet, Hong Kong, and Macao) – Macao" (March 2017) <www.state.gov/j/drl/rls/hrrpt/2016/eap/265334.htm>.

[47] Macao Special Administrative Region Legal Aid General Regime 2012, Law 13/2012, <https://bo.io.gov.mo/bo/i/2012/37/lei13_cn.asp>.

[48] Macao Legal Aid General Regime, art 7(2).

[49] UN Committee on the Elimination of Racial Discrimination, above n 45, at [50].

[50] Art 28(2).

[51] Macao Legislative Assembly First Permanent Committee, above n 36, comments to art 24.

[52] Macao Legislative Assembly First Permanent Committee, above n 36, comments to art 24.

accepted the Government's explanation. The Legislative Assembly also noted that art 32(1) of the Refugee Convention prohibits state parties from expelling a refugee who is lawfully in their territory except on grounds of national security and public order, and opined that the causes for the loss of refugee status under arts 24(2), (3) or (5) fall within the ambit of national security and public order; but it suggested that caution should be exercised when determining whether those causes exist.[53]

It is notable that the Refugee Status Regime includes an article on mass influx of refugees. Article 29 Exceptional Situations provides that:

> In cases where public order in the MSAR may be affected, namely in a situation of mass influx of refugees, the Chief Executive shall determine the measures to be taken, after a hearing with the Commission, the Security Council of the MSAR and the representative of UNHCR and obtaining, if necessary, the support and authorization of the Central People's Government.

This article leaves room for China's involvement in Macao's response to mass influx of refugees, even though the Macao Basic Law stipulates that "[t]he Government of the Macao Special Administrative Region may apply immigration controls on entry into, stay in and departure from the Region by persons from foreign states or regions".[54] The Legislative Assembly commented that it was right to listen to the Chinese Central Government's opinion in such situations because the Central Government is responsible for Macao's foreign affairs.[55] The Legislative Assembly also mentioned that granting refugee status could sometimes be very sensitive,[56] and agreed with the Macao Government that expelling refugees could also be extremely sensitive.[57] In another opinion relating to the Refugee Status Regime, the Assembly noted that granting refugee status is an extremely sensitive matter.[58]

The question of whether China has a legitimate role to intervene in the event of mass influx of refugees in Macao and Hong Kong deserves some discussion. Both the Hong Kong Basic Law and the Macao Basic Law

---

[53] Macao Legislative Assembly First Permanent Committee, above n 36, comments to art 28.

[54] Macao Basic Law, art 139 para 2.

[55] Macao Legislative Assembly First Permanent Committee, above n 36, comments to art 29.

[56] Comments to art 15.

[57] Comments to art 27.

[58] Macao Legislative Assembly First Permanent Committee "Opinion Number 2/II/2004" (21 February 2004) <www.al.gov.mo/file/colect/col_lei-01/cn/08/1-4.htm>.

provide that the Special Administrative Regions have high autonomy except for defence and foreign affairs.[59] Both Basic Laws authorise the Government of the Special Administrative Region to apply immigration control.[60] However, as demonstrated by the *Congo Asset* case,[61] the outer boundaries of the scope of the term "foreign affairs" in the Basic Laws may not have been definitively drawn. In 1999, a spokesperson of the Office of the Commissioner of the Ministry of Foreign Affairs of China in Hong Kong was asked whether handling Vietnamese refugees involved foreign affairs and was subject to the approval of the Chinese Ministry of Foreign Affairs.[62] The spokesperson did not answer that question directly, stating that the problem of Vietnamese refugees in Hong Kong resulted from the British Government's wrong policy of making Hong Kong a port of first asylum and that the central Chinese Government had been supporting and assisting Hong Kong to find a solution to the problem.[63] As the Chinese NPC Standing Committee has the power to interpret the Basic Laws,[64] in light of the Chinese official's ambiguous answer in 1999 and the existence of art 29 of the Macao Refugee Status Regime, it would seem that Beijing has not entirely excluded the possibility of intervention in Hong Kong and Macao's refugee policies in the event of mass influxes of refugees.

6.3   Current Challenges and Opportunities

In the fifteen years since Macao began screening asylum claims, Macao has not recognised a single refugee.[65] Despite the time frame stipulated in

---

[59]   Hong Kong Basic Law, art 13 cl 1 and art 14 cl 1; Macao Basic Law, art 13 cl 1 and art 14 cl 1.

[60]   Hong Kong Basic Law, art 154 cl 2; Macao Basic Law, art 139 cl 2.

[61]   *Democratic Republic of the Congo and Others v FG Hemisphere Associates LLC* [2011] HKCFA 43.

[62]   Office of the Commissioner of the Ministry of Foreign Affairs of the People's Republic of China in Hong Kong "gongshu fayanren jiu zhigang de yuenan chuanmin wenti da jizhewen" (17 June 1999) <www.fmprc.gov.cn/ce/cohk/chn/xwfb/gsxwg/2000/t40777 .htm> (translation: "Office of the Commissioner Answers Journalists' Questions regarding Vietnamese Refugees in Hong Kong").

[63]   Office of the Commissioner of the Ministry of Foreign Affairs of the People's Republic of China in Hong Kong, above n 62.

[64]   Hong Kong Basic Law, art 158; Macao Basic Law, art 143.

[65]   Marco Carvalho "Why Don't We Bring 100 Refugees to Macao and Help Them? – Paul Pun, President of the Association for Refugees' Welfare" (21 June 2019), <www.oclarim .com.mo/en/2019/06/21/why-dont-we-bring-100-refugees-to-macau-and-help-them-paul-pun-president-of-the-association-for-refugees-welfare/>.

the Refugee Status Regime, a refugee status application could take more than eight years to be processed.[66] As asylum seekers are not allowed to work, this forces them to depend on Macao Government benefits.

According to UNHCR, Macao has processed fewer than fifteen applications each year since 2009.[67] Nevertheless, that number does not include inadmissible applications, for which no statistics are publicly available. Although the Macao judiciary is empowered to review RSD-related decisions, as of June 2019 it has considered a very small number of RSD-related cases and has not quashed any decision on refugee status or admissibility of application for refugee status.[68] In a 2018 report, UNHCR noted that "the adjudication process for the pending asylum claims has stalled, with little to no progress recorded over the past years".[69] According to UNHCR:[70]

> One of the key obstacles observed is the inability of Government officials who make up the Refugee Commission to formally convene meetings due to other responsibilities. Other challenges appear to be resource-related, including the lack of suitable interpreters. UNHCR has frequently expressed views on this issue to the Commission, but there has been no action taken to date to rectify this.

Despite the Macao Government's zero recognition rate of refugees in the past fifteen years, it seems that the people of Macao have not lost the tradition of being supportive to the displaced. In Macao, NGOs such as the Macao Association of Refugees' Welfare and Caritas Macau are strong advocates for refugee rights and supporters to refugees. On the 2019 Refugee Day, Pun, President of the Macao Association of Relief of Refugees and the Secretary-General of Caritas, called for Macao to create a resettlement scheme for refugees recognised elsewhere: "We can send someone to these camps, to Jordan, for instance, and ask them how we can be of help. If some of them are willing to travel to the Far East, our doors must be open".[71]

---

[66] Carvalho, above n 65.

[67] See UNHCR Population Database <http://popstats.unhcr.org/en/time_series> accessed 28 June 2019. No statistics are available for 1996–2008.

[68] This is based on public information published on the website of the Macao judiciary, <www.court.gov.mo/zh/>.

[69] UNHCR *Submission by the United Nations High Commissioner for Refugees For the Office of the High Commissioner for Human Rights' Compilation Report: People's Republic of China and the Special Administrative Regions of Hong Kong and Macao* (March 2018) at 3 <www.refworld.org/docid/5b56ffde9.html>.

[70] UNHCR, above n 69, at 3.

[71] Carvalho, above n 65.

7

Conclusion and Recommendations

> You can have all the rights in the world, but if you can't enforce them, they are not worth much.
>
> Justice Ruth Bader Ginsburg[1]

7.1 China

7.1.1 China's Experience with Refugees

As an emerging destination and transit country for refugees, China's experience with incoming refugees in the past few decades has been characterised by large-scale inflows of refugees from neighbouring countries. The majority of those who have sought refuge in China are ethnic Han Chinese or are of the same ethnicity as an ethnic minority group in China that traditionally lives along border areas. It is well recognised that mass-influx refugee situations are particularly challenging for host countries and that states are more reluctant to recognise refugees in such situations.

The total number of refugees and asylum seekers in China arriving in non-mass-influx situations has generally been on the rise since the early 2000s, standing at just below 1,000 at the end of 2018. That number is low in comparison to that in many developed countries, but it represents a nearly 900 per cent increase from the number of refugees and asylum seekers in China in 2003.

It should be noted that China remains a country of origin of large numbers of refugees and asylum seekers. The Chinese Government criticised UNHCR for assisting certain groups of Chinese nationals in the 1950s and 1960s. More recently, it has sought repatriation of certain groups of refugees and asylum seekers of Chinese nationality from several countries, some of whom it claimed to be terrorists. The Chinese Government's need

---

[1] Ruth Bader Ginsburg, conversation with Joan Williams, University of California Hastings (September 2011) at 22:40, <www.youtube.com/watch?v=XA5KTkCGTWo&t=2916s>.

to pursue and justify its policy towards Chinese refugees and asylum seekers will inevitably influence its overall position on who merits refugee protection and how refugees and asylum seekers should be treated.

7.1.2 Chinese Refugee Law

Chinese law, as it currently stands, falls short of providing a sufficient legal framework for assessing refugee claims and safeguarding the principle of *non-refoulement* and the rights of refugees afforded by the Refugee Convention and Protocol. Despite having been a party to the Refugee Convention and Protocol since 1982, China has incorporated very few of the provisions of these instruments into domestic Chinese law, nor has it authorised the direct domestic application of these instruments. As a result, the Refugee Convention and Protocol generally are not enforceable in Chinese courts.

Chinese law provides no definition of a refugee. Article 32(2) of the 1982 Chinese Constitution allows the Chinese Government to grant asylum to foreigners who apply for it for political reasons. In comparison with the Convention definition, art 32(2) of the 1982 Constitution mentions nothing of the fear of persecution, which is essential to the Convention definition. In this sense, art 32(2) could be seen as less restrictive than the Convention definition. On the other hand, whereas the Convention definition recognises race, nationality, religion, political opinion and membership of a particular social group as grounds for a refugee's well-founded fear of persecution, "political reasons" (*zhengzhi yuanyin*) is the only ground for requesting asylum under art 32(2). There is no evidence that art 32(2) has been invoked, and the meaning and scope of the term "political reasons" under art 32(2) remains to be clarified.

Article 2(2) of the Counterterrorism Law excludes terrorist personnel, defined as persons who carry out terrorist activities or who are members of terrorist organisations under art 3 of the Counterterrorism Law, from refugee protection. Under the Counterterrorism Law, persons identified as terrorist personnel have no access to judicial review or independent external review. Blanket exclusion under art 2(2) of terrorists and members of terrorist organisations from refugee protection without assessing the individual's situation in accordance with established standards relating to art 1F of the Refugee Convention and appropriate procedural guarantees entails undue risk of *refoulement*.

Chinese law provides only limited legal protection for refugees against *refoulement* under art 8(3) of the Extradition Law, which prohibits the

Chinese Government from extraditing persons who have received asylum in China. Complementarily, arts 8(4) and 8(7) of the Extradition Law prohibit extradition of persons who have been or will probably be subjected to torture or other cruel, inhuman or humiliating treatment or punishment and persons who, for reasons of their race, religion, nationality, sex, political opinion or personal status, may face penal proceedings, punishment or unfair treatment in judicial proceedings. These articles, however, do not provide protection against *refoulement* by the Chinese Government in non-extradition situations.

Article 46 of the Exit–Entry Law is the first and only Chinese legal provision on the rights of refugees and asylum seekers. It allows persons who have been granted refugee status and whose refugee status application is being processed to stay in China. As UNHCR is currently the only organisation in China that processes refugee status claims, and claimants in China generally have to be in Beijing to submit their applications to UNHCR's only office in China, those who cannot travel to Beijing will have no access to UNHCR's RSD procedure and are thus excluded from the protection of art 46.

A few provisions in the Exit–Entry law, if constructively interpreted, could provide a legal basis for complementary humanitarian protection for refugees and asylum seekers. Article 31 of the Exit–Entry Law allows foreigners on short-term visas to apply for Chinese residence on the ground of humanitarian reasons. Articles 21 and 23 exempt foreigners who need to enter China urgently for humanitarian reasons and foreigners who need to enter China temporarily due to *force majeure* or other urgent reasons from normal visa requirements. However, as of June 2019 it is unclear how these articles are interpreted and applied in practice.

It should be noted that the Chinese Government has not always fully complied in a timely manner with existing legal provisions relating to refugees. Article 46 of the Exit–Entry Law, which explicitly allows refugees to obtain Chinese identity documents from Chinese public security authority, came into force on 1 July 2013, but UNHCR refugees were still unable to obtain Chinese identity documents as late as March 2018.[2]

---

[2] UNHCR *Submission by the United Nations High Commissioner for Refugees for the Office of the High Commissioner for Human Rights' Compilation Report: People's Republic of China and the Special Administrative Regions of Hong Kong and Macao* (March 2018) at 1 <www.refworld.org/docid/5b56ffde9.html>. The majority of Vietnamese refugees who arrived in the late 1970s and 1980s had been issued Chinese identity cards long before the Exit–Entry Law entered into force.

However, neither art 46 of the Exit–Entry Law nor any of the asylum- and refugee-related provisions in Chinese domestic law has been litigated before a Chinese court. The absence of the involvement of the legal profession and the judiciary in refugee protection in China is to the detriment of refugees in China.

On the positive side, the Chinese Government has demonstrated a growing interest in addressing refugee issues within a more formalised framework in recent years. For example, in 2008 a draft national refugee law was submitted to the country's top legislative body for its deliberation; in 2012 the Exit–Entry Law incorporated the first provision in Chinese law on the rights of refugees and asylum seekers; the NIA was created in 2018, and this is the first time the Chinese Government has had a department focusing on immigration affairs including refugee administration.

It is hopeful that the draft national refugee law will one day come into force and provide a comprehensive legal framework for RSD and treat- ment of refugees and asylum seekers in China. It is important that Chinese legislators and the Chinese judiciary must make sure refugees and asylum seekers in China can enforce their legal rights stated in statutes. Otherwise, the rights provided in the law would not be worth much to refugees and asylum seekers.

7.1.3   Chinese Refugee Policy

As there are few Chinese legal provisions on refugees and the Refugee Convention and Protocol are generally not enforceable domestically in China, the treatment of refugees in China is largely a matter of policy. After the Indochinese refugee crisis, the Chinese Government has had distinct policies for refugees and asylum seekers who arrive in mass- influx situations and those who do not. In the absence of a formal national RSD mechanism, the Chinese Government generally allows UNHCR's Beijing Office to process refugee status claims for those who came to China in non-mass-influx situations, but handles those who came in mass-influx situations without involving UNHCR or any main- stream international organisation.

In its response to mass influxes of refugees, the Chinese Government has consistently preferred a bilateral case-by-case approach. In the case of refugees from Vietnam, the Chinese Government's immediate response was to rely upon bilateral China–Vietnam agreements relating to the administration of Chinese residents in Vietnam and had many rounds of bilateral negotiations with the Vietnamese Government. In the case of

North Korean escapees, it referred to the 1998 China–North Korea bilateral agreement to justify its repatriation of North Korean escapees and strongly opposed the internationalisation of the issue. In the case of displaced Kokangs and Kachins, China relied on the 1997 China–Myanmar bilateral agreement to recognise them as border residents and allowed many of them to enter and remain in Yunnan province bordering Myanmar. It has also involved officials from the Kokang Special Region and the KIA to persuade displaced Kokangs and Kachins in Yunnan to return to Myanmar.

An important factor that appears to have influenced China's receptivity in mass-influx situations is the displaced persons' ethnic and cultural links to the Han Chinese. The majority of refugees from Vietnam and displaced Kokangs are of the same ethnicity as the Han Chinese who account for more than 90 per cent of China's entire population. They also speak or understand Mandarin Chinese and are generally familiar with the Han Chinese culture. These two groups received more favourable treatment than North Korean escapees and displaced Kachins, who are not ethnic Han and who have weaker cultural links to China's majority population.

Another important consideration underlying China's response to large-scale refugee influxes appears to have been China's political, diplomatic and strategic interest in the country of origin. The rapidly deteriorating China–Vietnam relation in the lead up to the Sino-Vietnamese War in February 1979 was an important reason for China's decision to internationalise the issue and recognise the displaced persons from Vietnam as refugees. North Korea's strategic location and its long-term close relation with China are critical to China's policy of denying refugee status to North Korean refugees and repatriating them. China's need to maintain good relations with the Myanmar Central Government, large Chinese investment in the hydropower industry in Kachin State, and the ethnic Kokang army's historic connection with Beijing are important factors that have shaped China's response to displaced Kokangs and Kachins in Yunnan province.

Generally speaking, the Chinese Government has been reluctant to recognise displaced foreigners as refugees in mass-influx situations. It has repeatedly tried to sidestep the Refugee Convention and Protocol and avoid international attention when handling refugees in mass-influx situations. For example, it routinely denies refugee protection to North Korean escapees and continues to repatriate them, despite evidence that many of them prima facie merit refugee protection. Even when it was willing to provide temporary refuge and humanitarian assistance, as it was in the case of the Kokangs in Yunnan, it still insisted that they were not refugees and blocked UNHCR and other mainstream international organisations from accessing and assisting them.

On the other hand, refugee status in China does not guarantee the full range of rights afforded by the Refugee Convention and Protocol. Of the refugees whose status has been recognised in China, namely the Indo-chinese refugees and UNHCR refugees, the former de facto enjoy the same socio-economic rights as Chinese nationals, whereas the latter are treated as foreigners in general, have no right to work and receive little support from the Chinese Government. Such differentiating treatment of refugees is inconsistent with art 3 of the Refugee Convention, which prohibits states from discrimination between and among refugees on the basis of race, religion or country of origin when applying the Convention. The Chinese Government also forcibly repatriated a number of UNHCR refugees in 1992 and 2008.

It is worth noting that the majority of the Vietnamese refugees in China were initially accepted and locally settled as Chinese nationals before they were recognised as refugees in August 1979. To some extent, Chinese authorities still view them as overseas Chinese nationals who returned to the motherland. That probably explains why they receive more favourable treatment than other refugees in China. In retrospect, the refugees themselves gained little from their refugee status, except perhaps for financial assistance from UNHCR; once they were recognised as refugees, they lost their Chinese nationality, which they could otherwise have kept. Now, UNHCR has been advocating for their naturalisation for more than ten years. The experience of the Vietnamese refugees in China is a reminder that, although refugee status is a powerful tool for refugees, it is sometimes possible to find an alternative solution which does not comprise any benefit that refugee status could afford for the refugees concerned and that such alternative solutions, when available, should not be ignored or dismissed.

7.2 Hong Kong and Macao

The Refugee Convention and Protocol have not been extended to Hong Kong. Hong Kong law gives no special status to refugees and asylum seekers and they are subject to Hong Kong immigration law provisions governing illegal immigrants. In practice, the Hong Kong Government generally respects the principle of *non-refoulement*, despite its firm position of not granting asylum to anyone.

The evolution of RSD procedures in Hong Kong since 2004 shows that an independent judiciary and vibrant civil society can play a vital role in safeguarding the rights of refugees and challenging the Government's refugee policy in a society where there is general respect for the rule of law. Following a series of court cases initiated by human rights lawyers and advocates, applications for *non-refoulement* protection based on the Refugee Convention and Protocol are now processed by the Hong Kong Government, rather than UNHCR; as a result, refugees are now provided with reasons for the denial or approval of their claims and can apply for judicial review of negative decisions, neither of which was available in the UNHCR-administered RSD procedure.

The evolution of RSD procedures in Hong Kong since 2004 also provides an example of a pragmatic and strategic approach to bringing positive changes when the Government strongly resists being bound by the Refugee Convention and Protocol. Over a period of ten years, through three different landmark cases, human rights lawyers and advocates gradually pushed for change in the procedures for assessing refugee status/*non-refoulement* claims applicable to three sub-groups of asylum seekers: first those who were also entitled to *non-refoulement* protection under the CAT, then those whose *non-refoulement* claims were grounded in absolute and non-derogatory rights under Hong Kong Bill of Rights Ordinance, and finally those whose *non-refoulement* claims were based on the Refugee Convention and Protocol.

Macao is bound by the Refugee Convention and Protocol and has enacted a local statute which provides a comprehensive framework for the recognition and loss of refugee status. The statute adopts a definition of refugees encompassing those who meet the Convention definition and those who fall under UNHCR's mandate. It allows judicial review of RSD decisions and gives refugees the same rights as Macao residents. Despite relatively small numbers of asylum seekers, the Macao Government often failed to meet the statutory provisions on the processing time frame and has not recognised a single refugee in the past fifteen years after it started processing refugee status claims. The example of Macao shows that even in a jurisdiction that is a party to the Refugee Convention and Protocol and has established a relatively reasonable statutory mechanism for RSD, refugee protection could still be set back by excessive delay in the process and a low recognition rate.

Comparing refugee protection in Hong Kong, Macao and China, a very obvious difference is the roles of the judiciary and civil society. In Hong Kong and Macao, NGOs openly advocate for and provide a wide range of support to refugees. Both allow judicial review of administrative decisions on refugee status and both provide publicly funded legal aid to refugee status claimants. In contrast, in China NGOs have been able to play only a very limited role in refugee support and advocacy. The Chinese legal profession and the judiciary have played almost no role in refugee protection in China. Additionally, refugees and asylum seekers in Hong Kong and asylum seekers in Macao, who have no right to work, receive social welfare provided by the local government. In contrast, UNHCR refugees and asylum seekers in China, who also have no right to work, receive little financial support from the Chinese Government.

There are commonalities between and among the refugee policies of the three jurisdictions. Hong Kong and China do not currently offer permanent local settlement to refugees, and Macao has not locally settled any refugees as it has not recognised any. While China denies refugee status to refugees in mass-influx situations, both Hong Kong and Macao have been criticised for their extremely low recognition rates, an issue that also exists in Korea and Japan, two other East Asian jurisdictions that have established their own RSD procedures.

7.3   Recommendations

As a party to the Refugee Convention and Protocol, China should take all necessary measures to ensure that its treatment of refugees is in accordance with its obligations under those instruments. In the immediate term, the Chinese Government should give UNHCR refugees access to the Chinese minimum living standards welfare system, refrain from *refoulement* of refugees and allow UNHCR to access freely all refugees and asylum seekers in China to conduct RSD. In the medium term, the Chinese Government should establish a statutory refugee protection mechanism to high standards of procedural fairness, including allowing legal representation during the screening process and judicial review, allow refugees to work in China and provide them with the opportunity to settle locally. In the long term, China may consider offering opportunities for refugees to resettle to China from third countries.

International organisations which have experience in working with China in relevant fields, such as UNHCR, should play a leading role in developing a more effective strategy for persuading the Chinese Government to improve refugee protection. For example, more attention should be paid to China's domestic law and policy that could potentially be relied upon to advocate for the improvement of the situation of refugees in China. Given that the Chinese Government currently regards refugees as a sensitive issue, advocates and non-governmental organisations could consider engaging and cooperating with organisations that traditionally do not focus on refugees but could possibly assist a certain group or type of refugees. For example, the topic of children's rights is generally perceived as neutral in China, and China has acceded to the UN Convention on the Rights of the Child. The fact that the Chinese Government has allowed refugee children in five provinces to attend local public school indicates a political willingness to improve the situation of refugee children. The UN Children's Fund (UNICEF), for example, could potentially make significant contribution to the protection of refugee children in China.

Essentially, the development of Chinese refugee law and policy is part of, and depends on, a broader process that China is going through as a developing country and an emerging world power. The improvement of refugee protection in China is interlinked with other challenges China faces in this process, including building a system based on the rule of law, reconciling its views on human rights and international law with those of the traditional world powers, and reshaping its perception of "self" and "others" in the era of globalisation. As refugee issues have resurfaced as a top global concern in recent years, China has demonstrated unprecedented interest in deepening its involvement in international refugee assistance projects and has indicated an interest in leadership in global refugee governance.[3] This presents an unprecedented opportunity for potential constructive dialogues about refugee protection between China and relevant international stakeholders. There is an old Chinese idiom "qiutong cunyi", meaning "seeking common ground while shelving differences". In the face of the global challenge of large-scale refugee movements, it is important and possible for China and relevant international stakeholders to find common ground through constructive dialogues,

---

[3] See Lili Song "China and the International Refugee Protection Regime: Past, Present and Potentials" (2018) 37(2) *Refugee Survey Quarterly* 139; Lili Song "Strengthening Responsibility Sharing with South–South Cooperation: China's Role in the Global Compact on Refugees" (2018) 30(4) *International Journal of Refugee Law* 687.

which may help international stakeholders to develop a more effective strategy for refugee advocacy in China and may also help China to reconsider its approach to refugee protection on its own soil. Indeed, if China aspires to leadership in global refugee governance, it will have to convince the international community that it upholds the core values of the refugee protection regime, including the *non-refoulement* principle, and protects refugees within its own borders in compliance with international standards, as any country that does not do this is unlikely to earn leadership in global refugee governance.

SELECT BIBLIOGRAPHY

A Cases

1 European Union

Cases C-57/09 and C-101/09 *Bundesrepublik Deutschland v B and D* [2011] Imm AR 190 (CJEU).

2 South Korea

Young Soon Lee SC 96 Nu 1221, 12 November 1996.

3 United Kingdom

Al-Sirri v Secretary of State for the Home Department [2012] UKSC 54, [2013] 1 AC 745.
DD (Afghanistan) v Secretary of State for the Home Department [2012] UKSC 54, [2013] 1 AC 745.
GP (South Korean Citizenship) North Korea CG [2014] UKUT 391 (IAC).
KK (Nationality: North Korea) Korea CG [2011] UKUT 92 (IAC).

4 Hong Kong

Alam Khan v Torture Claims Appeal Board / Non-Refoulement Claims Petition Office [2018] HKCFI 2138.
C and Others v Director of Immigration and Another [2013] HKCFA 21.
Democratic Republic of the Congo and Others v FG Hemisphere Associates LLC [2011] HKCFA 43.
FB v Director of Immigration [2008] HKEC 2072.
Secretary for Security v Sakthevel Prabakar [2004] HKCFA 43.

5 Macao

Court of Second Instance, *Apoio judiciário Pressupostos "Acesso ao direito e aos Tribunais"*, case 108/2003.

B Legislation

1 China

Constitution 1954.
Constitution 1975.
Constitution 1978.
Constitution 1982.
Counterterrorism Law 2015.
Criminal Law 1997.
Exit and Entry Administration Law 2012.
Extradition Law 2000.
Law on Administration of Entry and Exit of Aliens 1985.
Law on Legislation 2000.
Law on Public Servants 2005.
Nationality Law 1980.
Yunnan Province Administrative Rules of Entry–Exit of External Border Residents in the China–Myanmar Border Areas 1990.

2 European Union

Directive 2011/95/EU of the European Parliament and of the Council of 13 December 2011 on standards for the qualification of third-country nationals or stateless persons as beneficiaries of international protection, for a uniform status for refugees or for persons eligible for subsidiary protection, and for the content of the protection granted (recast) [2011] OJ L337/9.

3 South Korea

Constitution 1948.
Nationality Act 1948.
Protection of North Korean Residents and Support of Their Settlement Act 1997.

4 Hong Kong

Basic Law of the Hong Kong Special Administrative Region of the People's Republic of China 1990.
High Court Ordinance 1997.
Immigration (Amendment) Ordinance 2012.
Rules of the High Court 1998.

5 Macao

Basic Law of the Macao Special Administrative Region of the People's Republic of China 1993.

Macao Special Administrative Region General Legal Aid Regime 2013.

C Treaties

Agreement on Cooperation in the Work of Maintaining National Security and Social Orders at Border Areas between China and North Korea (signed 8 July 1998, entered into force 28 August 1998).

Agreement between the Government of the People's Republic of China and the Government of Nepal on Border Ports and Their Management Systems (14 January 2012).

Agreement between the Government of the People's Republic of China and Vietnam on Management of Land Borders (18 November 2009).

Agreement on China–Myanmar Border Management and Cooperation between China and Myanmar (signed 25 March 1997, entered into force 29 September 1997).

Agreement on the upgrading of the UNHCR Mission in the People's Republic of China to UNHCR branch office in the People's Republic of China, UNHCR–China 1899 UNTS 61 (signed 1 December 1995, entered into force 1 December 1995).

Agreement between the Government of the People's Republic of China and Vietnam on Management of Land Borders (18 November 2009).

Agreement between the Government of the People's Republic of China and the Government of Nepal on Border Ports and Their Management Systems (14 January 2012).

Chinese-North Korean Treaty on Friendship and Mutual Assistance (10 September 1961).

Convention of the Shanghai Cooperation Organisation against Terrorism 2815 UNTS 69 (opened for signature 16 June 2009, entered into force 14 January 2012).

Convention of the Shanghai Cooperation Organisation on Combating Extremism (opened for signature 9 June 2017).

Convention relating to the Status of Refugees 189 UNTS 137 (opened for signature 28 July 1951, entered into force 22 April 1954).

Joint Declaration of the Government of the United Kingdom of Great Britain and Northern Ireland and the Government of the People's Republic of China on the Question of Hong Kong (19 December 1984).

Joint Declaration of the Government of the Portuguese Republic and the Government of the People's Republic of China on the Question of Macau (13 April 1987).

Protocol relating to the Status of Refugees 606 UNTS 267 (opened for signature 31 January 1967, entered into force 4 October 1967).

The Ministry of Public Security of the People's Republic China and the Ministry of National Security of the Democratic People's Republic of Korea Protocol on Cooperation in the Work of Maintaining National Security and Social Order at Border Areas (8 July 1998).

Treaty between the Government of the People's Republic of China and the Government of Lao People's Democratic Republic (3 December 1993).

Treaty between the Government of the People's Republic of China and the Government of Mongolia on Border Management Mechanism (1 June 2010).

Treaty of Peace, Friendship and Commerce between France and China (9 June 1885).

Vienna Convention on the Law of Treaties 1155 UNTS 331 (opened for signature 23 May 1969, entered into force 27 January 1980).

D United Nations Materials

Commission of Inquiry on Human Rights in the Democratic People's Republic of Korea *Report of the commission of inquiry on human rights in the Democratic People's Republic of Korea* UN Doc A/HRC/25/63 (7 February 2014).

Commission of Inquiry on Human Rights in the Democratic People's Republic of Korea *Report of the detailed findings of the commission of inquiry on human rights in the Democratic People's Republic of Korea* UN Doc A/HRC/25/CRP.1 (7 February 2014).

Committee on Economic, Social and Cultural Rights *Implementation of the International Covenant on Economic, Social and Cultural Rights: Second periodic reports submitted by States parties under articles 16 and 17 of the Covenant – China* UN Doc E/C.12/CHN/2 (6 July 2012).

Committee on the Elimination of Discrimination against Women (CEDW) *Consideration of Reports Submitted by States Parties under Article 18 of the Convention on the Elimination of All Forms of Discrimination against Women: Combined Seventh and Eighth Periodic Report of States Parties – China* UN Doc CEDAW/C/CHN/7-8 (17 January 2013).

Committee on the Rights of the Child *Consideration of reports submitted by States parties under article 44 of the Convention: Third and fourth periodic reports of States parties due in 2009 – China* UN Doc CRC/C/CHN/3-4 (6 June 2012).

Conference of Plenipotentiaries on the Status of Refugees and Stateless Persons: Summary Record of the Twenty-second Meeting UN Doc A/CONF.2/SR.22 (26 November 1951).

Concluding observations on the fifth periodic report of China with respect to Hong Kong, China CAT/C/CHN-HKG/5 (3 February 2016).

Executive Committee of the Programme of the United Nations High Commissioner for Refugees *UNHCR Activities Financed by Voluntary Funds: Report for 1993–1994 and Proposed Programmes and Budget for 1995 – Part II Asia and Oceania – Section 4 – China* UN Doc A/AC.96/825/Part II/4 (16 August 1994).

Executive Committee of the Programme of the United Nations High Commissioner for Refugees *Forty-seventh session: Summary Record of the 509th Meeting* UN Doc A/AC.96/SR.509 (8 January 1997).

GA Res 51/75 (1997).

GA Res 52/132 (1998).

General Assembly Adopts Declaration for Refugees and Migrants, as United Nations, International Organization for Migration Sign Key Agreement UN Doc GA/11820 (19 September 2016).

Vitit Muntarbhorn *Question of the Violation of Human Rights and Fundamental Freedoms in Any Part of the World: Report of the Special Rapporteur on the Situation of Human Rights in the Democratic People's Republic of Korea* UN Doc E/CN.4/2006/35 (23 January 2006).

People's Republic of China *10th to 13th Periodic Reports on the Implementation of the International Convention on the Elimination of All Forms of Racial Discrimination* UN Doc CERD/C/CHN/13 (24 June 2008).

Report of the commission of inquiry on human rights in the Democratic People's Republic of Korea UN Doc A/HRC/25/63 (7 February 2014).

Report of the Commission to the General Assembly – Document A/5809: Report of the International Law Commission covering the work of its sixteenth session, 11 May–24 July 1964 [1964] vol 2 YILC 173.

Situation of human rights of Rohingya Muslims and other minorities in Myanmar: Report of the United Nations High Commissioner for Human Rights UN Doc A/HRC/32/18 (29 June 2016).

Special Rapporteur on the Situation of Human Rights in Myanmar *Situation of human rights in Myanmar* UN Doc A/70/412 (6 October 2015).

UNHCR *Guidelines on International Protection: Application of the Exclusion Clauses: Article 1F of the 1951 Convention relating to the Status of Refugees* UN Doc HCR/GIP/03/05 (4 September 2003).

UNHCR *Situation of Human Rights of Rohingya Muslims and Other Minorities in Myanmar: Report of the United Nations High Commissioner for Human Rights* UN Doc A/HRC/32/18 (28 June 2016).

United Nations General Assembly *Meeting on Refugees and Displaced Persons in South-East Asia, convened by the Secretary-General of the United Nations at Geneva, on 20 and 21 July 1979, and subsequent developments: Report of the Secretary-General* UN Doc A/34/627 (7 November 1979).

United Nations Human Rights Committee *Concluding Observations and Recommendations of the Human Rights Committee: Democratic People's Republic of Korea* UN Doc CCPR/CO/72/PRC (2001).

UNHCR *Submission by the United Nations High Commissioner for Refugees for the Office of the High Commissioner for Human Rights' Compilation Report: People's Republic of China and the Special Administrative Regions of Hong Kong and Macao* (March 2018).

Update on Regional Developments in Asia and Oceania UN Doc EC/46/SC/CRP.44 (19 August 1996).

UNHCR *Guidelines on International Protection: Application of the Exclusion Clauses: Article 1F of the 1951 Convention relating to the Status of Refugees* UN Doc HCR/GIP/03/05 (4 September 2003) at [25]–[29].

UN Committee on the Elimination of Racial Discrimination *Consideration of reports submitted by States parties under article 9 of the Convention: International Convention on the Elimination of All Forms of Racial Discrimination: 14th to 17th periodic reports of States parties due in 2015: Macao, China* CERD/C/CHN-MAC/14-17 (3 April 2017).

E Books and Chapters in Books

Eva Brems *Human Rights: Universality and Diversity* (Kluwer Law International, The Hague, 2001).

Allen Carlson and Ren Xiao *New Frontiers in China's Foreign Relations* (Lexington Books, Lanham (MD), 2011).

Alexander Casella *Breaking the Rules* (Editions du Tricorne, Geneva, 2011).

Pao-min Chang *Beijing, Hanoi, and the Overseas Chinese* (University of California Institute of East Asian Studies, Berkeley, 1982).

Jianfu Chen "Constitutional Judicialisation and Popular Constitutionalism in China: Are We There Yet?" in Guanghua Yu (ed) *The Development of the Chinese Legal System* (Routledge, Abingdon, 2011) 3.

Chinese Academy of Social Science Institute of Linguistics Dictionary Department *xiandai hanyu cidian* (The Commercial Press, Beijing, 1996) (translation: *Contemporary Chinese Language Dictionary*).

Jerome Alan Cohen and Hungdah Chiu *People's China and International Law: A Documentary Study* (Princeton University Press, Princeton, 1974) vol 1.

People's China and International Law: A Documentary Study (Princeton University Press, Princeton, 1974) vol 2.

Michael P Colaresi *Scare Tactics: The Politics of International Rivalry* (Syracuse University Press, Syracuse, 2005).

Sara E Davies *Legitimising Rejection: International Refugee Law in Southeast Asia* (Martinus Nijhoff, Leiden, 2008).

Jean-Francois Destexhe "Hong Kong and 1997: The Facts" in Werner Menski (ed) *Coping with 1997: The Reaction of the Hong Kong People to the Transfer of Power* (Trentham Books, Stoke-on-Trent (UK), 1995) 17.

David Feith *Stalemate: Refugees in Asia* (Asian Bureau Australia, Parkville, 1988).

Stephen Fitzgerald *China and the Overseas Chinese: A Study of Peking's Changing Policy, 1949–1970* (Cambridge University Press, Cambridge, 1972).

Chris Fraser *The Philosophy of the Mozi: The First Consequentialists* (Columbia University Press, New York, 2016).

Geoff Gilbert "Current Issues in the Application of the Exclusion Clauses" in Erika Feller, Volker Türk and Frances Nicholson (eds) *Refugee Protection in International Law: UNHCR's Global Consultations on International Protection* (Cambridge University Press, Cambridge, 2003) 425.

Guy S Goodwin-Gill and Jane McAdam *The Refugee in International Law* (3rd ed, Oxford University Press, Oxford, 2007).

Kelly M Greenhill *Weapons of Mass Migration: Forced Displacement, Coercion, and Foreign Policy* (Cornell University Press, Ithaca, 2010).

Stephan Haggard and Marcus Noland *Witness to Transformation: Refugee Insights into North Korea* (Peterson Institute for International Economics, Washington (DC), 2011).

Song Han *A Sunshine Home: Humanitarian Resettlement in Guangdong* (English ed, Lingnan Arts Publishing, Guangzhou, 1999).

yangguang jiayuan: rendao anzhi zai guangdong (Lingnan Arts Publishing, Guangzhou, 1999) (translation: *A Sunshine Home: Humanitarian Resettlement in Guangdong*).

Edvard Hambro *The Problem of Chinese Refugees in Hong Kong: Report Submitted to the United Nations High Commissioner for Refugees* (AW Sijthoff, Leiden, 1955).

Shiyuan Hao (translated by Xiaohua Tong) *How the Communist Party of China Manages the Issue of Nationality: An Evolving Topic* (Springer, Berlin, 2016).

James C Hathaway and Michelle Foster *The Law of Refugee Status* (2nd ed, Cambridge University Press, Cambridge, 2014).

Adam M Howard (ed) *Foreign Relations of the United States, 1977–1980: Volume 13 – China* (Department of State, Washington (DC), 1983).

Ivor C Jackson *The Refugee Concept in Group Situations* (Kluwer Law International, The Hague, 1999).

Ian Jeffries *North Korea: A Guide to Economic and Political Developments* (Routledge, London, 2006).

Political Developments in Contemporary China: A Guide (Routledge, Abingdon, 2010).

David Kranzler *Japanese, Nazis and Jews, the Jewish Refugee Community of Shanghai 1938–1945* (Yeshiva University Press, New York, 1976).

Kitchun Lam and Pakwai Liu *Immigration and the Economy of Hong Kong* (City University Press, Hong Kong, 1998).

Sheng Lang and Aili Wang *Commentary on the Counterterrorism Law of the People's Republic of China* (Law Press, Beijing, 2016).

Kirsteen Lau and others, *Non-Refoulement Law in Hong Kong* (LexisNexis, Hong Kong, 2017).

Jerry Z Li and Sanzhuan Guo "China" in Dinah Shelton (ed) *International Law and Domestic Legal Systems: Incorporation, Transformation, and Persuasion* (Oxford University Press, Oxford, 2011) 158.

Wang Li *Xianqin Waijiao Ciling Tanjiu* (World Knowledge Press, Beijing, 2008) (translation: *Research on Pre-Qin Diplomatic Languages*).

Xueju Li (ed) *Minzheng 30 nian* (China Society Press, Beijing, 2008) (translation: *Civil Affairs in the Past 30 Years*) cited in Shuying Liang *guoji nanmin fa* (Intellectual Property Publishing House, Beijing, 2009) at 281.

Zonggui Li *Between Tradition and Modernity: Philosophical Reflections on the Modernization of Chinese Culture* (Chartridge Books, Oxford, 2014).

Shuying Liang *guoji nanmin fa* (Intellectual Property Publishing House, Beijing, 2009) (translation: *International Refugee Law*).

"Refugee Protection in China: The Issue of Citizenship and Potential Solutions" in Angus Francis and Rowena Maguire (ed) *Protection of Refugees and Displaced Persons in the Asia Pacific Region* (Ashgate, Farnham (UK), 2013) 67.

Qing Ling *cong Yan'an dao lianheguo* (Fujian People's Press, Fuzhou, 2008) (translation: *From Yan'an to the United Nations*).

Xianbing Liu et al, *Aomen Jinxi* (2nd ed, Joint Publishing, Hong Kong 2009) 125 (translation: *Macao Past and Present*).

Guofu Liu *Chinese Immigration Law* (Ashgate, Farnham (UK), 2011).

zhongguo nanminfa (World Affairs Press, Beijing, 2015) (translation: *Chinese Refugee Law*).

Jianwei Luo and others *aomen falv xinlun (xia juan)* (Social Sciences Academic Press, Beijing, 2010) (translation: *New Essays on Macao Law, Volume II*).

Michael Marrus *The Unwanted: European Refugees in the Twentieth Century* (Oxford University Press, Oxford, 1985).

Sai Kaham Mong *Kokang and Kachin in the Shan State* (Institute of Asian Studies, Bangkok, 2005).

David Mozingo *Chinese Policy Toward Indonesia, 1949–1967* (Cornell University Press, Ithaca, 1976).

Vitit Muntarbhorn *The Status of Refugees in Asia* (Clarendon Press, Oxford, 1992).

Roda Mushkat *One Country, Two International Legal Personalities: The Case of Hong Kong* (Hong Kong University Press, Hong Kong, 1997).

Ma Ngok *Political Development in Hong Kong: State, Political Society, and Civil Society* (Hong Kong University Press, Hong Kong, 2007).

Hoàng Nguyên "Cong Jinbian dao Beijing" in [editor] *Zai Yuenan de huaren* (Foreign Languages Press, Hanoi, 1978) 11 (translation: "From Phnom Penh to Beijing" in *The Chinese in Vietnam*).

Randall Peerenboom *China Modernizes: Threat to the West or Model for the Rest?* (Oxford University Press, New York, 2007).

Peter C Perdue "Embracing Victory, Effacing Defeat: Rewriting the Qing Frontier Campaigns" in Diana Lary (ed) *The Chinese State at the Borders* (UBC Press, Vancouver, 2007) 105.

W Courtland Robinson *Terms of Refuge: The Indochinese Exodus and the International Response* (Zed Books, London, 1998).

Pamela Rotner Sakamoto *Japanese Diplomats and Jewish Refugees: A World War II Dilemma* (Praeger, Westport (CT), 1998).

Terence Chuntat Shum *Asylum-Seeking Journeys in Asia: Refugees in Hong Kong and Bangkok* (Routledge, Abingdon, 2019).

Alvin So "Hong Kong: Vibrant Civil Society Undergoing National Unification" in Akihiro Ogawa (ed) *Routledge Handbook of Civil Society in Asia*, (Routledge, Abingdon, 2017) 66.

Lili Song "zhongguo chujingrujingfa zhong de rendaozhuyi tiaokuan tanxi" in Huiyao Wang and Guofu Liu (eds) *liudong yu zhili: quanqiu rencai yimin yu yiminfa* (World Knowledge Press, Beijing, 2019) 162 (translation: "Exploring the Humanitarian Clauses in the Chinese Exit–Entry Administration Law" in *Movement and Management: International Talents, Migrants and Migration Law*).

Leo Suryadinata "China's Citizenship Law and the Chinese in Southeast Asia" in M Barry Hooker (ed) *Law and the Chinese in Southeast Asia* (Institute of Southeast Asian Studies, Singapore, 2002).

Jerzy Sztucki "Who is a Refugee? The Convention Definition: Universal or Obsolete?" in Frances Nicholson and Patrick Twomey (eds) *Refugee Rights and Realities* (Cambridge University Press, Cambridge, 1999).

UNHCR *The State of the World's Refugees: Fifty Years of Humanitarian Action* (Oxford University Press, Oxford, 2000).

   The State of the World's Refugees 2012: In Search of Solidarity (Oxford University Press, Oxford, 2000).

Francesco Vecchio *Asylum Seeking and the Global City* (Routledge, Abingdon, 2014).

Richard Louis Walker *The Multi-State System of Ancient China* (Shoe String Press, Hamden (CT), 1953).

Shuo Wang and Susan Shirk "The Media" in Nina Hachigian (ed) *Debating China: The US–China Relationship in Ten Conversations* (Oxford University Press, Oxford, 2015) 67.

Siulun Wong *Emigrant Entrepreneurs: Shanghai Industrialists in Hong Kong* (Oxford University Press, Hong Kong, 1988).

Qiushi Yuan *Xianggang huigui dashiji 1979–1997* (2ed, Joint Publishing, Hong Kong, 2015) (translation: *Historic Events Relating to Hong Kong's Return to China*).

Hong Zhou, Jun Zhang and Min Zhang *Foreign Aid in China* (Springer, Heidelberg, 2015).

Andreas Zimmermann and Claudia Mahlet "Article 1 A, para 2 1951 Convention" in Andreas Zimmermann (ed) *The 1951 Convention Relating to the Status of Refugees and its 1967 Protocol: A Commentary* (Oxford University Press, Oxford, 2011) 281.

Andreas Zimmermann and Philipp Wennholz "Article 1F 1951 Convention" in Andreas Zimmermann (ed) *The 1951 Convention Relating to the Status of Refugees and Its 1967 Protocol: A Commentary* (Oxford University Press, Oxford, 2011) 579.

F Journal Articles

Ramses Amer "Vietnam's Policies and the Ethnic Chinese since 1975" (1996) 11 *Sojourn: Journal of Social Issues in Southeast Asia* 76.

Tai Sung An "Vietnam: The Defection of Hoang Van Hoan" (1980) 7 *Asian Affairs* 288.

Brian Barbour "Protection in Practice: The Situation of Refugees in East Asia" (2012) 2 *Nanmin Kenkyu Journal* (translation: *Refugee Studies Journal*) 81 (Published in Japanese; English original available at: www.refugeestudies.jp/).

Kemal Bokhary "The Rule of Law in Hong Kong Fifteen Years after the Handover" (2012–2013) 51 *Columbia Journal of Transnational Law* 287.

Chan Kwok Bun "Hong Kong's Response to the Vietnamese Refugees: A Study in Humanitarianism, Ambivalence and Hostility" (1990) 18(1) *Southeast Asian Journal of Social Science* 94.

John Burns "Immigration from China and the Future of Hong Kong" (1987) 27(6) *Asian Survey* 661.

Shibing Cao "The Legal Status of Decisions and Judicial Interpretations of the Supreme Court of China" (2008) 3(1) *Frontiers of Law in China* 1.

Elaine Chan and Joseph Chan "Hong Kong 2007–2017: A Backlash in Civil Society" (2017) 39(2) *Asian Pacific Journal of Public Administration* 135.

Pao-min Chang "The Sino-Vietnamese Dispute over the Ethnic Chinese" (1982) 90 *The China Quarterly* 195.

Albert Chen "Constitutional Crisis in Hong Kong: Congressional Supremacy and Judicial Review" (1999) 33 *The International Lawyer* 1025.

Tung-Pi Chen "The Nationality Law of the People's Republic of China and the Overseas Chinese in Hong Kong, Macao and Southeast Asia" (1984) 5 *New York School J of International & Compararive Law* 281.

Lawrence Cox "The Failure of the People's Republic Of China to Extend the Refugee Convention to Hong Kong: The Contemporary Use of the 'Colonial Clause' by a Non-Colonial Power to Circumvent Human Rights Obligations" (2008) 4(2) *Journal of Migration and Refugee Issues* 80.

Mark Daly "Refugee Law in Hong Kong: Building the Legal Infrastructure" (2009) 9 *Hong Kong Lawyer* 14.

Shichao Deng and Lichang Huang "zhongguo yuenan guiguo nanqiao de anzhi yu shengchan shenghuo xianzhuang tanxi: yi Guangdong yangcun huaqiao gan-juchang weili" (2010) 58 *Ritsumeikan University Journal of Economics* 87 (translation: "Analysis on Reception of Overseas Chinese in Difficulty Returning from Vietnam and Their Present Work and Life Conditions: A Case Study of Guangdong Yang Village Overseas Chinese Mandarin Farm").

Rita Fan "Hong Kong and the Vietnamese Boat People: A Hong Kong Perspective" (1990) 2 (special issue) *International Journal Of Refugee Law* 144.

Daniel Fung "Foundation for the Survival of the Rule of Law in Hong Kong – The Resumption of Chinese Sovereignty" (1996) 1 *UCLA Journal of International Law & Foreign Affairs* 283.

Michael Godley "A Summer Cruise to Nowhere: China and the Vietnamese Chinese in Perspective" (1980) 4 *The Australian Journal of Chinese Affairs* 35.

Felix Gruenberger "The Jewish Refugees in Shanghai" (1950) 12 *Jewish Social Studies* 329.

Sanzhuan Guo "Implementation of Human Rights Treaties by Chinese Courts: Problems and Prospects" (2009) 8(1) *Chinese Journal of International Law* 161.

Enze Han "Geopolitics, Ethnic Conflicts along the Border, and Chinese Foreign Policy Changes toward Myanmar" (2017) 13 *Asian Security* 59.

Ju Hui Judy Han "Beyond Safe Haven: A Critique of Christian Custody of North Korean Migrants in China" (2013) 45 *Critical Asian Studies* 533.

Xiaorong Han "Spoiled Guests or Dedicated Patriots? The Chinese in North Vietnam, 1954–1978" (2009) 6 *International Journal of Asian Studies* 1.

"Exiled to the Ancestral Land: The Resettlement, Stratification and Assimilation of the Refugees from Vietnam in China" (2013) 10 *International Journal of Asian Studies* 25.

Keith Hand "Resolving Constitutional Disputes in Contemporary China" (2011) 7 *University of Pennsylvania East Asia Law Review* 51.

Arthur C Helton "Judicial Review of the Refugee Status Determination Procedure for Vietnamese Asylum Seekers in Hong Kong" (1991) 17(1) *Brook J Intl L* 263.

Elaine Lynn-Ee Ho "Interfaces and the Politics of Humanitarianism: Kachin Internal Displacement at the China–Myanmar Border" (2018) 31 *JRS* 407.

Eric Ip "Mapping Parliamentary Law and Practice in Hong Kong" (2015) 3(1) *CJCL* 97.

Jianhua Huang and Wenhua Ma "Yang Zhengxin yu eguo nanmin cuanrao Xinjiang shijian" (1994) 4 *Yili shifan xueyuan xuebao* 74 (translation: "Yang Zhengxin and the Influx of Russian Refugees in Xinjiang" *Journal of Yili Teachers' College*).

Oliver Jones "Customary Non-Refoulement of Refugees and Automatic Incorporation into the Common Law: A Hong Kong Perspective" (2009) 58(2) *International and Comparative Law Quarterly* 443.

Ronald C Keith and Zhiqiu Lin "Judicial Interpretation of China's Supreme People's Court as 'Secondary Law' with Special Reference to Criminal Law" (2009) 23 *China Information* 223.

Thomas E Kellogg "Constitutionalism with Chinese Characteristics? Constitutional Development and Civil Litigation in China" (2009) 7(2) *ICON* 215.

Agnes Ku "Immigration Policies, Discourses and the Politics of Local Belonging in Hong Kong (1950–1980)" (2004) 30(3) *Modern China* 326.

Ada Lai and Kerry Kennedy "Refugees and Civic Stratification: The 'Asian Rejection' Hypothesis and Its Implications for Protection Claimants in Hong Kong" (2017) 26(2) *Asian and Pacific Migration Journal* 206.

Tom Lam "The Exodus of Hoa Refugees from Vietnam and their Settlement in Guangxi: China's Refugee Settlement Strategies" (2000) 13 *Journal of Refugee Studies* 374.

Lihong Lan and Xiuxia Shi "Reflection on the Latest Progress in Chinese Legislation on International Migration" (2013) 8 *Frontiers of Law in China* 618.

Andrei Lankov "North Korean Refugees in Northeast China" (2004) 44 *Asian Survey* 856.

Puiyan Flora Lau and Iulia Gheorghiu "Vanishing Selves under Hong Kong's Unified Screening Mechanism, Cultural Diversity in China" (2018) 3(1) *Cultural Diversity in China* 21.

Kamyee Law and Kimming Lee "Citizenship, economy and social exclusion of mainland Chinese immigrants in Hong Kong" (2006) 36(2) *Journal of Contemporary Asia* 217 at 220.

Tang Lay Lee "Stateless Persons, Stateless Refugees and the 1989 Comprehensive Plan of Action – Part 2: Chinese Nationality and the People's Republic of China" (1995) 7 *International Journal of Refugee Law* 481.

Eric Yong-Joogn Lee "National and International Legal Concerns regarding Recent North Korean Escapee" (2001) 13 *International Journal of Refugee Law* 142.

Henry Litton "The Vietnamese Boat People Story: 1975–1999" (2001) 26(4) *Alternative Law Journal* 179.

Chengdu Liu "dui gongan churujing guanli bumen jiaqiang nanmin guanli de jidian sikao" (2000) 4 *Journal of Beijing People's Police College* 46 (translation: "Several Thoughts on Improving Refugee Administration by Border Exit and Entry Administration Department of Public Security System").

Yongwei Liu "guoji tiaoyue zai zhongguo shiyong xinlun" (2007) 2 *Jurists Review* 143 (translation: "New Thoughts on Application of International Treaties in China").

Gang Luo "Yunnan bianjing minzu diqu renkou feifa liudong fazhi duice yanjiu" (2011) 9 *Hebei Law Science* 184 (translation: "A Study on Legal Strategies for

Regulating Illegal Border Crossing in Yunnan Border Areas Inhabited by Ethnic Groups").

Christine Loh "Alive and Well but Frustrated: Hong Kong's Civil Society" 2007 (issue 2) *China Perspectives* 40.

Kelley Loper "Toward Comprehensive Refugee Legislation in Hong Kong? Reflections on Reform of the 'Torture Screening' Procedures" (2009) 39 *Hong Kong Law Journal* 253.

    "Human Rights, Non-refoulement and the Protection of Refugees in Hong Kong" (2010) 22(3) *International Journal of Refugee Law* 404.

Laura Madokoro, 'Borders Transformed: Sovereign Concerns, Population Movements and the Making of Territorial Frontiers in Hong Kong, 1949–1967', (2012) 25(3) *Journal of Refugee Studies* 407.

Chi Kwan Mark "The 'Problem of People': British Colonials, Cold War Powers, and the Chinese Refugees in Hong Kong, 1949–62" (2007) 41(6) *Modern Asian Studies* 1145.

Anthony Mason "The Rule of Law in the Shadow of the Giant: The Hong Kong Experience" (2011) 33 *Sydney Law Review* 623.

Roda Mushkat "Refuge in Hong Kong" (1989) 1(4) *International Journal of Refugee Law* 449.

Benjamin Neaderland "Quandary on the Yalu: International Law, Politics, and China's North Korean Refugee Crisis" (2004) 40 *Stanford Journal of International Law* 143.

Isabella Ng, Sharice Choi and Alex Chan "Framing the Issue of Asylum Seekers and Refugees for Tougher Refugee Policy: A Study of the Media's Portrayal in Post-colonial Hong Kong" (2019) 20 *Journal of International Migration and Integration* 593.

Michael Kingsley Nyinah "Exclusion under Article 1F: Some Reflections on Context, Principles and Practice" (2000) 12 (special issue) *International Journal of Refugee Law* 295.

Glen Peterson "To Be or Not to Be a Refugee: The International Politics of the Hong Kong Refugee Crisis, 1949–55" (2008) 36(2) *The Journal of Imperial and Commonwealth History* 171.

    "The Uneven Development of the International Refugee Regime in Postwar Asia: Evidence from China, Hong Kong and Indonesia" (2012) 25 *Journal of Refugee Studies* 326.

Michael Ramsden "Using International Law in Hong Kong Courts: An Examination of Non-Refoulement Litigation" (2013) 42 *Common Law World Review* 351 at 367.

Michael Ramsden and Luke Marsh "Refugees in Hong Kong: Developing the Legal Framework for Socio-Economic Rights Protection" (2014) 14 *Human Rights Law Review* 267.

James Rice "Hong Kong's policies relating to asylum-seekers: torture and the principle of non-refoulment" (2011) 28(2) *Pacific Basin Law Journal* 148.

Suzanne D Rutland "'Waiting Room Shanghai': Australian Reactions to the Plight of the Jews in Shanghai after the Second World War" (1987) 32 *The Leo Baeck Institute Year Book* 407.

Ronald Skeldon "Hong Kong and its Hinterland: A Case of International Rural-to-Urban Migration?" (1986) 5(1) *Asian Geographer* 1.

Lili Song "China and the International Refugee Protection Regime" (2018) 37(2) *Refugee Survey Quarterly* 139.

"Strengthening Responsibility Sharing with South–South Cooperation: China's Role in the Global Compact on Refugees" (2018) 28(4) *International Journal of Refugee Law* 687.

Leticia Ho-Ling Tang "The Situation of Asylum Seekers and Torture Claimants in Hong Kong" (2009) 3 *Hong Kong Journal of Legal Studies* 9.

Matthew J Walton "Ethnicity, Conflict, and History in Burma: The Myths of Panglong" (2008) 48 *Asian Survey* 889.

Jinrong Wang "On the Judicial Interpretation of China's Supreme People's Court" (1995) 3 *China L* 9 cited in Li Wei "Judicial Interpretation in China" (1997) 5 *Willamette Journal of International Law and Dispute Resolution* 87.

Yuanjun Wang "guanyu jianli woguo nanmin baohu falv zhidu de jidian sikao" (2005) 12 *Public Security Research* 46 (translation: "Several Thoughts on the Establishment of a Refugee Protection Mechanism in China").

Andrew Wolman "North Korean Asylum Seekers and Dual Nationality" (2013) 24 *International Journal of Refugee Law* 793.

Hanqin Xue and Qian Jin "International Treaties in the Chinese Domestic Legal System" (2009) 8(2) *Chinese Journal of International Law* 299.

Guohua Zeng "Guangxi nanqiao peixun gongzuo de lanshang xianzhuang he tiaoz-han" (2006) 2 *bagui qiaokan* 47 (translation: "Status Quo of and Challenges for Trainings of Nanqiao in Guangxi" *Overseas Chinese Journals of Bagui*).

Yu'e Zhou and Jiancheng Zheng "zai hua yinzhi nanmin yu guoji hezuo: yizhong lishi de fenxi he sikao" (2014) 3 *Southeast Asian Affairs* 41 (translation: "Indochinese Refugees in China and International Cooperation").

G Government Materials

Australian Senate Standing Committee on Foreign Affairs and Defence *Indochinese Refugee Resettlement – Australia's Involvement: Report from the Senate Standing Committee on Foreign Affairs and Defence* (1982).

Chinese State Council *Public Announcement 1982 NO14 Proposal on Reviewing, Discussing the Decision to accede to the Convention relating to the Status of Refugees and the Protocol relating to the Status of Refugee* (10 June 1982).

Chinese General Office of the State Council *Opinion on Resolving Issues of Hukou Registration for Persons with no Hukou* (guofaban [2015] No96, 14 January 2016).

Chinese Ministry of Public Security Security Management Bureau Reply to Jiangxi Province Resident ID Card Issuance Office's Enquiry about Whether to Issue ID Card to Refugees Returning to China 1989 (GONGSAN [1989]NO350).

Chinese Ministry of Public Security *Notice on Handling Illegal Entry and Illegal Stay of Aliens in accordance with Law* (1992).

  Notice on Taking Legal Actions Against Illegal Entry and Illegal Stay of Aliens (GONGTONGZI [1992] NO39, 9 April 1992).

Chinese State Council Office of Overseas Chinese Affairs *Party and State Leaders on Overseas Chinese Affairs* (internal files, 1992) cited in Jiancheng Zheng "From Nanqiao to Refugee: The Formation of China's Policy toward Indochinese Refugees, 1978–1979" (PhD Thesis, Jinan University, 2015).

Hong Kong Legislative Council Panel on Security *An Update on the Comprehensive Review of the Strategy of Handling Non-refoulement Claims: Proposals to Amend the Immigration Ordinance (Cap. 115)* LC Paper No. CB(2)529/18-19(03) (January 2019).

Hong Kong Security Bureau *Torture Claim Screening Mechanism: Enhanced Mechanism and Way Forward* LC Paper No. CB(2)370/09-10(03) (November 2009).

Hong Kong Security Bureau, Immigration Department and Social Services Department *Response to the Motion of the LegCo Panel on Security on Asylum Seekers and Torture Claimants* LC Paper No. CB(2)2994/05-06(01) (September 2006).

Hong Kong Legislative Council Secretariat *Judicial review and non-refoulement claims* ISSH11/18-19 (5 December 2018).

Hong Kong Security Bureau, Immigration Department and Social Welfare Department *Provision of Publicly-funded Legal Assistance and Humanitarian Assistance to Non-refoulement Claimants* LC Paper No. CB(2)581/18-19 (01) (January 2019).

Hong Kong Legislative Committee *Updated background brief prepared by the Legislative Council Secretariat for the meeting on 6 June 2017* LC Paper No. CB(2)1533/16-17(04) (27 March 2018).

Hong Kong Immigration Department *Notice to Persons Making a Non-refoulement Claim* (4 September 2017).

Hong Kong Legislative Council *Report of Subcommittee to Follow Up Issues Relating to the Unified Screening Mechanism for Non-refoulement Claims* LC Paper No. CB(2)874/18-19 (1 March 2019).

Letter of Intent between the Governments of the People's Republic of China and the Office of the United Nations High Commissioner for Refugees (8 May 1985).

Macao Legislative Assembly First Permanent Committee *Opinion 1/II/2004* (16 January 2004).

Macao Legislative Assembly First Permanent Committee *Opinion Number 2/II/ 2004* (21 February 2004).

The Supreme People's Court of China *Reply regarding the Real Estate Dispute between Fang Yishun, Fang Shengeng and the Central Production Team of Hengfeng Village, Wufeng Region, Qimen County* (FAMINZI[85] NO 4).

The People's Republic of China Ministry of Finance *Interim Implementation Rules for Management of State-owned Assets by Institutes Functioning Abroad* (CAIXING[2007]NO559).

United States Congressional-Executive Commission on China *The Plight of North Koreans in China: A Current Assessment: Roundtable before the Congressional-Executive Commission on China – One Hundred Eighth Congress – Second Session* (19 April 2004).

United States Department of State *2016 Human Rights Reports: China (includes Tibet, Hong Kong, and Macao) – Macao* (March 2017).

Office of the Commissioner of the Ministry of Foreign Affairs of the People's Republic of China in Hong Kong *gongshu fayanren jiu zhigang de yuenan chuanmin wenti da jizhewen* (17 June 1999) (translation: *Office of the Commissioner Answers Journalists' Questions Regarding Vietnamese Refugees in Hong Kong*).

Republic of Korea Ministry of Unification *Peace and Prosperity: White Paper on Korean Unification 2005* (2005).

Vietnamese Ministry of Foreign Affairs *Tuyên Bô´ của bô˙ ngoa˙ i giao nuỏ´c cô˙ ng hòa xã hô˙ i chủ nghı̃a Viê˙ t Nam vê` vâ´ n đê` nguỏ` i Hoa ỏ˙ Viê˙ t Nam* (Department of Culture and Information, 1978) (translation: *Declaration on the Issue of the Hoa People in Vietnam Issued by the Spokesperson of the Ministry of Foreign Affairs of the Socialist Republic of Vietnam*).

H Papers and Reports

Amnesty International *Myanmar: Investigate alleged rape and killing of two Kachin women* (ASA 16/006/2015, 22 January 2015).

Amnesty International and GlobeScan *Refugees Welcome Survey 2016: Views of Citizens Across 27 Countries – Topline Report from GlobeScan* (May 2016).

Asian-African Legal Consultative Organization Secretariat *The Status and Treatment of Refugees* (AALCO/48/PUTRAJAYA/2009/S 3, 2009).

Committee for Human Rights in North Korea *Lives for Sale: Personal Accounts of Women Fleeing North Korea to China* (2009).

Congressional-Executive Commission on China *2013 Annual Report* (10 October 2013).

Escaping North Korea: The Plight of Defectors – Hearing before the Tom Lantos Human Rights Commission House of Representatives – One Hundred and Eleventh Congress – Second Session (23 September 2010).

Euro-Burma Office *The Kokang Clashes – What Next?* (EBO Analysis Paper No 1, September 2009).

Executive Committee of the Programme of the United Nations High Commissioner for Refugees *General Conclusion on International Protection* (Conclusion No 79 (XLVII), 11 October 1996).

Hong Kong Bar Association *Security Bureau's Proposals to Enhance the Unified Screening Mechanism: Submission of the Hong Kong Bar Association* (2015).

Hong Kong Bar Association *Submissions of the Hong Kong Bar Association ("HKBA"): On Proposals to Amend the Immigration Ordinance (Cap 115) Pursuant to the Comprehensive Review on the Strategy of Handling Non-refoulement Claims* (2019).

Hong Kong University Centre for Comparative and Public Law *Submission to the United Nations Committee on the Elimination of all Forms of Racial Discrimination* (July 2018).

Human Rights Liaison Unit, Division of International Protection UNHCR *Submission by the United Nations High Commissioner for Refugees for the Office of the High Commissioner for Human Rights' Compilation Report – Universal Periodic Review: People's Republic of China* (March 2013).

Human Rights Watch *The Invisible Exodus: North Koreans in the People's Republic of China* (vol 14, no 8(C), November 2002).

Human Rights Watch *Isolated in Yunnan: Kachin Refugees from Burma in China's Yunnan Province* (June 2012).

International Crisis Group *A Tentative Peace in Myanmar's Kachin Conflict* (Asia Briefing No 140, 12 June 2013).

International Media Support *Conflict sensitive journalism: Handbook – Special Edition Myanmar* (September 2014).

Hanna B Krebs *Responsibility, legitimacy, morality: Chinese humanitarianism in historical perspective* (Overseas Development Institute, Humanitarian Policy Group Working Paper, September 2014).

CS Kuppuswamy *Challenging the Reconciliation Process: Myanmar's Ethnic Divide and Conflicts* (Institute of Peace and Conflict Studies, Issue Brief # 221, June 2013).

Law Society of Hong Kong *Non-refoulement Protection: The Government's Proposals to Amend the Immigration Ordinance – The Law Society's Submission* (February 2019).

Non-Refoulement Protection: The Government's Proposals to Amend the Immigration Ordinance (May 2019).

Law Society of Hong Kong and Hong Kong Bar Association *Joint Position Paper by the Law Society of Hong Kong and the Hong Kong Bar Association on the Framework for Convention against Torture ('CAT') Claimants and Asylum Seekers* (31 March 2009).

Joint submission of the Law Society of Hong Kong and the Hong Kong Bar Association to the Legislative Council Security Panel on framework for legal representation for torture claimant and asylum seekers (July 2009).

Rhoda Margesson, Emma Chanlett-Avery and Andorra Bruno *North Korean Refugees in China and Human Rights Issues: International Response and US Policy Options* (Congressional Research Service, Order Code RL34189, 26 September 2007).

Guang Pan *Shanghai: a Haven for Holocaust Victims* (The Holocaust and the United Nations Outreach Programme, Discussion Papers Series vol II, Discussion paper #6).

Sonya Sceats and Shaun Breslin *China and the International Human Rights System* (Chatham House, October 2012).

James D Seymour *China: Background Paper on the Situation of North Koreans in China* (January 2005).

UNHCR *Handbook on Procedures and Criteria for Determining Refugee Status under the 1951 Convention and the 1967 Protocol relating to the Status of Refugees* (HCR/IP/4/Eng/REV.1, reedited January 1992).

Information Note on Article 1 of the 1951 Convention (1 March 1995).

The International Protection of Refugees: Interpreting Article 1 of the 1951 Convention Relating to the Status of Refugees (April 2001).

Procedural Standards for Refugee Status Determination under UNHCR's Mandate (2003).

Fair and efficient asylum procedures: a non-exhaustive overview of applicable international standards (2 September 2005).

APC Regional Workshop – Refugee Status Determination (RSD) Discussion Paper: Refugee Status Determination Processes and Procedures in the Region (10 March 2009).

UNHCR Fonds 13 Records of the High Commissioner: Sub-fonds 2 Poul Hartling 1968–1987 (predominant 1977–1985) (2 September 2009).

Safe at Last? Law and Practice in Selected EU Member States with Respect to Asylum-Seekers Fleeing Indiscriminate Violence (July 2011).

UNHCR Regional Representation for China and Mongolia: Fact Sheet (September 2013).

UNHCR Regional Representation for China and Mongolia: Fact Sheet (September 2014).

Contributions to UNHCR: For Budget Year 2014 – As at 31 December 2014 (7 April 2015).

Rwanda: Emergency Update – Burundi Refugee Influx (16 June 2015).

Contributions to UNHCR for budget year 2015 (as at 31 December 2015).

Contributions to UNHCR for the budget year 2016 (as at 30 September 2016, in US dollars).

Submission by the United Nations High Commissioner for Refugees for the Office of the High Commissioner for Human Rights' Compilation Report: People's Republic of China and the Special Administrative Regions of Hong Kong and Macao (March 2018)

United States Committee for Refugees and Immigrants *US Committee for Refugees World Refugee Survey 1997 – China* (1 January 1997).

    US Committee for Refugees World Refugee Survey 1999 – China, (including Hong Kong and Tibet) (1 January 1999).

    US Committee for Refugees World Refugee Survey 2002 – China (Including Tibet) (10 June 2002).

United States Institute of Peace *China's Role in Myanmar's Internal Conflicts: USIP Senior Study Group Final Report* (No 1, September 2018).

K Yhome *Understanding China's Response to Ethnic Conflicts in Myanmar* (Observer Research Foundation, Occasional Paper 188, April 2019).

I Unpublished Papers

Luong Nhi Ky "The Chinese in Vietnam – A Study of Vietnamese-Chinese Relations with Special Attention to the Period 1862–1961" (PhD Thesis, University of Michigan, 1963).

Allan Mackey and Maya Bozovik "Asian Perspectives and Realities in Asylum Protection and Associated Human Rights" (Presented at the 11th World Conference of the IARLJ, Athens, Greece, 29 Nov–1 Dec 2017).

Jiancheng Zheng "From Nanqiao to Refugee: The Formation of China's Policy toward Indochinese Refugees, 1978–1979" (PhD Thesis, Jinan University, 2015).

J Internet Materials

"bianmin: taoguo guojing quemei taoguo zhadan" (22 March 2015) <https://xw.qq.com/cmsid/2015032201508900> (translation: "Border Residents: Fleeing Across Borders but Still Cannot Escape Bombs").

"China Urges Kachins to Return to Myanmar and Join Peace Process" (8 March 2019) <www.rfa.org/english/news/myanmar/china-kachins-03082019173425.html>.

"Myanmar Government Bombs Fall in China's Yunnan, Sparking Forest Fires" (12 March 2015) <www.rfa.org/english/news/china/bombs-03122015112650.html>.

"shipai mianbei zhanhuopang de zhongguo xiaozhen: zhaoyang chifan" (25 November 2016) <www.wenxuecity.com/news/2016/11/25/gossip-127663_print.html> (translation: "Scenes from a Chinese Little Town Close to War: Eating and Sleeping as Usual").

Amnesty International "Refugees Welcome Survey 2016 – The Results" (19 May 2016) <www.amnesty.org/en/latest/news/2016/05/refugees-welcome-survey-results-2016/>.

Archives Portal Europe "Malayan People's Army 10th Regiment Archives" (no date) <www.archivesportaleurope.net/ead-display/-/ead/pl/aicode/NL-AmISG/type/fa/id/http_COLON__SLASH__SLASH_hdl.handle.net_SLASH_10622_SLASH_ARCH02799>.

The Australian "A hypocritical, hollow critique" (21 February 2014) <www.theaustralian.com.au/opinion/editorials/a-hypocritical-hollow-critique/story-e6frg71x-1226834198413?nk=435b3b55a6999c3aea51f56645fd3005>.

David Barboza "China Passes Japan as Second-Largest Economy" *The New York Times* (15 August 2010) <www.nytimes.com/2010/08/16/business/global/16yuan.html?pagewanted=all&_r=0>.

Hannah Beech "China's Uighur Problem: One Man's Ordeal Echoes the Plight of a People" (28 July 2011) *Time* <http://world.time.com/2011/07/28/chinas-uighur-problem-one-mans-ordeal-echoes-the-plight-of-a-people/>.

"China Accuses Burmese Military of Fatal Bombing Across Border" (16 March 2015) *Time* <http://time.com/3745604/china-burma-kokang-myanmar/>.

Beijing Youth Daily "paodan luoru 10 tianlai zhongguo zhengfu ruhe yingdui" (23 March 2015) <http://news.ifeng.com/a/20150323/43393886_0.shtml> (translation: "How the Chinese Government Has Responded since the Bombs Fell Ten Days Ago").

Bureau of Exit and Entry Administration of the MPS "churujing bianfang jiancha zongzhan ji xiashu churujing bianfang jianchazhan" (3 July 2008) <www.mps.gov.cn/n16/n84147/n84165/1291480.html> (translation: "Exit–Entry Inspection Head Station and Exit–Entry Stations under It").

Burma Link "Patterns of State Abuse" (27 October 2016) <www.burmalink.org/background/burma/human-rights-violations/patterns-of-state-abuse/>.

David Campanale and Joel Gunter "North Korean man begs China not to deport wife and young son" (11 November 2017) <www.bbc.co.uk/news/world-asia-41952298>.

Marco Carvalho "Why Don't We Bring 100 Refugees to Macao and Help Them? – Paul Pun, President of the Association for Refugees' Welfare" (21 June 2019) <www.oclarim.com.mo/en/2019/06/21/why-dont-we-bring-100-refugees-to-macau-and-help-them-paul-pun-president-of-the-association-for-refugees-welfare/>.

Alexander Casella "Time for China to make legal preparations for acceptance of refugees" (28 May 2013) *Global Times* <www.globaltimes.cn/content/785010.shtml#.U1tSpSgoyZY>.

Huaquan Chen "cong nanmin dao guomin: chongxin Shenshi yuenan guiqiao jianit tequ 30nian" (20 August 2012) <http://zh.cnr.cn/2100zhfw/syyw/201208/t20120820_510637382_1.shtml> (translation: "From Refugees to

Nationals: Rethinking the Participation of Returned Overseas Chinese from Vietnamese in Developing the Special Zone in the Past 30 Years").

Shaoming Chen "rujia lunli yu guoji nanmin wenti" (23 May 2017) <www.rujiazg .com/article/11257> (translation: "Confucian Ethics and International Refugee Issues").

Luo Cheng "Statement by Mr LUO Cheng of the Chinese Delegation at the Third Committee of the 64th Session of the UN General Assembly, on Refugees (Item 41)" (3 November 2009) <www.china-un.org/eng/hyyfy/t624524.htm>.

Eric Cheung "People's Daily blames pro-democracy camp for helping 'fake refugees' abuse system in Hong Kong" (14 December 2016) <www.hongkongfp .com/2016/12/14/peoples-daily-blames-pro-democracy-camp-helping-fake-refugees-abuse-system-hong-kong/>.

China Human Rights Studies Association "zhongguo jiaru le naxie guoji renquan gongyue he yidingshu" (27 March 2006) <http://theory.people.com.cn/GB/ 49150/49152/4239175.html> (translation: "Which International Human Rights Treaties and Protocols Has China Ratified?").

China Net "China's Current Legislation Structure" (2003) <www.china.org.cn/ english/kuaixun/76212.htm>.

China News "gaige kaifang 30 nian: huzhao cong cengceng shenpi dao anxu shenling" (4 November 2008) <www.chinanews.com/gn/news/2008/11-04/ 1436222.shtml> (translation: "Thirty Years of Reform and Open-up: Obtaining A Passport as You Need No More Strict Approval Procedures").

"Miandian keqin wuzhuan zan bu pohuai zhongmian youqi guandao deng zhongguo huiying" (6 June 2011) <www.chinanews.com/gj/2011/06-16/ 3115812.shtml> (translation: "Burma's Kachin Army Has Not Ruined China–Myanmar Oil and Gas Pipes, Awaiting China's Response").

"jilin sheng gongan jiguan qieshi jiejue wu hukou renyuan luohu wenti" (11 August 2017) <www.jl.chinanews.com/hyhc/2017-08-11/24565.html> (translation: "Jilin Provincial Public Security Authorities Dutifully Solve the Issue of Hukou Registration for People without Hukou").

Chinese Christian Journalist Association "keqin nanmin jiuzhu: keqin chongtu lishi beijing fenxi" (9 April 2012) <www.chinaaid.net/2012/04/blog-post_ 9.html> (translation: "Assistance of Displaced Kachins: Historical Analysis of the Kachin Conflict").

Chinese State Council Information Office "2012 zhongguo renquan shiye de jinzhan" (14 May 2012) <http://news.xinhuanet.com/politics/2013-05/14/ c_115758619.htm> (translation: "2012 Progress of Human Rights in China").

Roberta Cohen "Legal Grounds for Protection of North Korean Refugees" (13 September 2010) Brookings <www.brookings.edu/research/opinions/2010/09/ north-korea-human-rights-cohen>.

Mark Daly "Refugee and Non-Refoulement Law in Hong Kong: The Introduction of the Unified Screening Mechanism" (October 2014) <www.hk-lawyer.org/content/refugee-and-non-refoulement-law-hong-kong-introduction-unified-screening-mechanism>

Peter Danchin "Article 5" Columbia Center for Teaching and Learning <http://ccnmtl.columbia.edu/projects/mmt/udhr/article_5/development_2.html>.

Khin Khin Ei (translated by Khin Maung Nyane and written in English by Paul Eckert) "Myanmar Says Kokang Rebels Getting Help from China's Side of Border" (26 February 2015) <www.rfa.org/english/news/myanmar/ye-htut-kokang-02262015162400.html>.

Embajada de la República Popular China en la República Oriental del Uruguay "Foreign Ministry Spokesperson Hong Lei's Regular Press Conference on June 16, 2011" (17 June 2011) <http://uy.china-embassy.org/eng/fyrth/t832130.htm>.

Embassy of the People's Republic of China in the Hellenic Republic "Foreign Ministry Spokesperson's Press Conference on January 16, 2003" (3 August 2004) <http://gr.china-embassy.org/eng/xwdt/xw2003/xw200301/t145873.htm>.

Embassy of the People's Republic of China in the Republic of Zimbabwe "Foreign Ministry Spokesperson Hong Lei's Regular Press Conference on May 22, 2012" (23 May 2012) <http://zw.china-embassy.org/eng/fyrth/t935031.htm>.

Chenggang Fan and Shiwei Shao "dao zhongguo qu: zhongmian bianjingxianshang de shiwan keqin nanmin" (17 January 2013) *Southern Weekly* <www.infzm.com/content/85250> (translation: "Go to China: The 100 Thousand Displaced Kachins on the China–Myanmar Border").

LZ Fan "zhongtai hezuo yindu xianfan zao lianheguo nanminshu ganshe zhongfang ti yanzheng jiaoshe" The Global Times (25 November 2015) <http://world.huanqiu.com/exclusive/2015-11/8044932.html> (translation: "China Protested against UNHCR's Interference in Extradition of Criminal Suspects from Thailand to China").

Shuchen Fang "zai hebeisheng sanheshi shenghuo de bajisitan nanmin shi zenme huishi" (25 June 2017) <www.sohu.com/a/151888273_354194> (translation: "Facts about Pakistan Refugees Living in Sanhe City, Hebei Province").

Susanna Fischer "A Brief Introduction to the Legal System of China" (2002) <http://faculty.cua.edu/fischer/ComparativeLaw2002/bauer/China-main.htm>.

Free Burma Rangers "Burma Army Offensive in Waingmaw Township Continues" (4 October 2016) <www.burmalink.org/burma-army-offensive-waingmaw-township-continues/>.

Wang Guangya "Remarks by HE Mr Wang Guangya, Vice Minister of Foreign Affairs of China, at the Opening Ceremony of the Third APC Mekong

Sub-regional Meeting on Refugees, Displaced Persons and Migrants" (8 August 2002) <www.fmprc.gov.cn/eng/wjdt/zyjh/t25088.htm>.

"Statement by HE Mr Wang Guangya, Vice Foreign Minister of the People's Republic of China, at the Ministerial Meeting of States Parties to the 1951 Convention Relating to the Status of Refugees (12 December 2001)" (25 November 2003) <http://pg.china-embassy.org/eng/zt/rqwt/t46963.htm>.

Wu Haitao "Statement by Ambassador WU Haitao at the Security Council Briefing by the United Nations High Commissioner for Refugees" (2 November 2017) <www.china-un.org/eng/hyyfy/t1511072.htm>.

Fang Haochen "zhongguo weihe hui jieshou guoji nanmin? Tamen guode zenmeyang?" (26 June 2017) <www.ims.sdu.edu.cn/info/1014/8699.htm> (translation: "Why Does China Accept International Refugees? How Is Their Life in China?").

Yafei He "Statement by Ambassador Yafei HE on the 61st UNHCR Excom" (4 October 2010) <www.china-un.ch/eng/hom/t758725.htm>.

"Statement by HE Ambassador HE Yafei at the intergovernmental event at the ministerial level of Member States of the United Nations to commemorate the 60th anniversary of the 1951 Convention relating to the Status of Refugees and the 50th anniversary of the 1961 Convention on the Reduction of Statelessness" (9 December 2011) <www.china-un.ch/eng/hom/t885656.htm>.

Hanna Hindstrom "Burma's Transition to Civilian Rule Hasn't Stopped the Abuses of Its Ethnic Wars" (1 April 2016) *Time* <http://time.com/4277328/burma-myanmar-suu-kyi-ethnic-wars/>.

Human Rights Watch "'Untold Miseries': Wartime Abuses and Forced Displacement in Burma's Kachin State" (March 2012) <www.hrw.org/report/2012/03/20/untold-miseries/wartime-abuses-and-forced-displacement-burmas-kachin-state>.

"China: Refugees Forcibly Returned to Burma – Thousands of Kachin at Risk From Conflict, Abuses, Aid Shortages" (24 August 2012) <www.hrw.org/news/2012/08/24/china-refugees-forcibly-returned-burma>.

"Nepal: Increased Pressure from China Threatens Tibetans – Authorities Increase Surveillance and Abuses Against Refugees" (1 April 2016) <www.hrw.org/news/2014/04/01/nepal-increased-pressure-china-threatens-tibetans>.

"China: Redoubling Crackdowns on Fleeing North Koreans: Human Rights Watch Documented 41 North Koreans Detained by China in Summer 2017" (3 September 2017) <www.hrw.org/news/2017/09/03/china-redoubling-crackdowns-fleeing-north-koreans>.

Zhang Hui "Famous people are quitting their social media accounts to avoid abuse from netizens" (19 September 2018) *Global Times* <www.globaltimes.cn/content/1120244.shtml>.

Kris Janowski "UNHCR seeks access to North Koreans detained in China" (21 January 2003) <www.unhcr.org/3e2d81b94.html>.

Guoqing Jiang "guojifa yu guojitiaoyue de jigewenti" (29 April 2000) <www.npc .gov.cn/npc/xinwen/2000-04/29/content_1459914.htm> (translation: "Several Issues of International Law and International Treaties").

Song Jing "Vietnamese refugees well settled in China, await citizenship" (10 May 2007) <www.unhcr.org/464302994.html>.

Terril Yue Jones "China warns UN against 'irresponsible remarks' on North Koreans" (3 June 2013) <www.reuters.com/article/2013/06/03/us-korea-north-china-idUSBRE95209W20130603>.

Kachin News "Kachin IDPs reach over 40,000 due to civil war in Northern Burma" (2 September 2011) <www.kachinnews.com/news/2040-kachin-idps-reach-over-40000-due-to-civil-war-in-northern-burma.html>.

Kachin News Group "War Snowballs: Kachin Refugees Influx to China Border" (24 June 2011) <www.kachinnews.com/news/1955-war-snowballs-kachin-refugees-influx-to-china-border.html>.

Kachinland News "China Closes Border as Thousands Flee Ongoing War" (11 April 2014) <http://kachinlandnews.com/?p=24308>.

Sally Kantar "Ghost Villages Await the Return of Kokang Refugees" (12 May 2016) <www.newsdeeply.com/refugees/articles/2016/05/12/ghost-villages-await-the-return-of-kokang-refugees>.

Ba Kaung "Kachin State Refugees Face Uncertain Future" (1 July 2011) <www2 .irrawaddy.org/article.php?art_id=21612>.

Manya Koeste "Chinese Netizens on World Refugee Day: 'Don't Come to China'" (23 June 2017) <www.whatsonweibo.com/chinese-netizens-world-refugee-day-dont-come-china/>.

Amy Sawitta Lefevre and Pairat Temphairojana "UN agency protests Thailand's deportation of Chinese refugees" (19 November 2015) <www.reuters.com/ article/us-china-thailand-refugees/u-n-agency-protests-thailands-deportation-of-chinese-refugees-idUSKCN0T70J720151118>.

Michael A Lev "China aggressively pursues asylum-seeking N. Koreans" (28 October 2004) Chicago Tribune <http://articles.chicagotribune.com/2004-10-28/news/ 0410280226_1_north-koreans-south-korean-consulate-refugee-crisis>.

Daming Li and others "zhonghan yin 'tuobeizhe' gekong duizhi" (23 February 2012) <http://news.xinhuanet.com/world/2012-02/23/c_122744929.htm> (translation: "Tension between China and South Korea Due to 'North Korean Escapees'").

Hansen Li (ed) "jiena guoji nanmin: chuyu liyi, yuanyu daoyi" (27 February 2012) <http://news.cntv.cn/special/thinkagain/refugee/index.shtml> (translation: "Acceptance of International Refugees: Out of Interest, Originated in Humanity").

Huagang Li "liuluo de guogan – 2018 zhongmian bianjing guogan nanmin sheng-cun kunjing" (26 August 2018) *Kokang123* <www.kokang123.com/thread-37177-1-1.html> (translation: "Kokang in Exile – Difficult Life of Kokang Refugees on the China–Myanmar Border in 2018").

Lianhe Zao Bao "weibi zhanhuo mianbei pingmin fentao yunnan" (14 January 2017) <www.zaobao.com.sg/news/sea/story20170114-713261> (translation: "Escaping Warfare: Civilians from Northern Myanmar Fled to Yunnan Province").

Lan Lin "Beijing zanting qianfan chaoxian nanmin" (18 April 2012) *Radio France International* <www.chinese.rfi.fr/%E4%B8%AD%E5%9B%BD/20120418-%E5%8C%97%E4%BA%AC%E6%9A%82%E5%81%9C%E9%81%A3%E8%BF%94%E6%9C%9D%E9%B2%9C%E9%9A%BE%E6%B0%91> (translation: "Beijing Suspended Repatriation of North Korean Refugees").

Xin Lin (translated by Luisetta Mudie) "Myanmar Army Holds Three Chinese Nationals on Suspicion of Spying" (14 May 2015) <www.rfa.org/english/news/china/myanmar-china-05142015125627.html>.

"List of North Korean Refugees and Humanitarian Workers Seized by Chinese Authorities" <www.seoultrain.com/content/resources/the_list.htm>.

Guofu Liu "zhongguo weilai raobuguo nanmin yiti" (23 February 2012) <http://news.xinhuanet.com/world/2012-02/23/c_122744895.htm> (translation: "China Cannot Avoid Refugee Issues in the Future").

Hongxiong Liu "zhengdong zhongyang de 'dataogang' fengchao" (1 August 2010) <www.people.com.cn/GB/198221/198819/198857/12308776.html> (translation: "The 'Great Escape to Hong Kong' that Shocked the Central Government").

Jun Liu "30,000 ming guogan nanmin tashang miandian guitu" (16 September 2009) *China Weekly* <www.chinaweekly.cn/bencandy.php?fid=60&id=4491> (translation: "30,000 Kokang Refugees on Their Way Home").

Lun Min Maung "Myanmar apologises to China over cross-border bombing" (3 April 2015) *Myanmar Times* <www.mmtimes.com/national-news/13884-myanmar-apologises-to-china-over-cross-border-bombing.html>.

Miluyuzijiang "mainbei zhanluo guogan nanmin taodao zhongguo nansan zai nanminying jianku duri" (23 October 2018) <https://mbd.baidu.com/newspage/data/landingshare?context=%7B%22nid%22%3A%22news_9058935335342101040%22%2C%22sourceFrom%22%3A%22bjh%22%7D&type=gallery> (translation: "War in Northern Myanmar Drove Kokang Refugees into China's Nansan Having a Difficult Time in Refugee Camps").

Ministry of Civil Affairs of the People's Republic of China "minzhengbu zhuyao zhize" <www.mca.gov.cn/article/zwgk/jggl/zyzz/> (translation: "Main Duties and Responsibilities of Ministry of Civil Affairs").

Ministry of Commerce, People's Republic of China "China and UNHCR Sign the Assistance Agreement to Meet Refugee Challenges" (30 September 2017)

<http://english.mofcom.gov.cn/article/newsrelease/significantnews/201710/ 20171002654087.shtml>.

Ministry of Foreign Affairs of the People's Republic of China "Main Responsibilities of the Ministry of Foreign Affairs of the People's Republic of China" <www.fmprc.gov.cn/eng/wjb/zyzz/>.

"Dai Bingguo Meets with UN High Commissioner for Refugees Guterres" (3 September 2010) <www.fmprc.gov.cn/eng/wjb/zzjg/gjs/gjsxw/t738076 .shtml>.

"Foreign Ministry Spokesperson Hong Lei's Regular Press Conference on February 25, 2015" <www.fmprc.gov.cn/mfa_eng/xwfw_665399/s2510_ 665401/2511_665403/t1240548.shtml>.

"Wang Yi: Both Temporary and Permanent Solutions Should Be Adopted to Eliminate Root Causes in Addressing Syrian Refugee Issue" (28 October 2015) <www.fmprc.gov.cn/mfa_eng/zxxx_662805/t1310429.shtml>.

"Wang Yi Talks about Issue of Refugees in the Middle East" (24 June 2017) <www.fmprc.gov.cn/mfa_eng/zxxx_662805/t1473802.shtm>.

Mizzima "China offers cash to Kachin refugees willing to return" (9 March 2019) <http://mizzima.com/article/china-offers-cash-kachin-refugees-willing-return>.

Luisetta Mudie "Kachin Forced Back to Burma" (24 August 2014) <www.rfa.org/ english/news/china/kachin-08242012105036.html/>.

Myanmar Peace Monitor "International Response to Myanmar's Ethnic Conflict" <www.mmpeacemonitor.org/1504>.

Seth Mydans "20 Uighurs Are Deported to China" *The New York Times* (19 December 2009) <www.nytimes.com/2009/12/20/world/asia/20uighur.html? _r=0>.

Saw Yan Naing "Kachin Conflict Sparks Refugee Situation" (15 June 2011) <www2.irrawaddy.org/article.php?art_id=21495>.

Shan Nan "Beijing chaichu yingdi qianfan guogan nanmin" (1 September 2009) <www.asianews.it/news-zh/%E5%8C%97%E4%BA%AC%E6%8B%86%E9% 99%A4%E8%90%A5%E5%9C%B0%E9%81%A3%E8%BF%94%E6%9E%9C %E6%95%A2%E9%9A%BE%E6%B0%91-16205.html> (translation: "Beijing Removed Camps and Repatriated Kokang Refugees").

National Diet Library, Japan "Tokuda, Kyuichi" <www.ndl.go.jp/portrait/e/datas/ 407.html?cat=119>.

Stephanie Nebehay "China deports refugees ahead of Olympics: UN" (9 April 2008) <www.reuters.com/article/2008/04/08/us-china-un-refugees-idUSL08 6328120080408>.

The New Humanitarian "Myanmar: Border guard plan could fuel ethnic conflict" (29 November 2010) *Reliefweb* <https://reliefweb.int/report/myanmar/ myanmar-border-guard-plan-could-fuel-ethnic-conflict>.

"Kachin refugees in China in need" (27 June 2012) <www.thenewhumanitarian .org/news/2012/06/27/kachin-refugees-china-need>.

Grace Ng "Red Tape Foils Green Card Dreams in China" (4 April 2012).

Nang Noom "China restricts border access as Kokang exodus continues"
(2 March 2015) <www.unhcr.org/cgi-bin/texis/vtx/refdaily?pass=52fc6fbd5
&id=54f56b385>.

Jane Perlez "Fearing the Worst, China Plans Refugee Camps on North Korean
Border" *The New York Times* (online ed, New York, 11 December 2017)
<www.nytimes.com/2017/12/11/world/asia/china-north-korea-border.html>.

Jianyi Piao and Zhipei Li "chaoxian 'tuobeizhe' wenti de guojihua yanbian jiqi
yingxiang" (13 August 2012) <http://iaps.cass.cn/news/523644.htm>
(translation: "The Internationalization of the Issue of North Korean
'Escapees' and Its Influence").

James Pomfret "Relief camp in China swells as thousands flee conflict in Myanmar"
(13 March 2017) <www.reuters.com/article/us-myanmar-insurgency-china-
refugees/relief-camp-in-china-swells-as-thousands-flee-conflict-in-myanmar-
idUSKBN16K0JW>.

Long Qiao "Guogan laojie zaifa wuzhuang chongtu yunnan guanbi nansan zhen
nanminying" (7 March 2015) <www.rfa.org/mandarin/yataibaodao/junshi
waijiao/ql2-03072015122210.html> (translation: "Fresh Armed Conflict in
Laukai in the Kokang Region, Yunnan Closing Refugee Camps in Nansan
Town").

Vivian Tan "Chinese schools offer primary education for urban refugees"
(22 November 2013) <www.unhcr.org/en-au/news/latest/2013/11/528f66086/
chinese-schools-offer-primary-education-urban-refugees.html>.

"China can play key role in solving refugee crises – UNHCR chief" (8 June 2017)
<www.unhcr.org/en-au/news/latest/2017/6/593946b64/china-play-key-role-
solving-refugee-crises-unhcr-chief.html>.

Khin Oo Tha "China Reportedly Urging Kokang Refugees to Return" (9 March
2015) <www.irrawaddy.com/news/burma/china-reportedly-urging-kokang-
refugees-to-return.html>.

That's Beijing "I'm an Asylum Seeker Living in Beijing. Here's What My Life is
Like" (12 July 2017) <www.thatsmags.com/beijing/post/19734/an-asylum-
seekers-firsthand-account-of-life-in-china>.

The Economist "The Kachin dilemma: Over the border, the Kachin conflict causes
headaches for China" (2 February 2013) <www.economist.com/news/asia/
21571189-over-border-kachin-conflict-causes-headaches-china-kachin-
dilemma>.

"The Han that Rock the Cradle" (12 March 2015) <www.economist.com/news/
asia/21646248-kokang-conflict-causes-problems-china-too-han-rock-cradle>.

Permanent Mission of the People's Republic of China to the United Nations Office
at Geneva and Other International Organizations in Switzerland "China's
Relationship with United Nations High Commissioner for Refugees

(UNHCR)" (16 April 2004) <www.china-un.ch/eng/rqrd/jblc/t85094.htm>.

"zhongguo daibiao Ren Yisheng gongcan zai lianheguo nanmin zhiweihui di65ci huiyi yibanxing bianlun zhongde fayan" (2 October 2014) <www.china-un.ch/chn/hyyfy/t1197675.htm> (translation: "Statement of Chinese Representative Ren Yisheng at 65th UNHCR ExCom Meeting").

"Ma Zhaoxu Called for Durable Solution to the Global Issue of Refugees" (5 October 2016) <www.china-un.ch/eng/dbtzyhd/t1403595.htm>.

Piaobotanggula "guogan, jinye wumian weini qidao" (28 August 2009) Tianya Forum <http://bbs.tianya.cn/post-news-141112-1.shtml> (translation: "Kokang, Praying for You in This Sleepless Night").

Zhuang Pinghui "More foreigners moving to China for work, study finds" (15 June 2018) <www.scmp.com/news/china/society/article/2151057/more-foreigners-moving-china-work-study-finds>.

Project MAJE, Mekong Network "The North War: A Kachin Conflict Compilation Report" (2011) <www.projectmaje.org/kachin_2011.htm>.

Radio Free Asia "Criticism over Deportation" (5 June 2011) <www.rfa.org/english/news/uyghur/refugee-06052011164247.html>.

"UNHCR Refuses to Shed Light" (6 June 2011) <www.rfa.org/english/news/uyghur/refugees-06062011190817.html>.

"mianbei zhanhuo chongran dapi nanmin taowang zhongguo" (21 November 2016) <www.rfa.org/cantonese/news/myanmar-civilwar-11212016083635.html> (translation: "Armed Conflict Resumed in North Myanmar: Large Numbers of Refugees Fled to China").

Reuters "Indochinese refugees may get Chinese citizenship" (1 June 2007) <www.reuters.com/article/us-china-indochina-idUSPEK9279520070601>.

Righteous Kokang "guogan gaikuang" <www.righteouskokang.com> (translation: "Basic Facts of Kokang").

Li Ruohan "97% of Chinese would reject receiving refugees: online poll" (20 June 2018) <www.globaltimes.cn/content/1107731.shtml#.W0PeY6hoR9Q.twitter>.

School of Asian Pacific Study of Sun Yat-Sen University "2012 nian zhongshan daxue moni lianheguo dahui nanmin anzhi yu nanmin quanli baozhang beijing wenjian" (19 April 2012) <http://saps.sysu.edu.cn/xsyd/zsdxmnlhg/96477.htm> (translation: "2012 Sun Yat-Sun University Moot UN Meeting on Refugee Settlement and Rights Protection Background Document").

Shan Herald Agency for News "Kokang Capital Falls: 'Not Shoot First' Policy under Fire" (26 August 2009) <www.shanland.org/index.php?option=com_content&view=article&id=2695:kokang-capital-falls-not-shoot-first-policy-under-fire&catid=86:war&Itemid=284>.

Shan Human Rights Foundation "Killing, beheading and disappearance of villagers instill fear of return among Kokang refugees" (11 May 2015)

<www.shanhumanrights.org/index.php/news-updates/212-killing-beheading-and-disappearance-of-villagers-instill-fear-of-return-among-kokang-refugees>.

Shanghai Jiaotong University "jiaoda zhiyuanzhe zai Yunnan bianchun anquan duguo guogan zhanshi" (24 September 2009) <http://topics.sjtu.edu.cn/newsnet/shownews.php?id=22669> (translation: "Jiaotong University Volunteers Survived Kokang War").

Yao Shaojun "Statement by Counsellor YAO Shaojun during the General Debate on the Item of Refugees at the Third Committee of the 72nd Session of the General Assembly" (2 November 2017) <www.china-un.org/eng/hyyfy/t1507214.htm>.

Sidiki Sheriff "Asylum Registration in China" (1 March 2014) <https://rightsinexile.tumblr.com/post/78227619023/asylum-registration-in-china>.

Nancy Shwe (translated by Sarah Jackson-Han) "Kokang Fighters Flee to China" (31 August 2009) <www.rfa.org/english/news/myanmar/kokang-08312009061953.html>.

Sohu News "waiguoren ruhe dedao zhongguo 'bihu'" (18 December 2013) <http://news.sohu.com/s2013/dianji-1291/> (translation: "How Can Foreigners Receive Asylum in China").

Mae Sot "Myanmar's ethnic problems" (29 March 2012) <www.thenewhumanitarian.org/report/95195/briefing-myanmar%E2%80%99s-ethnic-problems>.

State Council Information Office of the People's Republic of China "Yunnan Sheng zhengfu jiu dangqian zhongmian bianjing jushi juxing xinwen fabuhui" (31 August 2009) <www.scio.gov.cn/xwfbh/gssxwfbh/xwfbh/yunnan/200908/t398584.htm> (translation: "Yunnan Government Holds Press Conference on Situation on China–Myanmar Border").

Youpeng Su "zai yunnan lingyiduan de guogan, wo tanfang zhanzheng yinying xia de shenghuo" (24 November 2017) <http://kongbei.io/archives/15889> (translation: "At Kokang at the Other End of Yunnan, I Visited Life under the Shadow of War").

Tacheng Municipality "Tacheng de waiguo qiaomin" (20 July 2011) <www.xjtcsh.gov.cn/tcgk/rwsl/201107/t4028a8ab3145442001314701c94f04dd.html> (translation: "Foreign Sojourners in Tacheng").

UNHCR "UNHCR Regional Representation in China" <www.unhcr.org.hk/unhcr/en/about_us/China_Office.html>.

"Seven North Korean asylum seekers arrive in Seoul" (30 June 2001) <www.unhcr.org/3b4049cb1.html>.

"China: Concerns over deportation" (8 April 2008) <www.unhcr.org/47fb4ed42.html>.

"China: UNHCR calls for access to Myanmar refugees" (4 September 2009) <www.unhcr.org/news/briefing/2009/9/4aa108159/>.

"UNHCR reaches Kachins sent back from China" (7 September 2012) <www.unhcr.org/5049cdba9.html>.

"Government Contributions to UNHCR" (2014) <www.unhcr.org/cgi-bin/texis/vtx/page?page=49e487cd6&submit=GO>.

UNHCR Hong Kong "Regional Representation in China" <www.unhcr.org/hk/en/134-china.html>.

"Regional Representation in China" (10 March 1999) <www.unhcr.org/hk/en/134-china-2.html>.

UNHCR UK "North Koreans leave China" (15 March 2002) <www.unhcr.org/uk/news/briefing/2002/3/3c91d7ba15/north-koreans-leave-china.html>.

United Nations Treaty Collection "Convention relating to the Status of Refugees" <https://treaties.un.org/Pages/ViewDetailsII.aspx?src=TREATY&mtdsg_no=V-2&chapter=5&Temp=mtdsg2&clang=_en>.

"Protocol relating to the Status of Refugees" <https://treaties.un.org/Pages/ViewDetails.aspx?src=IND&mtdsg_no=V-5&chapter=5&clang=_en>.

United States Committee for Refugees and Immigrants "World Refugee Survey" (2009) <www.refugees.org/resources/refugee-warehousing/archived-world-refugee-surveys/2009-wrs-country-updates/china.html>.

Voice of America "Aid Groups Say China is Expelling Kachin Refugees" (23 June 2011) <http://blogs.voanews.com/breaking-news/2011/06/23/aid-groups-say-china-is-expelling-kachin-refugees/>.

Max Walden "Online polls show 97pc of Chinese reject accepting refugees" (22 June 2018) <https://asiancorrespondent.com/2018/06/online-polls-show-97pc-of-chinese-reject-accepting-refugees/>.

Ann Wang "The forgotten refugees of Kokang" (8 March 2016) <https://frontiermyanmar.net/en/the-forgotten-refugees-kokang>.

"Myanmar refugees in China caught between political fault lines" (16 March 2016) <www.thenewhumanitarian.org/feature/2016/03/16/myanmar-refugees-china-caught-between-political-fault-lines>.

Philip Wen "Myanmar's Kokang refugees caught between army, aged warlord and a pipeline to China" (27 March 2015) *The Sydney Morning Herald* <www.smh.com.au/world/myanmars-kokang-refugees-caught-between-army-aged-warlord-and-a-pipeline-to-china-20150327-1m95pg.html>.

Lawi Weng "Analysis: A Window Opens for China to Nudge Myanmar Army Forward on Peace Process" (23 November 2017) <www.irrawaddy.com/news/burma/analysis-window-opens-china-nudge-myanmar-army-forward-peace-process.html>.

"Army Shelling Seen Signaling Start of New Offensive in Kachin, Shan States" (14 December 2017) <www.irrawaddy.com/news/burma/army-shelling-seen-signaling-start-new-offensive-kachin-shan-states.html>.

Hilary Whiteman "Scenarios for Snowden: Escape, arrest, asylum" (21 June 2013) <https://edition.cnn.com/2013/06/20/world/asia/snowden-scenarios-hong-kong/index.html>.

Edward Wong "China Is Disputing Status of Uighurs in Cambodia" *The New York Times* (17 December 2009) <www.nytimes.com/2009/12/18/world/asia/18xinjiang.html>.

Edward Wong and Poypiti Amatatham "Ignoring Protests, Thailand Deports about 100 Uighurs Back to China" *The New York Times* (10 July 2015) <http://cn.nytimes.com/asia-pacific/20150710/c10uighur/enus/>.

Huan Wu "zhongmian bianjing nanmin er'tong jiuxue zaiyu dizhi" (1 April 2017) <http://news.dwnews.com/china/news/2017-04-01/59808561.html> (translation: "Refugee Children on the China–Myanmar Border Face Difficulty Going to School Again").

Xinhua "mingji 'yongjiao toupiao' de lishi jingshi" (4 November 2013) <http://news.xinhuanet.com/politics/2013-11/04/c_117988157.htm> (translation: "Remembering the Historic Lesson of 'Voting with Foot'").

"14,000 Myanmar Border Residents Flocking to China Relocated" (3 March 2015) <http://usa.chinadaily.com.cn/world/2015-03/03/content_19701937.htm>.

"Over 60,000 Myanmar refugee arrivals in China since conflict outbreak" (7 March 2015) <https://reliefweb.int/report/china/over-60000-myanmar-refugee-arrivals-china-conflict-outbreak>.

"Chinese FM discusses Myanmar in border province after bombing" (17 March 2015) <http://en.people.cn/n/2015/0317/c90883-8864529.html>.

"Reform meeting tables healthcare, environmental, hukou proposals" (10 December 2015) <www.scio.gov.cn/m/32618/Document/1458841/1458841.htm>.

"yidaiyilu guojihezuo gaofengluntan chengguo qingdan (quanwen)" (16 May 2017)   <www.xinhuanet.com/world/2017-05/16/c_1120976848.htm> (translation: "List of Achievements of the Belt-and-Road Forum for International Cooperation (Full Text)")

"China Proposes three-phase solution to Rakhine issue in Myanmar: FM" (20 November 2017) <http://news.xinhuanet.com/english/2017-11/20/c_136764392.htm>.

Yan Xu "jiemi: miandian gongchandang xingwang shimo yu jiaoxun" (2 December 2012) <http://dangshi.people.com.cn/GB/85039/13375304.html> (translation: "Secret Revealed: The Rise and Fall of the Burma Communist Party and Its Lessons").

Zhijun Xu "guogan, qiangsheng weishei er'ming" (15 April 2017) <www.ifengweekly.com/detil.php?id=3803> (translation: "Kokang, Gunfire for Whom?").

Yang Yang "beijing fengsuo bianjing nanmin zhong jingxian daliang junren" (14 January 2017) <http://news.dwnews.com/global/news/2017-01-14/59794169.html> (translation: "Beijing Closed Norders; Many Soldiers amongst Refugees").

Ke Yousheng "Statement by Mr. KE Yousheng, Adviser of the Chinese Delegation, at the Third Committee of the 62nd Session of the General Assembly, on the

Report of UNHCR (Item 42)" (8 November 2007) <www.china-un.org/eng/xw/t380695.htm>.

Yunnan Civil Affairs "duiwai hezuo chu 2009 nian gongzuo zongjie he 2010 nian gongzuo jihua" (8 March 2010) <http://yunnan.mca.gov.cn/article/ztzl/mzgzh/cszj/201003/20100300060711.shtml> (translation: "Office of External Cooperation 2009 Work Report and 2010 Work Plan").

Xiong Zhang "guogan nanmin zai zhongguo" (8 September 2009) <http://qzone.qq.com/blog/622006396-1252371403> (translation: "Kokang Refugees in China").

K Newspaper and Magazine Articles

"Cargo Ships and 'Refugees' – Vietnamese Authorities Export 'Refugees' in a Planned Way" *Beijing Review* (Beijing, 22 December 1978).

Laurie Chen and Yujing Liu "Explainer: How Hong Kong Has for Decades Been A a Magnet for Refugees and Migrants" *South China Morning Post* (online ed, Hong Kong, 23 December 2017)

Yinghong Cheng "magong zongshuji Chen Ping de chuanqi rensheng" *Phoenix Weekly* (online ed, Hong Kong, 16 October 2013) (translation: "The Legendary Life of the Former Secretary General of the Malayan Communist Party, Chen Ping").

"China Compelled to Terminate Economic and Technical Aid to Viet Nam" *Beijing Review* (Beijing, 14 July 1978).

Buzhi Ding, Zhen Xu and Jialin Liang "yige yi cunzai 30 nian de chenmo qunti: 30 wan nanmin zai zhongguo" (2009) *Nanfang zhoumo* (online ed, Guangzhou, China, 15 October 2009) (translation: "A Silent Community That Has Existed for 30 Years: 300 Thousand Refugees in China").

Jon Gordon "FYI: What happened to Hong Kong's Vietnamese refugee community?" *South China Morning Post* (online ed, Hong Kong, 15 June 2008).

Guangxi Zhuang Autonomous Region Local Chronicle Commission "guangxi tongzhi: qiaowuzhi" (online ed, Guangxi People's Press, 1996) (translation: "Guangxi Chronicle: Overseas Chinese Affairs Chronicle").

"huyu guojishang youxiao zhizhi yuenan shuchu nanmin" *People's Daily* (Beijing, 30 June 1979) (translation: "Calling the International Community to Effectively Stop Vietnam from Exporting Refugees").

Cui Jia "Refugees look to end life in limbo" *China Daily* (online ed, Beijing, 1 June 2016).

Meilian Lin "Home away from home" *Global Times* (online ed, Beijing, 22 December 2013).

Jay Mathews "Refugees Worry South China: Thousands of Refugees from Vietnam Produce Uneasiness in South China" *The Washington Post* (Washington, 16 July 1978).

"Myanmar apologises for bombs that killed five in China's Yunnan province" *South China Morning Post* (online ed, Hong Kong, 3 April 2015).

Mark O'Neill "Scourge of War" *Macao Quarterly* (Macao, July 2011) 43.

Jane Perlez "Myanmar's Fight with Rebels Creates Refugees and Ill Will With China" *The New York Times* (online ed, New York, 21 March 2015).

"qianglie kangyi yuenan buduan ba yuenan jumin qugan dao woguo jingnei" *People's Daily* (Beijing, 6 January 1979) (translation: "Strong Opposition to Vietnam Expelling Vietnamese Residents into China").

Renmin Ribao Commentator "Lies Cannot Cover up Facts" *Beijing Review* (Beijing, 16 June 1978).

Elisabeth Rosenthal "China in Campaign to Expel Koreans Who Enter Illegally" *The New York Times* (online ed, New York, 31 May 2000).

"9 More North Koreans Seek Asylum in Seoul Embassy in Beijing" *The New York Times* (online ed, New York, 12 June 2002).

Xiao Shao "shenghuo zai zhongguo de waiguo nanmin" *Baixing* (Beijing, March 2004) (translation: "Foreign Refugees Living in China" *Ordinary People*).

"Sino-Vietnamese Negotiations At Vice-Ministerial Level" *Beijing Review* (Beijing, 4 August 1978).

Spokesman of the Overseas Chinese Affairs Office of the State Council "Statement on Viet Nam's Expulsion of Chinese Residents" *Beijing Review* (Beijing, 2 June 1978).

"Statement by Spokesman of Consular Department of Chinese Foreign Ministry" *Beijing Review* (Beijing, 30 June 1978).

"Viet Nam Slams Door on Negotiations" *Beijing Review* (Beijing, 6 October 1978).

Jing Wan "nanmin wenti yizhi zai fasheng, bushi zhe jiushi na" *Southern Weekly* (online ed, Guangzhou, 8 July 2011) (translation: "Refugee Problems Always Happen, Either Here or Elsewhere").

"Who Is to Blame? – Why ships sent by China to bring back persecuted Chinese residents in Viet Nam are lying at anchor off its territorial sea" *Beijing Review* (Beijing, 7 July 1978).

Edward Wong "China Forces Ethnic Kachin Refugees Back to a Conflict Zone in Myanmar's North" *The New York Times* (online ed, New York, 23 August 2012).

"Chinese Deny Forcing Refugees to Myanmar" *The New York Times* (online ed, New York, 25 August 2012).

Hongwei Ying "Guogan jiannan rongru miandian" *Time Weekly* (online ed, Beijing, 17 January 2013) (translation: "Kokang Painfully Integrate into Myanmar").

"yuenan dangju canwu rendao de lesuo" *People's Daily* (Beijing, 30 November 1978) (translation: "The Vietnamese Authorities' Inhumane Extortion").

Jing Zhang "zhongguo weishenme bushe nanminying" *China Society Magazine* (Beijing, May 2002) (translation: "Why China Did Not Establish Refugee Camps").

"zhizhi yuenan dangju yilingweihe de fandong zhengce" *People's Daily* (Beijing, 20 January 1979) (translation: "Stop Vietnam's Policy").

L News Releases

Fortify Rights "China: Protect Ethnic Kachin Refugees Fleeing War in Northern Myanmar – Prevent forced returns, allow humanitarian agencies unfettered access to displaced communities" (news release, 13 January 2017).

INDEX

For EU product safety concerns, contact us at Calle de José Abascal, 56–1º, 28003 Madrid, Spain or eugpsr@cambridge.org.